Communicating Corporate Ethics on the World Wide Web

METROPOLITAN COLLEGE
OF NEW YORK LIBRARY
75 Varick Street 12th Fl.
New York, NY 10013

European University Studies

Europäische Hochschulschriften
Publications Universitaires Européennes

Series V
Economics and Management

Reihe V   Série V
Volks- und Betriebswirtschaft
Sciences économiques, gestion d'entreprise

Vol./Bd. 2952

PETER LANG
Frankfurt am Main · Berlin · Bern · Bruxelles · New York · Oxford · Wien

Irene Pollach

Communicating Corporate Ethics on the World Wide Web

A Discourse Analysis of Selected Company Web Sites

PETER LANG
Europäischer Verlag der Wissenschaften

Bibliographic Information published by Die Deutsche Bibliothek
Die Deutsche Bibliothek lists this publication in the Deutsche Nationalbibliografie; detailed bibliographic data is available in the internet at <http://dnb.ddb.de>.

Zugl.: Wien, Wirtschafts-Univ., Diss., 2002

Gedruckt auf alterungsbeständigem,
säurefreiem Papier.

ISSN 0531-7339
ISBN 3-631-50695-3
US-ISBN 0-8204-6417-1
© Peter Lang GmbH
Europäischer Verlag der Wissenschaften
Frankfurt am Main 2003
All rights reserved.

All parts of this publication are protected by copyright. Any utilisation outside the strict limits of the copyright law, without the permission of the publisher, is forbidden and liable to prosecution. This applies in particular to reproductions, translations, microfilming, and storage and processing in electronic retrieval systems.

Printed in Germany 1 2 4 5 6 7

www.peterlang.de

*Integrity is what we do, what we say,
and what we say we do.*

~ Don Galer ~

Preface and Acknowledgments

This book seeks to illuminate how companies use language to present themselves as ethical players and how corporate Web sites function as instruments of external corporate communication. The roots of this work are clearly interdisciplinary, drawing chiefly from the disciplines of corporate communication, applied linguistics and corporate ethics.

As is the case with all Internet-related research, the findings presented in this book might already be outdated by the time it goes to print. The World Wide Web is always in a state of flux and can never be captured in a snapshot. In fact, all Web sites examined in this book changed visually or content-wise in the course of my research. Although accounting for the changes would have strengthened my arguments, I continued my analysis with my pre-existing data, as trying to keep up with the fast pace of the World Wide Web quickly becomes a labor of Sisyphus. Despite these limitations, the insights this book provides are well suited to aid communication professionals in designing more effective messages for ethics Web pages.

This book would not have turned out the way it did without the support of a few individuals along the way.

First, I am indebted to W. Michael Hoffman, Director of the Center for Business Ethics at Bentley College, for having me at the Center and for sharing his insights about corporate ethics. His contributions were pivotal to developing the research framework.

As this work was originally submitted as a doctoral dissertation at the Vienna University of Economics and Business Administration in Austria, I would like to thank my supervisor Professor Richard J. Alexander for introducing me to the world of linguistics, and my second supervisor Professor Bodo B. Schlegelmilch for allowing me to go on this journey.

The journey was a long and lonely one, so I am grateful to my colleagues at the Department of Business English at the Vienna University of Economics and Business Administration for persuading me to participate in "extracurricular" activities as well.

Finally, I would like to express my gratitude to my parents for encouraging and supporting me throughout the years.

Table of Contents

1 Introduction 15
2 Research Design 17
2.1 Research Questions 17
2.2 Unit of Analysis: Corporate Web Sites 18
2.3 Research Strategy: Case Studies 20
   2.3.1 Justification for the Strategy Chosen 21
   2.3.2 Sample Selection and Cross-Case Analysis 22
   2.3.3 Data Collection and Structure of the Analysis 24
2.4 Method of Data Analysis: Discourse Analysis 25
   2.4.1 The Ideational Function 27
   2.4.2 The Interpersonal Function 28
   2.4.3 The Textual Function 30
   2.4.4 Context 32

3 Business Ethics vs. Corporate Social Responsibility 33
3.1 Business Ethics: Preventing Harm 34
   3.1.1 Motives and Stimuli 34
   3.1.2 Creating an Ethical Climate 35
      3.1.2.1 Top Management Commitment 35
      3.1.2.2 Organizational Culture 36
      3.1.2.3 Reward and Discipline Systems 37
      3.1.2.4 Internal Reporting Mechanisms 37
   3.1.3 The Institutionalization of Corporate Ethics 38
      3.1.3.1 Ethics Codes 39
         3.1.3.1.1 The History of Ethics Codes 40
         3.1.3.1.2 Characteristics of Effective Ethics Codes 40
      3.1.3.2 Ethics Ombudspersons 43
      3.1.3.3 Ethics Committees 43
      3.1.3.4 Ethics Officers 44
      3.1.3.5 Ethics Hotlines 45
      3.1.3.6 Ethics Training Programs 46
      3.1.3.7 Ethics Audits 47
      3.1.3.8 Recent Trends in Ethics Programs 48

3.2 Corporate Social Responsibility: Doing Good 49
3.2.1 Historical Framework Since 1900 50
3.2.2 The Rationale for Corporate Social Responsibility 53
3.2.3 Manifestations of Corporate Social Responsibility 54
3.2.3.1 Corporate Philanthropy and Community Involvement 54
3.2.3.2 Statements of Mission, Vision, and Values 58
3.2.3.2.1 Mission and Vision Statements 58
3.2.3.2.2 Corporate Credos 60
3.2.3.3 Corporate Social Reporting and Auditing 61
3.3 Summary of Key Points 62

4 The Business-Ethics Paradigm 63
4.1 Case 1: *BellSouth Corp.* 63
4.1.1 Background to the Company 63
4.1.2 Discourse Analysis 64
4.1.2.1 The Ideational Function 64
4.1.2.2 The Interpersonal Function 71
4.1.2.3 The Textual Function 78
4.2 Case 2: *Lockheed Martin Corp.* 79
4.2.1 Background to the Company 79
4.2.1.1 Company Profile 79
4.2.1.2 Overcharges, Illegal Payments and Arms Export 79
4.2.1.3 The Defense Industry Initiative 81
4.2.1.4 Lockheed Martin's Ethics Program in the Media 81
4.2.2 Discourse Analysis 82
4.2.2.1 The Ideational Function 82
4.2.2.2 The Interpersonal Function 86
4.2.2.3 The Textual Function 92
4.3 Intra-Paradigm Analysis 95

5 The Corporate-Social-Responsibility Paradigm 97
5.1 Case 3: *Ben & Jerry's Homemade, Inc.* 97
5.1.1. Background to the Company 97
5.1.1.1 Company Profile 97
5.1.1.2 Caring Capitalism 98
5.1.1.3 Reputation Threats 101
5.1.1.3.1 The Takeover by Unilever 101
5.1.1.3.2 Dioxin and the Eco-Pint Scandal 102
5.1.1.3.3 The Rainforest-Crunch Scandal 103

    5.1.2 Discourse Analysis 104
        5.1.2.1 The Ideational Function 104
        5.1.2.2 The Interpersonal Function 110
        5.1.2.3 The Textual Function 115
5.2 Case 4: *McDonald's Corp*.. 119
    5.2.1 Background to the Company... 119
        5.2.1.1 Company Profile 119
        5.2.1.2 McDonald's Corporate Symbols and Icons................................... 122
        5.2.1.3 McDonald's Reputation Threats.. 123
            5.2.1.3.1 The McLibel Case 123
            5.2.1.3.2 Junk Food 125
            5.2.1.3.3 McJobs 126
            5.2.1.3.4 Waste Production 127
            5.2.1.3.5 Labor Issues in China 128
            5.2.1.3.6 Anti-McDonald's Web Sites 129
    5.2.2 Discourse Analysis 131
        5.2.2.1 The Ideational Function 131
        5.2.2.2 The Interpersonal Function 136
        5.2.2.3 The Textual Function 144
5.3 Intra-Paradigm Analysis 146

6 The BE & CSR Paradigm..149

6.1 Case 5: *Nike, Inc.*.. 149
    6.1.1 Background to the Company... 149
        6.1.1.1 Company Profile 149
        6.1.1.2 Nike's Corporate Icons and Symbols 150
        6.1.1.3 Nike's Image Threats... 151
            6.1.1.3.1 Operation PUSH 151
            6.1.1.3.2 Labor Issues in Asia.. 152
            6.1.1.3.3 Anti-Nike Campaigns on the Internet 156
    6.1.2 Discourse Analysis 158
        6.1.2.1 The Ideational Function 159
        6.1.2.2 The Interpersonal Function 167
        6.1.2.3 The Textual Function 170
6.2 Case 6: *Levi Strauss & Co.* 173
    6.2.1 Background to the Company... 173
        6.2.1.1 Company Profile 173
        6.2.1.2 Levi Strauss & Co.'s Corporate Symbols and Icons 174
        6.2.1.3 Social Responsibility at Levi Strauss & Co.................................. 175
        6.2.1.4 Levi Strauss & Co.'s Image Threats... 176

  6.2.2 Discourse Analysis 179
    6.2.2.1 The Ideational Function 179
    6.2.2.2 The Interpersonal Function 184
    6.2.2.3 The Textual Function 191
6.3 Intra-Paradigm Analysis 194

7 Cross-Case Analysis 197
7.1 The Ideational Function across Cases 197
  7.1.1 Content 197
    7.1.1.1 Reputation 198
    7.1.1.2 Image Threats 198
    7.1.1.3 Ethics Codes 199
    7.1.1.4 Ethics Statements 200
    7.1.1.5 Philanthropy 201
  7.1.2 Persuasive Appeals 201
    7.1.2.1 Appeal to Source Credibility 202
      7.1.2.1.1 Integrity as a Heritage 202
      7.1.2.1.2 Membership in Ethics-Related Associations 203
    7.1.2.2 Appeal to Reason 203
      7.1.2.2.1 CEO Statements 204
      7.1.2.2.2 Honors, Awards and Magazine Rankings 205
      7.1.2.2.3 Concrete Examples 206
      7.1.2.2.4 External Monitoring and Auditing 207
      7.1.2.2.5 Alignment with Science 207
      7.1.2.2.6 Feedback Mechanisms 208
      7.1.2.2.7 Links to External Ethics Sites 209
    7.1.2.3 Appeal to Emotions 209
7.2 The Interpersonal Function across Cases 209
  7.2.1 Personal Address 210
  7.2.2 Viewpoint 211
  7.2.3 Stakeholders 211
7.3 The Textual Function across Cases 213
  7.3.1 Links on Home Page 213
  7.3.2 Menus 214
  7.3.3 Crosslinks 214

8 Conclusion 217

Bibliography 219

List of Tables

Table 1: Relevant Situations for Different Research Strategies 21
Table 2: *Fortune 500* Rankings of Case Companies in 2001 23
Table 3: Case Companies and Corporate-Ethics Paradigms 24
Table 4: Corpus Sizes.. 25
Table 5: Collocations with *Violation* 67
Table 6: Breakdown of References to BellSouth.. 71
Table 7: Breakdown of References to Lockheed Martin 86
Table 8: Breakdown of References to Ben & Jerry's.. 110
Table 9: Restaurant Growth at McDonald's from 1955 to 2001 120
Table 10: Breakdown of References to McDonald's 136
Table 11: Breakdown of References to Nike 167
Table 12: Breakdown of References to Levi Strauss & Co. 184
Table 13: Content across Cases 197
Table 14: Appeals to Reason across Cases 204
Table 15: The Interpersonal Function across Cases 210
Table 16: Stakeholders across Cases 211
Table 17: The Textual Function across Cases 213

List of Exhibits

Exhibit 1: Nike's Response to an Information Request 19
Exhibit 2: Reebok's Response to an Information Request................................. 19
Exhibit 3: Ben & Jerry's Statement of Mission.. 106

List of Figures

Figure 1: Societal Expectations and Business Conduct 52
Figure 2: Contents of Mission Statements 59
Figure 3: Cohesion among Lockheed Martin's Web Pages 94
Figure 4: Cohesion among Ben & Jerry's Web Pages 116
Figure 5: Anti-McDonald's Ads 125
Figure 6: Cohesion among McDonald's Web pages 145
Figure 7: Examples of the Swoosh 150
Figure 8: "Just do it" as a Punch Line 156
Figure 9: What Does Nike Pay its People? 157
Figure 10: Anti-Nike Logos 158
Figure 11: Cohesion among Nike's Web Pages 171
Figure 12: Cohesion among Levi Strauss & Co.'s Web Pages 193

1 Introduction

At the outset of the twenty-first century, corporate ethics in the United States is evolving into three separate paradigms that ethically concerned companies may adopt: Business ethics (BE), corporate social responsibility (CSR) and BE & CSR, a combination of the two. Companies involved in BE seek to ensure compliance with legal regulations and raise their ethical standards by institutionalizing ethics within their organizations, which has led to the development of corporate phenomena such as ethics officers, ethics committees and ethics training. Examples include companies that rely heavily on government contracts, which they would not be awarded if they were caught acting illegally. CSR, which draws on the notion that businesses have the responsibility to give something back to the community, encompasses activities such as corporate philanthropy and community involvement. Companies concerned with CSR attempt to project the image of a good corporate citizen. Companies in the BE paradigm also engage in corporate philanthropy but giving plays a rather insignificant role for these companies and thus their philanthropic activities are less visible in the media than those of CSR companies. Companies in the BE & CSR paradigm put more or less equal weight on BE and CSR. Examples include Nike and Levi Strauss & Co., which were forced to implement stringent sourcing guidelines within their supply chain when the media shed light on the poor labor standards of their foreign suppliers. The codes they have implemented are a clear manifestation of the BE paradigm. At the same time, they also belong to the CSR paradigm, as they publicly pride themselves on these efforts and present themselves as ethical players to the general public (Hoffman 2001; Altham 2001: 11).

The research approach of this study is based on Hoffman's (2001) distinction between the three corporate-ethics paradigms. This book explores how companies communicate their ethical stance on their Web sites by applying the linguistic method of discourse analysis to six case studies. The sample consists of two companies from each of the three paradigms. Chapter 2 focuses on the research approach before Chapter 3 discusses the BE and the CSR paradigms in more detail, but not the BE & CSR paradigm, as the latter is merely a combination of the former two. Chapters 4 to 6 contain the case studies of BellSouth, Lockheed Martin, Ben & Jerry's, McDonald's, Nike and Levi Strauss & Co. Ultimately, the cross-case analysis in Chapter 7 synthesizes the findings from the individual cases, identifying and discussing strategies the case companies use in communicating corporate ethics with regard to the research questions posed in Chapter 2.

2 Research Design

The research conducted in this book is based on the distinction between the business-ethics paradigm, the corporate-social-responsibility paradigm and the paradigm combining the two. Chapter 2 sets out to outline the research design of the study, including research questions, sample selection and data analysis.

2.1 Research Questions

There is consensus that corporate ethics statements are frequently used as PR tools in external corporate communication (cf. Baker 1993: 264; Bowie 1978: 235, Gaines 1994: 22, Seeger 1997: 192). However, the communicative strategies companies use to present themselves as ethically concerned companies with a view to enhancing their reputations or even positioning themselves as ethical players in business appears to be hitherto unexplored.

The relatively small incorporation of linguistics into business-communication research is surprising, given that the business community spends fortunes on language, e.g. in advertising, public relations, employee communication, customer relationship management, or internal reporting (Czerniawska 1997: 7). Stevens (1994: 68) also notes the minimal incorporation of linguistics into business-communication research. In particular, she points to business ethics as a field that requires more linguistic attention. In her review of ethical code studies, she concludes that

> "we need to spend more time evaluating corporate codes as messages. Most of the questions about how codes function as messages remain unanswered. ... We need to explore the more exegetic aspects of these texts and analyze their messages more rhetorically rather than relying so heavily on content analysis. ... We need to focus more intensely on the effectiveness of these messages and analyze how codes use language to express values and beliefs" (Stevens 1994: 68).

Farrell and Farrell (1998) did so in their study of the language of business codes of ethics. Their linguistic analysis revealed that the language used in most codes of conduct is not very reader-friendly, as it establishes a strong authoritarian tone through the overuse of passives, normalization and modality. Sanderson and Varner (1984) also examined the language of ethics codes and found the majority of codes to be written in legalese, containing "many long sentences, interrupted by phrases, relative clauses, and explanatory remarks" (Sanderson and Varner 1984: 31). Apart from their studies, the language of corporate ethics seems to be relatively uncharted territory. This research seeks to fill this gap by exploring how companies communicate their ethical stance by closely examining the linguistic idiosyncrasies of the messages companies convey. The unit of analysis is ethics-related messages on corporate Web sites (see Section 2.2). The primary objective of this research is to illuminate how ethics Web pages function as instruments of external corporate communication. The in-depth analysis conducted seeks to answer the following subsidiary research questions:

- What themes are addressed and what persuasive appeals are used in these messages?
- In what form do companies include their stakeholders in these messages?
- How are these messages organized?

2.2 Unit of Analysis: Corporate Web Sites

The plethora of print media and TV channels available across the globe makes it impossible to closely follow a company's ethical discourse at all levels. Instead of examining the entirety of media available, corporate Web sites were singled out as the unit of analysis in the underlying piece of research. Dunfee and Werhane (1997) gave the impetus to confine the analysis to corporate Web sites, asserting that

> "[m]ore and more companies are putting their codes of conduct on the World Wide Web. The Web is a new tool by which firms attempt to create reputations as responsible, caring firms" (Dunfee and Werhane 1997: 1592).

Accordingly, this book investigates how companies communicate their ethical stance on their Web sites.

Since the mid-1990s corporate Web sites have become "multimedia manifestations for corporate communication" (Goodman 1998: 1-2). This trend is readily understandable, given that the World Wide Web with its enormous reach is available around the clock to audiences spread around the globe. It provides unlimited space for masses of content in color, motion and audio. Additionally, the WWW is interactive, menu-driven and relatively inexpensive (Newsom, Turk, and Kruckeberg 1999: 399). Thus, Web sites offer clear advantages over printed company material in terms of space and availability, and they must be the most widely read company documents nowadays. What is more, they are frequently available in English, thereby fostering the hegemony of English as a global language.

Web sites seem to increasingly replace traditional forms of corporate communication such as company information kits, company brochures or leaflets. In April 2001, I sent an information request to Nike Inc. and asked for company brochures or similar material. As a reply, Nike sent me its annual report accompanied by a leaflet saying that additional company information is available on the company's Web sites at <http://www.nike.com> and <http://www.nikebiz.com>. Nike's original leaflet is shown in Exhibit 1. Reebok Inc. responded to the same request by sending its annual report along with a business card pointing out that further information about Reebok can be found on the company's Web site. Exhibit 2 displays the original reply from Reebok.

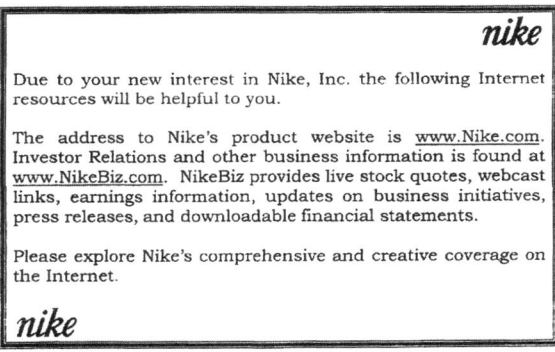

Exhibit 1: Nike's Response to an Information Request

Exhibit 2: Reebok's Response to an Information Request

The examples of Nike and Reebok suggest that the WWW has become *the* medium for corporate self-presentation, thereby superseding printed forms of external corporate communication, excluding however annual reports. Since reading from computer screens takes considerably longer than reading from paper, the content of a Web site cannot be simply duplicated from material that was formerly distributed on paper. Not only the visual design needs to be modified when publishing printed company material on the WWW, but also the writing style has to be optimized for online readers. Typically, users merely scan text on the screen, so bulleted lists, subheadings, and short paragraphs serve well to break text blocks into smaller sections. Also, long texts should be split up and published on several shorter pages (Nielsen 2000: 101; 103-104).

Another major difference between printed text and Web pages is that Internet users are forced to select the sequence of information, as the whole text is published on individual pages and users can only see one page at a time. Printed text, by contrast, is linear and does thus not require readers to choose the sequence of information (Van Berkel and de Jong 1999: 32; 37). Hence, reading nonlinear text on the WWW is a more complex activity than reading printed material, because users need to remember their location in the Web of pages and constantly need to decide which pages to see next. At the same time, they need to keep track of the pages they have already seen. Only a consistent design and navigational aids (e.g. menus) help users develop a mental image of how the Web site is organized and what information it contains. Only then can users understand the contents (Van Berkel and de Jong 1999: 29-30).

As Web sites and Web pages are central terms in the analysis to follow, their meanings need to be clarified beforehand. A Web site consists of one or more Web pages, i.e. individual documents written in hypertext markup language (HTML). Material merely made available for download, e.g. .pdf files, does thus not qualify as a Web page. The home page is the opening Web page of a Web site, i.e. the very first page visitors see when they enter the company's Web address in their browser interface.

2.3 Research Strategy: Case Studies

Research in a relatively new field is most insightful when conducted qualitatively in the form of case studies. Therefore, case studies are the research strategy chosen to answer the research questions posed. Yin (1984: 23) defines case studies as "an empirical inquiry that

- investigates a **contemporary** phenomenon within its real-life context; when

- the **boundaries** between **phenomenon** and **context** are not clearly evident; and in which
- **multiple** sources of evidence are used" (Yin 1984: 23; boldface added).

The main strengths of case studies are that they allow us to focus on specific situations and organizations and that they are able to integrate various forms of evidence, e.g. documents, interviews, observations and artifacts (Yin 1984: 20).

2.3.1 Justification for the Strategy Chosen

Research in the social sciences can be conducted in a variety of ways, including experiments, surveys, archival analyses, histories, and case studies. Table 1 juxtaposes these five research strategies to three questions regarding (1) the nature of the research questions, (2) the investigator's control over behavioral events, and (3) the time frame of the phenomena studied (contemporary vs. historical) (Yin 1984: 13).

	Research Question	Control Over Events	Contemporary Events
Experiment	how, why	yes	yes
Survey	who, what, how many	no	yes
Archival analysis	who, what, how many	no	yes/no
History	how, why	no	no
Case Study	how, why	no	yes

Table 1: Relevant Situations for Different Research Strategies
(Adapted from: Yin 1984: 17)

This juxtaposition aids in identifying the most suitable research strategy for a given research problem. The gray shadings in Table 1 relate to the research problem addressed, indicating that the answers in the table cells hold true for the underlying research problem. As Table 1 shows, case studies are the most appropriate research strategy for studies that address the questions "how" and "why", that do not require control over behavioral events, and that focus on contemporary events in a real-life context (Yin 1984: 13). Since all this applies to the phenomenon examined, the research problem addressed warrants the use of case studies. As for the use of case studies in the field of business ethics or corporate ethics, Brigley (1995: 219) points out that

> "the case-study approach is more appropriate to inquiries into the complex, diverse contents and contexts of business ethics. Investigatory case study in particular can do much to rectify the inadequacies of the prevailing positivist paradigm" (Brigley 1995: 219).

These strengths notwithstanding, the use of case studies as a research strategy has been met with criticism on two major grounds. One of the prejudices against case studies is that they lack rigor, because the findings are frequently biased and based on dubious evidence. This is, however, not a potential pitfall of case studies only. Biases may also influence the outcome of experiments or the conduct of surveys. Another concern uttered about case studies relates to the external validity of results. It has been argued that case studies provide too little a basis for generalizing results to theories (Yin 1984: 21). Brigley (1995: 225) argues that judgments of validity are strongly impacted by the research paradigm adopted. One may arrive at valid, reliable results through the study of cases, only positivists will never consider these results valid. Yin (1984: 21) asserts that there is no difference at all between experiments and case studies regarding the possibilities for generalization, and he goes on to conclude that case studies are in no way an inadequate research strategy.

To counter the criticism of limited generalizability, the use of multiple cases is a viable strategy (Brigley 1995: 223). The comparative analysis across multiple cases clearly enhances external validity, i.e. makes for more generalizable results. However, multiple cases need to be compared on a more abstract level to partly eliminate the individual peculiarities of each actor and each setting (Hubermann and Miles 1994: 435).

2.3.2 Sample Selection and Cross-Case Analysis

The rationale for the cases selected was that the companies chosen are in need of presenting themselves as ethical companies to divert attention away from potential points of attack. This piece of research studies and compares a total of six cases, which were selected purposively rather than randomly to ensure that the cases offer both typicality and variety, as suggested by Stake (1994: 243). Table 2 presents an overview of the six case companies and their *Fortune 500* ranks in the year 2001. Apart from Ben & Jerry's, which was taken over by Unilever in 2000, all companies are major players in their respective industries.

Case Subjects	Industry	Overall Rank	Industry Rank
BellSouth	Telecommunications	82	3
Lockheed Martin	Aerospace & Defense	77	3
Ben & Jerry's	Food	Not listed	Not listed
McDonald's	Food Services	139	1
Nike	Apparel	204	1
Levi Strauss & Co.	Apparel	383	3

Table 2: *Fortune 500* Rankings of Case Companies in 2001

The sample of the six case subjects includes two companies from each of the three corporate-ethics paradigms introduced in Chapter 1. Originally, the paradigms these companies belong to either emerged from research by Hoffman (2001) and Altham (2001) or was determined based on my own judgment. The intra-paradigm analyses (see Sections 4.3, 5.3 and 6.3) confirm that the companies actually belong to the paradigms they were assigned to initially.

To make for adequate intra-paradigm comparability, the two companies representing one paradigm face the same stigma, which emerges from the industry they belong to. A stigma is understood as a negative perception the public has of the industry. Both BellSouth (Case 1) and Lockheed Martin (Case 2) represent the business-ethics paradigm and are members of the *Ethics Officer Association* (EOA 2002b). They do not belong to the same industry, but they both do a substantial amount of business with U.S. government agencies. The challenge they face is that the business-to-government segment has often been under attack for unethical business practices, e.g. overcharges on government contracts or bribery to secure contracts. The close media scrutiny of these scandals is primarily due to the fact that these business deals are financed with taxpayers' money. Ben & Jerry's (Case 3) and McDonald's (Case 4) represent the corporate-social-responsibility paradigm and are both members of *Business for Social Responsibility*. Ben & Jerry's was even among the founding members (Business for Social Responsibility 2002c; 2002d;). Ben & Jerry's and McDonald's belong to the food and food-service industries, respectively, and produce and sell food that may endanger human health. The stigma attached to Cases 3 and 4 is thus food safety. Apparel companies Nike (Case 5) and Levi Strauss & Co. (Case 6), both also members of *Business for Social Responsibility* (Business for Social Responsibility 2002d), originate from an industry that is notorious for overseas sweatshop scandals. Driven by fierce competition, all major industry players have moved production to low-wage countries, where apparel and shoes are often produced under poor labor conditions. Table 3 gives the case companies, their respective paradigms, the ethics organizations they are a member of and the stigmas they face.

Case Subjects	Paradigm	Organization	Stigma
BellSouth	Business Ethics (BE)	EOA	Bribery and overcharges
Lockheed Martin		EOA	
Ben & Jerry's	Corporate Social Responsibility (CSR)	BSR	Food safety
McDonald's		BSR	
Nike	BE & CSR	BSR	Sweatshop labor
Levi Strauss & Co.		BSR	

Table 3: Case Companies and Corporate-Ethics Paradigms

After discussing each case and each paradigm separately, a cross-case analysis is conducted in Chapter 7 that synthesizes the findings from all six cases. For this inter-paradigm analysis, a variable-oriented strategy has been adopted, which seeks to identify "themes that cut across cases" (Hubermann and Miles 1994: 436). The inter-paradigm analysis thus focuses on similarities across paradigms rather than differences between them, leaving aside company-specific and industry-specific characteristics.

2.3.3 Data Collection and Structure of the Analysis

The sources used to research the companies' backgrounds include news reports, material provided by public interest groups and NGOs, and material furnished by the case companies. In view of the inherent bias in company information this triangulation of data is vitally important to gain multiple perspectives (Stake 1994: 241).

The prime sources for the analysis are ethics-related Web pages found on the Web sites of the case subjects. These pages form the corpora for the linguistic analysis. A corpus is defined as a collection of texts available in machine-readable format and "maximally representative of the language variety under consideration" (McEnry and Wilson 1996: 21; 24). The corpora thus include all Web pages of the company Web sites that focus on corporate ethics to a reasonably large extent. However, the corpora of BellSouth and Nike contain only a representative selection of their ethics-related Web pages in order to make for adequate comparability within the sample. Table 4 shows the number of ethics-related pages included in each corpus and the total number of words each corpus contains.

Case	Web Pages	Word Totals
BellSouth	17	5,745
Lockheed Martin	10	1,897
Ben & Jerry's	9	4,747
McDonald's	12	2,823
Nike	17	6,203
Levi Strauss & Co.	8	5,361

Table 4: Corpus Sizes

These Web pages were transformed into text files for computer-assisted analysis but kept as printouts as well to preserve the visual design. The linguistic analyses were facilitated by *WordSmith Tools,* a software for textual analysis. *WordSmith Tools* creates alphabetical word lists and word frequency lists, which can be adjusted for inflectional affixes of tense and number (i.e. plural forms and verb inflections) and derivational affixes (e.g. responsib-*le*, responsib-*ility*) to provide better results. Apart from this quantitative analysis, *WordSmith Tools* is also helpful in identifying collocations and displaying particular words in their co-text.

Each case analysis is divided into two sections, viz. *Background to the Company* and *Discourse Analysis*. The background includes a company profile and an account of ethical issues the company has been involved in that may have harmed its reputation. The discourse analyses are critical linguistic investigations of the text corpora, which also seek to establish links between the context and the discourse.

2.4 Method of Data Analysis: Discourse Analysis

The Web pages are analyzed by drawing on the linguistic method of discourse analysis. Discourse analysis focuses on "the use of language for communication in context" (Georgakopoulou and Dionysis 1997: viii). Fairclough and Wodak (1997) make the point that "[d]iscourse is not produced without context and cannot be understood without taking the context into consideration" (Fairclough and Wodak 1997: 276). In view of the importance of the context in which discourse occurs, discourse is considered a social activity. Discourse analysis therefore focuses not only on texts but also on the participants involved, the situations in which discourse occurs and the social structures that have an influence on how participants make meaning of the texts (Stillar 1998: 12).

Texts are a realization of discourse (Stillar 1998: 12). They always "exhibit some kind of unity or texture that enables them to be (socially) recognizable as a whole" (Stillar 1998: 11). As for Web pages, hyperlinks take on this function of uniting several individual pieces of text into one unit. Therefore, in the underlying analysis, all ethics-related pages are incorporated into one single corpus for each analysis. Stillar (1998) also points out that text

> "is a meaningful unit, an instantiation of meaning-making resources, including such 'material' resources as voice quality in spoken texts or font choice in written texts because these, too, are meaning-making resources" (Stillar 1998: 11).

For the underlying piece of research, this means that not only the texts on the Web pages but also visual elements, e.g. font face, font size and images, are included in the analysis, if they are meaning-carrying units.

Stillar's (1998) method of discourse analysis will be relied on in the research conducted. His functional approach to discourse analysis is largely based on the works of Fairclough (1989; 1992) and Halliday (1978; 1994). The sections below outline Stillar's (1998) approach to discourse analysis, which will be applied in the in-depth investigations in Chapters 4 to 6. The rationale for choosing Stillar's (1998) functional approach to discourse analysis is that "the object of analysis for a social and functional discourse analysis is language activity — actual texts occurring in real contexts" (Stillar 1998: 20), which is well-suited for the analysis conducted.

Stillar (1998: 20-21) uses Halliday and Hasan's (1976: 26) categorization of language into three functions, which are interdependent and exhibited by all message-carrying units in a text:

- The **ideational** function: "*Text is always about something*"
- The **interpersonal** function: "*Text is always to and from somebody*"
- The **textual** function: "*Text always exhibits structure and organization*"

In the underlying piece of research, the ideational function concerns the content of the Web pages. The interpersonal function concerns the companies whose Web sites are examined and their stakeholders, who need to be convinced of the company's sound ethics. With Web sites, the notion of text structure takes on a broader meaning, denoting not only the organization of the text within a Web page but also the embedding of individual pages within the whole Web site, which is realized through hyperlinks.

2.4.1 The Ideational Function

Language has the resources to construct content by construing experience. Ideational structures in texts thus represent "things, concepts, relations, and events and their circumstances" (Stillar 1998: 20). Stillar (1998) uses four categories to label these representations:

a) **Process type and participant roles:** This category represents events, relations, and the participants involved in the events and relations. The analysis of the process type is meant to reveal how language (i.e. the text) constructs experience and reality. Processes can be broken down into action processes (an agent performs an action), mental processes (a processor "mentalizes" a phenomenon, e.g. seeing, liking, understanding, saying), or relational processes (realized by linking verbs[1]). These events and processes are realized in clauses, nominal groups, or nouns (Stillar 1998: 22-23; 25).

b) **Circumstances:** Language resources are able to attach circumstantial function such as time, place, manner, purpose, reason, and role to processes and participants. These functions may be realized in the form of single words (e.g. adverbs), prepositional phrases, or dependent clauses (Stillar 1998: 26).

c) **Time and perspective:** In the English language, time and perspective are not exclusively constructed through grammatical tense and aspect, respectively. Present tense, for example, does not necessarily realize the present, but may also realize the future, which one only knows when looking at the whole sentence or the broader context. Similarly, to correctly interpret perspective, one needs to look at the context of the phrase. Circumstantial elements (see above) also help in shaping these temporal relations, but do not suffice. Rather, Stillar (1998) regards time and perspective as semantic relations that emerge from the "position of the text's point of writing" (Stillar 1998: 27).

d) **Concept taxonomies:** Ideational content and meaning is also created through the clustering and hierarchical arrangement of lexical items. Lexical items in a text are "content" words or phrases. Typically, they "cluster in different ways in text depending on their relationship to the situation of which the text is a part" (Stillar 1998: 27). Lexical items relate to concept taxonomies in that concepts

> "label the items realized by lexical items because in a particular instance of text, the significantly meaningful features of each lexical item are conditioned by the text and its context" (Stillar 1998: 28).

---

[1] E.g. *be, have, seem, appear, become,* etc.

Possibly, a set of lexical items denotes different concepts with different hierarchical arrangements in different texts and contexts. For example, the lexical items *high* and *low* may belong to a lot of different concepts and are likely to co-occur with different nouns in different texts and contexts (Stillar 1998: 28).

2.4.2 The Interpersonal Function

Interpersonal language resources are able to constitute identities and relationships among the participants in the discourse, as the addressers take on roles themselves and assign roles to their addressees. This way, language constructs **relational** meaning. In addition, language enables the addressers to express attitudes towards or evaluations of the addressees or the content of the discourse. Such messages convey **positional** meaning (Stillar 1998: 20; 32). Stillar (1998: 34) outlines four categories of interpersonal resources, all of which convey positional meaning, relational meaning, or both.

a) **Speech function:** The four categories of speech function are statements, questions, commands, and exclamations. They assign roles to the participants in the discourse (Stillar 1998: 34).

b) **Modality:** When modality refers to the functions of language resources that express the addresser's attitude toward the content of the text, they convey positional meaning (Stillar 1998: 35). When modality appears in language elements that construct "forms of interaction by assigning permission, obligation, and so on, to listeners and readers" (Stillar 1998: 35), they have relational meaning. These two forms of modality are also referred to as epistemic and deontic modality (cf. Greenbaum and Quirk 1990: 60). Fairclough (2001: 105) labels them expressive and relational. Modal verbs and modal adverbs in particular function to realize positional or relational meaning in texts (Stillar 1998: 35), but modality can also be conveyed in simple present tense form. A proposition in simple present tense expresses the "categorical commitment of the producer to the truth of the proposition" (Fairclough 2001: 107). Therefore, a proposition and its negation form two "categorical extremes", between which all propositions with modal verbs fall (Fairclough 2001: 107). For example, the proposition *They are the industry leader* and the negative proposition *They are not the industry leader* are the extremes of a spectrum that contains propositions like *They may/could/must be the industry leader*.

c) **Attitudinal lexis:** Attitudes are mainly expressed through adjectives, adverbs, linking verbs, reporting verbs, or verbs expressing possibility or probability (Stillar 1998: 36-38). Among the various subclasses of adjectives, only qualitative adjectives[2] (e.g. *good, bad*) and emphasizing adjectives (e.g. *absolute, perfect*) exhibit an interpersonal function, as they express the estimation of the writer/speaker, thus conveying positional meaning. Similarly, adverbs of degree (e.g. *absolutely, unbelievably*) and adverbs of manner perform an interpersonal function and construct positional meaning by expressing the writer's/speaker's evaluation (Stillar 1998: 36-37). In addition, linking verbs and reporting verbs perform an attitudinal function by constructing positional interpersonal meanings (Stillar 1998: 37). Linking verbs include, for example, *appear, look,* or *seem* and communicate subjective evaluations. Reporting verbs communicate the reasons for speaking/writing. They include *admit, dispute, plead, promise, refuse,* etc. (Stillar 1998: 37). Lastly, there are verbs which function similarly to modal verbs in that they express possibility, probability, or desirability, e.g. *think, believe,* or *suppose*. If these merely convey the writer's/speaker's assessment of a situation, they have positional value. If these verbs are used for reasons of politeness, they have relational value (Stillar 1998: 38).

d) **Sentence adjuncts:** Basically, sentence adjuncts come in the form of links, topics, attitudinals, and vocatives. Links (e.g. *furthermore, moreover*) perform a textual function, while topics (e.g. *technically, as for X, in terms of X*) perform an ideational function. Only attitudinals and vocatives perform an interpersonal function (Stillar 1998: 38-39). Attitudinals convey positional interpersonal meaning in that they express the addresser's attitude towards the content of the text. Examples include adjuncts like *interestingly, strikingly,* or *surprisingly* or adjuncts that express possibility, certainty, or probability, e.g. *maybe, certainly* or *possibly*. Vocatives, e.g. as in *This is for you, John*, may convey relational or positional meaning. They perform a relational function when they hail an addressee. Alternatively, vocatives may play a positional role, as the level of formality chosen conveys the addresser's attitude towards and opinion of the addressee (Stillar 1998: 39).

Fairclough (2001: 106) makes the point that the pronouns *we* and *you* also have relational values. *We* occurs either as exclusive *we*, including only the writers/speakers but not the audience, or as inclusive *we*, embracing the writer/speaker and the audience (Fairclough 2001: 106). The latter "retains the inclusionary warmth of implied 1st person involvement" (Greenbaum and Quirk

---

[2] Qualitative adjectives can be modified by words like *very* or *rather* and can be used in comparative or superlative structures (Stillar 1998: 36).

1990: 115). The pronoun *you* in mass-media communication is often not an audience address form but rather the addresser's attempt to express solidarity with an anonymous audience (Fairclough 2001: 106-107). In this case, *you* has generic reference, analogous to inclusive *we*, and could be replaced with *one* in a more formal context (Greenbaum and Quirk 1990: 115).

2.4.3 The Textual Function

Language resources are able to structure information, to put special emphasis on parts of a text, to create cohesion within the text and, ultimately, to link the text with its context (Stillar 1998: 21; 45). This ability to organize messages is referred to as the textual function. Messages need to be organized in order to realize the ideational function and the interpersonal function of texts. Stillar (1998: 46) introduces two categories of textual language resources: themes and cohesion.

Themes are devices capable of structuring the message at the sentence level. The theme of a sentence is, in most basic terms, what the sentence is about. In English, the sentence element that occurs in first position is the theme of the sentence. A declarative sentence in active voice "thematizes" the agent, whereas the same sentence in passive voice "thematizes" the "done to" (Stillar 1998. 46). As for questions, the *wh*-word in information questions or the auxiliary in yes/no questions are the themes of the sentences. Similarly, commands are "thematized" merely by the verb in first position. Multiple themes in a sentence are possible, but only if an adjunct (e.g. *However* or *Unfortunately*) occurs in first position. The theme then includes not only the adjunct but also the sentence element immediately after the adjunct. Textual analysis is, however, not concerned with the themes of isolated sentences. Rather, it focuses on the thematic development throughout the text to get an idea of how information is structured in the text (Stillar 1998: 47-48).

While themes are textual elements within a sentence, cohesion is a device used to relate sentences or parts thereof to other parts of the text, thereby giving the text some sort of unity (Stillar 1998: 46). This relation between elements in the text is established through presupposition. A presupposed element can only be correctly interpreted through the element that presupposes it. Thus, presupposition makes more of a text than just a collection of isolated words or sentences — it creates cohesion (Halliday and Hasan 1976: 4). Halliday and Hasan (1976: 6) distinguish between grammatical cohesion and lexical cohesion.

Lexical cohesion is created through reiterations (e.g. repetitions or synonyms) and collocations[3] (Halliday and Hasan 1976: 279) and is thus related to concept taxonomies (see above) (Stillar 1998: 51- 52). Grammatical cohesion occurs in the following forms:

- Cohesion through **reference** occurs when the writer/speaker uses personal pronouns, demonstrative pronouns or comparative words (e.g. *same*, *similar*, *other*) that refer to a referent specified earlier in the text (e.g. *John* ← *he*) (Halliday and Hasan 1976: 31; 76).
- With **substitution**, elements such as *one* may substitute for the word omitted (Halliday and Hasan 1976: 89).
- **Ellipsis** means that a word is omitted but "recoverable in previous text" (Stillar 1998: 49). It is thus a "substitution by zero" (Halliday and Hasan 1976: 143).
- **Conjunction** relates a sentence to previous text, either implicitly or through linking words (e.g. *and*, *furthermore*, *nevertheless*, *subsequently*, etc.) (Halliday and Hasan 1976: 227; 231; 233).

It is worth noting that a cohesive text is not necessarily one that makes sense. A text may well contain a sufficient number of cohesive links between sentences and still be meaningless. Also, a text may make only sense to people who share a certain background knowledge (e.g. assumptions, expectations, experiences), but may be meaningless to others who do not have this background knowledge. The ability to establish links between the text and "the world", i.e. to understand the meaning of a text, is referred to as coherence (Fairclough 2001: 65; Yule 1996: 141).

In the analysis to follow, the text corpora are too long to conduct an analysis at the sentence level. Thematic structure is therefore only discussed when it is particularly prominent. I look instead at cohesive devices such as menus and cross-reference hyperlinks, also called crosslinks. These are understood as hyperlinks embedded in a text block that point to other Web pages with related contents (Van Berkel and de Jong 1999: 35). This definition of crosslinks thus excludes menu items and links within pages (e.g. "Back to top"). Furthermore, visual consistency helps maintain cohesion among Web pages. Such visual cues include colors, text format, text headings and the continuous repetition of a menu frame (Van Berkel and de Jong 1999: 30; 34; 38).

---

[3] A collocation is a pair of words that tends to co-occur at greater-than-random chance in a certain language (Stillar 1998: 51).

When discussing text cohesion, the lack thereof merits discussion as well. Fairclough (2001) found lists in particular to reduce text cohesion. Lists are "reader-friendly" devices to structure texts and highlight important points. However, list items typically represent whole arguments without being further explained or discussed, thus lacking cohesion. By listing merely keywords, authors inevitably equalize the importance of the list items and may even conceal important differences between them. As the order of list items does not matter at all, removing one item does not change much. Only the "cumulative effect" these minimalist arguments bear is of importance. Still, lists can be effective means of persuasion and can enhance the acceptability of a message, e.g. by listing examples to support a claim (Fairclough 2001: 14-15; 28; 45; 53; 162).

2.4.4 Context

The three functions of language resources discussed in the above sections do not suffice to uncover the meaning of a certain text, as "text always occurs in a context that enables it to function ideationally, interpersonally, and textually" (Stillar 1998: 52). Context is thus not understood as the linguistic co-text of a certain text, but rather as the "physical context", i.e. the situational, nonlinguistic surroundings of a text (Yule 1996: 129; Halliday and Hasan 1976: 21). In the case studies to follow this nonlinguistic context is discussed in the sections titled *Background to the Company*.

Negative statements merit discussion as well in connection with context. Essentially, negations evoke corresponding positive assertion and contest them. Thus, speakers/writers who make negative statements are "implicitly taking issue with the corresponding positive assertions" (Fairclough 2001: 128). For example, a company claiming *We do not use child labor* implicitly contests the charge that its products are made with child labor and has probably even been accused of using child labor. Thus, negative forms must always be interpreted in terms of the underlying positive statement (Fairclough 2001: 127-128), although a negative proposition does not necessarily mean that the corresponding positive proposition really exists, but the positive form must at least be possible and the speaker/writer must have encountered the positive form somehow (Hodge and Kress 1993: 145).

3 Business Ethics vs. Corporate Social Responsibility

The business-ethics (BE) approach and the corporate-social responsibility (CSR) approach result in three different paradigms companies may belong to, viz. BE, CSR and BE & CSR. This chapter explores only the former two paradigms, as the BE & CSR paradigm is merely a combination of the former two. Before looking at the BE paradigm and the CSR paradigm in detail, the main differences between these two paradigms will be pointed out.

Altham (2001: 10) identifies four main differences between BE and CSR. First, they have divergent aspirations. While BE seeks to prevent harm, CSR tries to do good. Second, BE and CSR differ in their strategic directions. While BE is a rather reactive strategy, e.g. when ethics officers resolve existing problems, CSR takes a proactive approach, enhancing corporate reputation. CSR has proved effective as a marketing and positioning tool to enhance corporate reputation or defend reputation against public criticism and charges (Altham 2001: 10). The third major difference between the BE paradigm and CSR paradigm is the stakeholder groups they focus on (Altham 2001: 10). Basically, corporate stakeholders can be subdivided into stakeholders that are vital to the survival of the organization and stakeholders that affect the organization and are affected by it (Freeman and Reed 1983). BE is directed at the former group, which includes employees, customers, suppliers and shareholders. CSR, in turn, adheres to a broader definition of stakeholders and recognizes business' responsibility to the local communities and society as a whole. Thus, CSR is concerned with one big, heterogeneous stakeholder group — the public at large (Altham 2001: 10-11). This makes stakeholder management inherently difficult, as there is a multiplicity of interests that have to be taken into consideration (Izraeli and BarNir 1998: 1190). Ultimately, BE companies differ from CSR companies in that they are represented by different associations. Companies in the BE paradigm are typically members of the *Ethics Officer Association* (EOA), whereas CSR companies are members of *Business for Social Responsibility* (BSR). The two organizations do not cooperate in any way, as they serve different *clientèles* (Hoffman 2001).

3.1 Business Ethics: Preventing Harm

At its core, business ethics is intended to ensure compliance with legal regulations by implementing early-warning mechanisms within the organization. The corporate ethics program subsumes these early-warning mechanisms, which seek to identify compliance problems as early as possible or prevent them outright (Hoffman 2001; Altham 2001: 10). Ethics programs are part of every organization, either because they have been explicitly created or because they are inherent in the organizational culture. Broadly, an ethics program consists of values, policies and activities, all of which are either implicit or explicit components of the ethics program. Implicit parts encompass the organizational culture, management behavior, reward systems and performance appraisal systems. Explicit components, in turn, include ethics codes, policy manuals, employee orientation programs, employee training materials and ethics seminars. (Brenner 1992: 391; 393; 398). This section first looks at the motives and stimuli of the BE approach, then focuses on the implicit elements and lastly discusses the institutionalization of the explicit elements within the organization.

3.1.1 Motives and Stimuli

In the past decades, the media's attention to business ethics has increasingly made people aware of unethical business practices. To counter the pressure from the media and public-interest groups, businesses have begun to institutionalize ethics within their organizations (Morf, Schumacher, and Vitell 1999: 265). In the 1970s, incidents such as kickbacks and bribery in the defense industry and above all Watergate stimulated corporate and academic interest in business ethics (DeGeorge 1987: 202). The Foreign Corrupt Practices Act (FCPA) was enacted in 1977 to put a halt to questionable payments made by U.S. companies to foreign officials for the purpose of obtaining business. An investigation by the Securities and Exchange Commission in the mid-1970s had turned up the fact that bribery of foreign officials was common practice in corporate America and over 400 companies admitted to having bribed foreign officials. U.S. Congress then passed the FCPA "to restore public confidence in the integrity of the American business system" (U.S. Department of Justice 2002). Violating the FCPA can result in large fines for the company and a prison sentence for the employees involved. In addition, the company may be debarred from public tenders in the future. In view of these severe consequences, many U.S. companies operating internationally have implemented comprehensive compliance programs in order to prevent their employees from making such illegal payments to obtain business (U.S. Department of Justice 2002). In 1991 only, the United States Sentencing Commission enacted the U.S. Federal

Sentencing Guidelines to foster ethical business conduct. The Sentencing Guidelines stipulate that the fines for corporate illegal and unethical behavior be reduced, if the companies in question (1) have effective ethics programs in place, (2) report the crime on their own, (3) cooperate in the investigation and (4) accept responsibility for the act. For the fine to be reduced at all, merely one of the above aspects suffices. If, however, all of the above apply, the fine is reduced substantially. Also, the company's size and its prior criminal history play an important role in determining the fine (Hartman 1998: 317). The rationale behind the Sentencing Guidelines is that companies which commit themselves to ethical business conduct should not suffer the dear consequences of one employee's ethical lapse. The Federal Sentencing Guidelines thus motivate corporations to establish internal control mechanisms and design ethics programs to prevent and detect employee misconduct and to reduce the potential liability arising from the Guidelines (Morf, Schumacher, and Vitell 1999: 265; France 1996: 27; Kamen 1993: 10; Dunfee and Werhane 1997: 1591).

3.1.2 Creating an Ethical Climate

Instilling ethics in an organization requires a set of non-obvious mechanisms that foster an ethical climate and convey the idea that the company takes ethics seriously and does not just pay lip service to ethical conduct. These mechanisms include top management commitment to corporate ethics, an ethical organizational culture, disciplining violators of ethics standards and facilitating the reporting of ethical misconduct. The sections below will consider these in turn.

3.1.2.1 Top Management Commitment

Top management sets "the moral tone of an organization" (Carroll 1989: 124), as it is top management's actions and behavior that deliver messages about acceptable conduct to all employees. Therefore, the CEO and other high-ranking executives need to demonstrate ethical behavior and constantly "stress the importance of sound ethical principles and practices" (Carroll 1989: 124), as only

> "a chief executive officer who projects a strong ethical concern, who lets employees know what is expected as they do their work, and who personally puts these ethical attitudes into practice establishes a positive ethical tone throughout the entire company" (Frederick, Davis, and Post 1988: 68).

If the organizational culture reflects top management's values and actions, top managers serve as role models for all organizational members (Ferrell and Fraedrich 1997: 86), as all human beings are strongly influenced by the behavior of others (Jose and Thibodeaux 1999: 135). When launching a corporate ethics program, it is critical to its success that top management be involved in the institutionalization process (Steiner and Steiner 2000: 227). Izraeli and BarNir (1998: 1191) point out that institutionalization efforts carry a symbolic meaning to employees. If top management allocates resources to corporate ethics, employees perceive management to be committed to the ethical norms set forth in corporate ethics policies and are more likely to adhere to these ethical norms.

A survey conducted by Thomas and Simerly (1994: 964-965) suggests that the functional background of the CEO is a key determinant of the company's ethical culture. Their survey indicates that companies with outstanding social performance are led by CEOs with backgrounds in output functions (e.g. marketing), whereas companies with poor social performance are managed by CEOs with backgrounds in throughput functions, such as engineering.

3.1.2.2 Organizational Culture

The main factors shaping decision making in ethically ambiguous situations are not only an individual's values but also organizational culture. Organizational culture, or corporate culture, denotes the set of values, beliefs, norms, assumptions, practices, and goals that are shared by all members of an organization. Organizational culture is the glue that holds all members of the organization together and distinguishes them from other organizations, thereby conveying a sense of identity for them (Bromley 1993: 196; Ferrell and Fraedrich 1997: 100). Corporate cultures evolve over time and often cultures reflect the values of company founders ("Culturing change": 65). This is why corporate cultures often clash when companies merge (Murphy 1998: 4). The ethical climate is a component of corporate culture that forms the ethical conscience of the organization (Ferrell and Fraedrich 1997:101). An organization's ethical climate is said to have a stronger impact on employee behavior than formal ethics policies or codes (Murphy 1998: 1). However, the values on which corporate cultures are based are not necessarily morally right. Corporate cultures might thus conflict with employees' personal value systems. For example, if corporate cultures support unethical conduct, new employees whose personal values conflict with such a corporate culture will find it hard to become integrated unless they are willing to act unethically as well. Similarly, the integration of new hires with questionable ethics into a strong ethical culture may prove difficult as well (Ferrell and Fraedrich 1997: 100).

3.1.2.3 Reward and Discipline Systems

Since individuals tend to repeat behavior that is rewarded, organizations should make sure they have implemented reward systems that honor ethical behavior and avoid rewarding unethical behavior. Likewise, they should seek to penalize unethical behavior and avoid punishing ethical behavior (Sims 1991: 504; Navran 1997:121). Organizational reward systems must not honor good results that were achieved by questionable means, as other employees will act in a like manner as soon as they have learned "the real organizational rules". A well-executed reward system contributes to the achievement of the organization's ethical goals (Hill, Metzger, and Dalton 1992: n.p.).

It is imperative that companies respond forcefully to employee misconduct, irrespective of the hierarchical level the employee is at (Carroll 1989: 133). Companies need to have procedures for disciplining employees who have violated the companies' ethics policies. Standard forms of employee discipline include counseling, the issue of warnings, suspension without pay, demotion and dismissal. Clearly, the nature and extent of the misconduct determine the discipline, so that decisions on disciplines have to be taken on a case-by-case basis (The Defense Industry Initiative 2000: 42-43). If the misconduct is not only unethical but also criminal, companies should cooperate with law enforcement authorities. Covering up the issue could backfire severely if it is uncovered and exposed in the news media (Carroll 1989: 133).

3.1.2.4 Internal Reporting Mechanisms

Employees often do not know how to react when they observe unethical acts. Therefore, companies provide whistle-blowing mechanisms, so that employees know how to report such incidents without having to fear retaliation (Carroll 1989: 133-134). Steiner and Steiner (2000: 228) report a general unwillingness among employees to blow the whistle, as they distrust the anonymity of reporting mechanisms and fear retaliation. Especially if the allegations are proven wrong, the person reporting the ethical misconduct is in trouble and often forced to leave the company. But even it the allegations are correct, the person reporting may suffer from retaliatory measures taken by the wrongdoer, e.g. holding the whistle blower back from promotion or pay increases. Sadly, ethical misconduct is often not reported at all in order not to jeopardize one's career prospects. Whenever an ethical violation is suspected, it is crucial to have an objective hearing process and to protect the person reporting. Ideally, the company code of ethics also includes specifications about reporting suspected misconduct (Brooks 1989: 124).

3.1.3 The Institutionalization of Corporate Ethics

Institutionalization within an organization occurs if a particular behavior displayed by two or more individuals over time becomes "a part of the daily functioning of the organization" (Sims 1991: 494). The institutionalization of ethics refers to the process of building ethics into the organizational structure. Fundamental to the institutionalization process is the psychological contract between employer and employees. Every employee who joins an organization enters into this psychological contract with the organization. This contract is made up of explicit or implicit reciprocal expectations between the organization and its employees, based on the exchange of contributions from both parties, with the employer contributing inducements to compensate employees for commitment to the organization. Employee commitment refers to their identification with the organization. This commitment stems from the employees' belief in the organization's mission and values, their willingness to make an effort to achieve the organization's goals, and their desire to stay with the organization. Employee commitment and organizational culture are mutually reinforcing, which means that high levels of employee commitment result in a strong organizational culture and vice versa. It is certainly possible that the expectations the employer and the employees have about each other's contributions do not perfectly match, in which case the contract is violated. This would be the case if an ethically committed organization detects employee misconduct or, vice versa, a morally upright employee discovers that the organization encourages unethical behavior. If, however, employees' and employer's ethical expectations under the psychological contract match, this will lead to greater institutionalization of ethics within the organization (Sims 1991: 495-499). To this end, Sims (1991: 503-504) recommends ethical screening in the employment process to avoid hiring people with questionable personal ethics, which prevents a mismatch of the expectations underlying the psychological contract.

To shape and enhance organizational culture in a manner that makes it conducive to ethical behavior within the organization, businesses have adapted their organizational structures by integrating a variety of internal control and counseling mechanisms (Morf, Schumacher and Vitell 1999: 265). The following sections discuss seven such mechanisms.

3.1.3.1 Ethics Codes

The cornerstone of every ethics program is an ethics code. In general, no distinction is made between codes of ethics, ethics codes, ethical codes, and codes of conduct. Milton-Smith (1999: 23), however, argues for a distinction between codes of ethics and codes of conduct. His admittedly obscure point is still worth quoting in full:

> "Whereas a code of ethics will generally express the values that the organization aspires to uphold, the code of conduct outlines the behaviour needed to practise them in a particular context" (Milton-Smith 1999: 23).

This distinction is not widely supported and will thus not be relied on. Broadly, codes of ethics/conduct are defined as

> "a statement setting down corporate principles, ethics, rules of conduct, codes of practice or company philosophy concerning responsibility to employees, shareholders, consumers, the environment or any other aspects of society external to the company" (Langlois and Schlegelmilch 1990: 522).

Setting the company's ethical expectations, codes usually define not only the limits of acceptable conduct, but also the consequences of misconduct by employees (Navran 1997: 120; Redeker 1990: 83) to discourage unethical employee behavior and possibly prevent regulatory legislation (Carroll 1989: 129). Ethics codes may be released by industry associations, professional bodies, or individual corporations (Smith 1995: 91). Broadly, ethics codes serve five main purposes:

> (1) "to explain the company's philosophy of ethics,
> (2) to provide information on legal and ethical issues,
> (3) to provide guidance for complex ethical issues,
> (4) to provide a set of enforceable rules, and
> (5) to serve as a public relations statement on company ethics"
>   (Sanderson and Varner 1984: 29).

Sanderson and Varner's (1984) last point has also been repeatedly stressed in the literature. Many times ethics codes have been considered PR documents and mere exercises in public relations (cf. Baker 1993: 264, Bowie 1978: 235; Sanderson and Varner 1984: 29; Murphy 1998: 5; Munro 1997: 97), as well as "window dressing" (Bowie 1978: 235; Kamen 1993: 10; Shaw 1991: 174), or "an image thing" (Kamen 1993: 10). This point has already been raised in Chapter 2, when outlining the problem statement of the research conducted.

3.1.3.1.1 The History of Ethics Codes

Corporate ethics codes are not a phenomenon of the past decades but emerged more than a century ago. Benson (1982: 42) describes their development in three stages. Initially, around 1900, codes were merely brief statements spelling out general business ideals. Later, in the early 1950s, they were modified as to also make reference to antitrust laws. In the 1980s, ethics statements became detailed policies covering numerous areas of concern (Benson 1982: 42), not least because both the Watergate scandal in 1975 and the enactment of the Foreign Corrupt Practices Act in 1977 had spurred the growth of corporate ethical codes (Stevens 1994: 63). A fourth stage might be added to Benson's (1982: 42) classification of 1982, as ethics codes have, in the meantime, not only become *de rigueur* but are also increasingly used as a vehicle in external corporate communication (see above). It is worth noting that codes have always been more widely used in the U.S. than in Europe (Langlois and Schlegelmilch 1990). A 1979 survey among Fortune 100 companies revealed that only about 75% of them had ethics codes then (White and Montgomery 1980 quoted in Sims 1991: 494). But there is consensus that virtually all major corporations have ethics codes in place today (Carroll 1989: 129). At some point, companies realized that codes of ethics were not a panacea for preventing ethical misconduct (Stevens 1999: 113). Rather, the implementation of an ethics code is only the first step towards instilling ethics in the organization. To create an ethical organization, the values contained in the code must permeate the whole organization (McDonald 2000: 174). This may be achieved by a series of complementary institutionalization mechanisms, which are discussed in later sections of this chapter.

3.1.3.1.2 Characteristics of Effective Ethics Codes

Redeker (1990: 83-84) identifies four main characteristics of ethics codes, including notice, discretion, risk and tone. Notice means that codes provide general notice to all organizational members, making them aware of the organization's expectations as to ethical standards. It stands to reason that the quality of the notice rises with the level of detail the code bears. Similarly, the level of detail obviously determines the amount of discretion for interpreting and applying the code. The risk involved for the employees also depends on the level of detail, as detailed rules reduce the employee's risk of unconsciously violating the code. Lastly, the language of the code strongly impacts the message sent. A message conveyed in the form of guidelines and directions is likely to be better received than a message containing prohibitions (Redeker 1990: 83-84). Sanderson and Varner (1984: 30) suggest structuring codes as follows. First, there should be a section on why the company needs a code at all, why the company commits itself to ethical business conduct, and how the company intends to punish misconduct. The main part should contain enforceable rules regarding topical areas such as general decision guidelines, company objectives, and business principles. Lastly, codes should contain a section on interpretations to facilitate enforcement (Sanderson and Varner 1984: 30). Numerous inherent weaknesses have made many critics question the effectiveness of codes of ethics. In the following, a taxonomy of critical issues is offered.

Employee Involvement at All Levels
There is an inherent conflict of interest associated with codes of ethics, if they are developed by those to be primarily regulated, viz. upper management (Dienhart and Curnutt 1998: 327). Therefore, employees from various hierarchical levels of the organization should be involved in the formulation of the code (Post, Lawrence, and Weber 1999: 135).

Revisions
Once created, codes should be regularly reviewed and updated. They must not be cast in stone, but adapted to a changing business environment (Milton-Smith 1999: 23; Murphy 1998: 8). Newly emerged ethical issues such as the authorized use of software or e-mail policies should be included in the codes as well (The Defense Industry Initiative 2000: 2).

Clear Language
Effective ethics codes do not simply contain "platitudes about honesty, integrity, respect, teamwork, and fairness" (Steiner and Steiner 2000: 227), but give guidance in case of ethical conflicts employees might encounter at work. The practical value of an ethics code is clearly limited if it contains only "meaningless language" and "semantically foggy *clichés*" (Baker 1993: 279-280) only. If used at all, abstract moral terms should be clearly defined to avoid ambiguity (Dienhart and Curnutt 1998: 327). Care is to be taken when "translating the non-linguistic areas of an organization" (Czerniawska 1997: 186), i.e. values, into language, as this might result in a mismatch of words and deeds.

Rewards and Penalties
Effective codes state rewards for compliance to encourage ethical behavior and point out penalties for code violations to discourage misconduct (Steiner and Steiner 2000: 228-229). Compliant behavior should be taken into account in the

corporate reward structure, as far too often managers are not motivated to take decisions in compliance with the corporation's code, since compliant behavior might harm financial results (Sethi 2000: 487). Sanctions for code violations might, for example, include discontinuing business with suppliers that offer kickbacks, dismissing employees who accept bribes, or discharging employees who download pornographic material from the Internet (Steiner and Steiner 2000: 228-229). Codes that do not include sanctions are in danger of being only weakly enforced, if at all. The danger inherent in weak enforcement is that especially companies that claim to uphold lily-white moral standards appear all the more hypocritical, if the media discover non-compliance with these high moral standards. The ensuing unfavorable media coverage inevitably jeopardizes corporate reputation (Murphy 1998: 5; Kamen 1993: 10).

Cross-Cultural Flexibility

Companies operating in various countries around the globe must acknowledge local values and adapt certain elements of their ethics programs — including their ethics codes — to other cultural settings (Cohen and Nelson 1994: 148; 152-153). Companies claiming to uphold the same set of values in all their operations around the globe appear extremely incredible (Howard 1998: 173). Examples of cultural flexibility include the issue of equal employment opportunities for men and women, which is perceived differently in Western countries and Islamic countries. Likewise, gift giving is a customary practice in most Asian countries, but a matter of moral concern for Western companies doing business in Asia (McDonald 2000: 174).

Adequate Communication

Ethics codes should be communicated to all internal and external stakeholders of the organization. Communication vehicles such as pamphlets, booklets, company newsletters, or the World Wide Web are used to communicate ethics codes to all employees. Particularly in multinational corporations ethics codes should also be available in multiple languages (Murphy 1998: 5-7).

Specificity

Ethics codes have been criticized for being too general in nature and thus unhelpful, as they do not pertain to the particular settings of the industry, let alone the company. Also, codes tend to consist of codified rules based on federal law, so that they are bound to fail when it comes to giving guidance on ethical problems. Clearly, they can never allow for all ethical problems that employees may encounter on the job, but every effort should be made to make the code's provisions as specific as possible (Murphy 1998: 5; Sethi 2000: 487; France

1996: 27). In addition, codes typically address all employees, without distinguishing among executives, clerical workers and manual workers. The latter two are unlikely to be involved in bribery, insider trading or antitrust acts, as they make less far-reaching decisions on their jobs. Rather, unethical acts of lower-level employees include protracted absenteeism, non-compliance with quality standards, lying, or passing a colleague's idea off as their own. Therefore, it seems that typical codes address managers only (Greengard 1997b: n.p.; Sanderson and Varner 1984: 30). Customized codes targeted at different departments or hierarchical levels might help. Similarly, different codes for different types of business partners will prove helpful, e.g. a supplemental code covering business deals with the federal government (The Defense Industry Initiative 2000: 12).

Uniqueness
Companies may find it tempting to simply copy another organization's ethics code, but the code's uniqueness and its reflection of the organizational culture are key to being accepted by employees (McDonald 2000: 172-173). In reality, however, corporate codes are anything but unique. It seems that any code can be "easily transposed to any of its competitors ... in any other field and have just as much applicability" (Howard 1998: 92).

3.1.3.2 Ethics Ombudspersons

The role of ethics ombudspersons is to handle ethics complaints confidentially and to resolve ethical problems within the organization. Ombudspersons are neutral parties rather than agents of the organization. Their key function is to give advice and they become active only when they are called upon (Dunfee and Werhane 1997: 1591). Employees who are reluctant to discuss delicate issues with their supervisors might be willing to refer to ombudspersons instead (Post, Lawrence, and Weber 1999: 136). In practice, this function is rare and often fulfilled by ethics committees, ethics officers or ethics hotlines instead.

3.1.3.3 Ethics Committees

Another mechanism is the establishment of standing ethics committees, ideally composed of both board members and lower-ranking employees with rotating committee membership (McDonald 2000: 182). The appointment of an ethics committee signals to all internal and external stakeholders that the company takes ethics seriously. Ethics committees instill ethics in top management, which are typically concerned with company-policy setting and may need to be made aware of ethical matters (Frederick, Davis and Post 1988: 70; Sims 1991: 494). The ethics committee is called upon to investigate grievances and code violations, to punish wrongdoers, or to review and update the code if and when the need arises (Shaw 1991: 174). The committee may also issue newsletters on its decisions to illustrate its interpretations of the ethics code in ethically gray areas (Sims 1991: 504). If a company has not undertaken any prior ethics initiatives, the ethics committee may act as an initial task force that establishes the organizational infrastructure necessary to manage ethics within the organization (Navran 1997: 120).

3.1.3.4 Ethics Officers

A more recent phenomenon in the field of corporate ethics is the appointment of ethics officers (EO). The position of ethics officers was virtually non-existent on the organizational chart until the mid-1980s, but gradually became more common, and by 1996 over a third of U.S. corporations had ethics officers (Post, Lawrence and Weber 1999: 136). This increase is also reflected in the membership figures of the *Ethics Officer Association* (EOA), which was founded in 1991 only and has more than 800 corporate members as of 2002 (EOA 2002a). Despite this large number of ethics officers, a 1999 survey of ethics officers by Morf, Schumacher and Vitell (1999: 265; 270) revealed that there was no formal training for ethics officers yet. A survey of *Fortune 1000* service and industrial firms in 1999 showed that ethics-officer responsibilities were most frequently assigned to members of legal departments. Separate ethics offices proved to be less common. A minority of companies had these responsibilities assigned to departments like internal auditing, human resources, and general administration. To boot, the majority of these companies had ethics responsibilities shared between two or more employees (Weaver, Treviño and Cochran 1999: 288). Ethics officers are primarily concerned with

- "creating and maintaining a company's guiding values, principles, and business practices",
- "investigating alleged violations of the law",
- "evaluating the company's adherence to its formal ethics code" and
- "advising top management as to various moral and ethical issues" (Morf, Schumacher and Vitell 1999: 265).

Izraeli and BarNir (1998: 1191-1192) have identified five necessary requirements for effective ethics officers. First, an effective ethics officer must have acquired insider status by the time he becomes appointed, which means that he must have become a member of the organization well before his appointment. Having been an organizational member for some time enhances the EO's credibility. At the same time, the EO's status in the organizational hierarchy must enable him to have easy access to top management, which gives him an image of authority. The second important condition is independence and autonomy. Only an ethics officer who is independent of senior executives and free of any pressure is able to promote corporate ethics. In addition, the ethics officer must act professionally at all times. Only then will employees respect him and provide him with essential information. Also, to effectively deal with problems, the EO must also be familiar with organizational issues such as corporate culture and social norms within the organization. Ultimately, an effective EO must have some background knowledge of ethics theory and experience in dealing with ethical dilemmas (Izraeli and BarNir 1998: 1191-1192). McDonald (2000: 182) rightly notes that confidentiality is vital when dealing with delicate issues such as corporate ethics, so ethics officers must also be trustworthy, morally upright individuals (McDonald 2000: 182).

3.1.3.5 Ethics Hotlines

Many companies have established anonymous in-house reporting and advice systems, e.g. telephone or e-mail systems, in order to foster communication among employees and the ethics office. Employees who encounter ethically ambiguous situations and feel incapable of dealing with them by themselves may anonymously call or e-mail the ethics hotline to discuss these dilemmas or ask questions about their own decisions. Employees are more likely to resolve such dilemmas in a manner compliant with company policy if they receive sufficient support. The downside of such open communication channels is, however, that employees might shift responsibilities for business decisions in ethically ambiguous situations on to the hotline. Employees can turn to ethics hotlines not only to obtain assistance and advice but also to report suspected ethical misconduct, which the ethics office will then investigate (McDonald 2000: 183). However, Weaver, Treviño and Cochran (1999: 290) have found call rates on ethics hotlines to be very low.

3.1.3.6 Ethics Training Programs

Ethics training is a formal program designed (1) to familiarize employees with company policy on ethical issues (Frederick, Davis, and Post 1988: 71), (2) to make them aware of the ethical implications of their day-to-day decisions (McDonald 2000: 175) and (3) to provide them with the ability to apply ethical analysis to the dilemmas they may encounter at work (Delaney and Sockell 1992: 721). Companies that include ethics-training programs in their personnel development programs send a clear message to their employees that top management is fully committed to ethical behavior, even if that means forgoing business opportunities. It is pivotal to the success of all ethics training that such programs be voluntarily established. If companies conduct ethics training merely to abide by legal requirements, e.g. the 1991 U.S. Federal Sentencing Guidelines (see Section 3.1.1), the training program is probably carried out with little dedication and therefore unlikely to encourage ethical decision-making among employees (Delaney and Sockell 1992: 725).

In their 1992 study on ethics training programs, Delaney and Sockell (1992) found that only few companies actually conducted such programs. The reluctance to institutionalize ethics training can be put down not only to the high costs of the programs but above all to the costs of ethical behavior, which is often more expensive for the company than unethical behavior (Delaney and Sockell 1992: 726). Their study also revealed that ethics training had a positive effect on employee's assessment of moral behavior. Employees exposed to ethics training were more likely not to take unethical actions when confronted with a serious ethical dilemma than were employees who had not received any ethics training (Delaney and Sockell 1992: 725).

In general, however, there is no consensus whether ethics training actually succeeds in impacting on ethics awareness and moral reasoning. McDonald and Donleavy (1995: 840-841) cite a great many studies that have been conducted on the effectiveness of ethics courses, some of which found that ethical training had no significant effect on individuals and some of which suggest the contrary. An argument put forward to explain why ethics training is ineffectual is that participants' ethical attitudes have developed over time as a result of their cultural backgrounds and religious upbringings and can thus not be easily changed (McDonald and Donleavy 1995: 841). Conversely, others argue against such static personal values, claiming that attitudes and values are constantly in a state of flux as a result of "emotional, behavioural or cognitive interventions" (McDonald and Donleavy 1995: 844).

Effective means of teaching ethics emphasize on-the-job problems rather than far-fetched scenarios. Teaching methods should enable participants to consider the viewpoints of all stakeholders involved in the ethical issue and should make participants aware of the effects of their actions on others. This helps participants to gain a broader perspective of the issue, which fosters their awareness of ethical dilemmas they may encounter (McDonald 2000: 178; Sims 1991: 504). Typical vehicles and methods used for ethics training include:

- Watching and discussing commercially available video tapes in the field of business ethics (McDonald 2000: 177),
- acting out ethical dilemmas in the form of role plays (McDonald 2000: 177),
- discussing case studies based on events that have actually happened in the company (Frederick, Davis, and Post 1988: 71),
- playing ethics-related board games (The Defense Industry Initiative 2000: 24), and
- computer-based training modules using the Internet, Intranets or CD-ROMs (The Defense Industry Initiative 2000: 24).

Attention should not only be paid to the selection of adequate training methods and content but also to the selection of appropriate trainers. Ethics training has proved more effective if done by in-house managers rather than outside trainers, as the former lend the training program more authenticity (Steiner and Steiner 2000: 228). If corporate managers are used as trainers, it is vital that they attend train-the-trainer sessions beforehand (McDonald 2000: 177).

Finally, there are a number of dangers inherent in teaching ethics that trainers need to consider in order to enhance the learning process. First, trainers must make sure at all times that they do not indoctrinate or impose their own values on their trainees. Trainees should merely be made aware of how the company intends to deal with certain ethical issues rather than be brainwashed (McDonald and Donleavy 1995: 846). Moreover, trainers should constantly point out that ethical dilemmas do typically not have a black or white solution (McDonald 2000: 178), although this may make the goals of the training program appear ambiguous (McDonald and Donleavy 1995: 845). Lastly, trainers should also discuss practical issues, e.g. how to obtain guidance and assistance when in doubt or how the company sanctions ethical lapses (McDonald 2000: 178).

3.1.3.7 Ethics Audits

Companies institute ethics audits as a way to assess the ethical gap between the ethics polices and the company's daily performance. If the audit uncovers deviations of actual performance from the company's ethical aspirations, strategies can be adopted to close this gap by preventing opportunities for unethical behavior (Frederick, Davies, and Post 1988: 71; Gray 1996: 188). In the course of these audits employees are asked critical questions on their perception of corporate values and on whether these conflict with their personal values (Hill, Metzger and Dalton 1992: n.p.). Ideally, the auditors initiate an open dialogue with employees and their discussions focus on specific examples of corporate life (Gray 1996: 188). Hill, Metzger and Dalton (1992) idealize the outcome of an ethics audit as follows:

> "A well-executed ethics audit could yield significant returns in greater goal alignment, improved corporate performance and employee morale, and reduced exposure to the kind of incidents that damage companies' reputations and saddle them with substantial exposure to legal liability" (Hill, Metzger and Dalton 1992: n.p.).

Since the outcome of an ethics audit is largely dependent on employees' willingness to talk honestly about their personal ethics on the job, it is doubtful whether the results of an audit are valid and whether they mirror the state of ethics in the organization.

3.1.3.8 Recent Trends in Ethics Programs

Recently observed trends and newly developed techniques in the field of business ethics include the following (The Defense Industry Initiative 2000: 1):

- There is a tendency to replace the name ethics "hotline" with "helpline" to stress that employees may turn to these hotlines primarily to obtain help and guidance.
- Increasingly, companies reward employees with ethics awards and prizes in recognition of their ethical achievements.
- In their efforts to ensure ethical business conduct along the supply chain, businesses have begun to establish supplier-outreach programs to help their suppliers implement ethics program.
- Companies offer more and more Web-based training modules on either the Internet or the corporate Intranet.

3.2 Corporate Social Responsibility: Doing Good

The relationship between business and the community is twofold. For one, business is capable of making significant contributions to the community, be it in the form of employee volunteerism or be it simply monetary support of education, culture or welfare programs. On the other side of the coin, business is potentially harmful to the community, e.g. through air and water pollution, plant closings, consumer deception or employee exploitation (Carroll 1989: 299). Corporate social responsibility (CSR) draws on this two-way relationship between business and society, claiming that business has "responsibilities to society that go beyond the production of goods and services at a profit" (Buchholz and Rosenthal 1998: 5). Implied in this definition is an obligation of companies "to participate in a positive social way in the community ... in which they live and work beyond simply making a profit" (Garbett 1988: 113-114). In this context, community is not necessarily confined to the local community, i.e. the town or city in which the company resides. Owing to modern communication technology and rapid transport systems the relevant community may refer to a whole region, a nation or even the entire world (Garbett 1988: 114).

Proponents of CSR argue that CSR is in the self-interest of companies, as it enhances the quality of life, which the whole society benefits from. Also, socially responsible behavior may anticipate regulations, as there would be no need for stringent government regulation, if all companies voluntarily acted responsibly, (Starling 1995: 506). CSR has one clear advantage for companies that is hard to overlook — it benefits the bottom line, since a socially responsible company is attractive to consumers (Starling 1995: 506). This is what Fombrun (1996: 70) calls the *responsibility principle*, which holds that the more socially concerned a company appears to its audience, the better its reputation will be and the greater the company's financial success will be (Fombrun 1996: 70).

Despite its positive effects, corporate social responsibility has been met with harsh criticism from economists. They argue that CSR is economically inefficient and expensive for companies, thereby weakening their competitive positions. According to economist Milton Friedman (1970), the money companies allocate to CSR activities, be it because required by law or be it voluntarily, belongs to the company's owners, i.e. its shareholders. It could be reinvested or distributed among the shareholders instead of being spent on social causes. Giving it away is thus an undue tax on shareholders. It should be up to them whether this money is spent on giving to the community, e.g. philanthropy, or whether it is distributed among shareholders (Friedman 1970: 12; Starling 1995: 505-506).

3.2.1 Historical Framework Since 1900

When business faced mounting criticism and distrust from the general public around the turn of the twentieth century, businesses began to use their power and their money to give something back to society, as business leaders started to recognize that business had a responsibility to society (Post, Lawrence and Weber 1999: 59). This notion is based on two fundamental ethical principles: (1) the stewardship principle and (2) the charity principle. The stewardship principle requires business leaders to do good to society and in particular to those in need. This obligation arises from the fact that businesses exercise enormous control over society's resources and this influence makes business leaders stewards of society. This stewardship principle has evolved into the modern stakeholder theory (cf. Freeman and Reed 1983). The second fundamental principle is the charity principle, according to which wealthier members of society — not necessarily businessmen — should give to the needy. This idea was taken up by businessmen and has evolved into the modern concept of corporate philanthropy (Post, Lawrence and Weber 1999: 60-62).

In the early 1900s contemporary concepts of public welfare, e.g. Social Security, Medicare or unemployment pay, had not been legally established yet. At that time, wealthy business leaders started to donate enormous amounts of money to support the poor, to fund educational institutions or to endow public libraries (Post, Lawrence and Weber 1999: 60). A case in point is steelmaker Andrew Carnegie, who was a pioneer philanthropist, founding his first charitable foundation in 1901 and established many other foundations thereafter. On the whole, Andrew Carnegie funded more than 2,500 libraries. At this time his ideas of charitable foundations were rather uncommon, which makes him a pioneer in the field of corporate philanthropy (Wulfson 2001: 135; DeLong 2001). But other entrepreneurs followed suit. Other prominent foundations of the first half of the twentieth century include the *J.D. Rockefeller Foundation*, established in 1913 by tycoon John D. Rockefeller (Wulfson 2001: 136) and automaker Henry Ford's *Ford Foundation*, established in 1936 (Iacocca 2001). Ford also set up programs to support the well-being of his employees by attending to their recreational and health needs (Post, Lawrence and Weber 1999: 59). Henry Ford strongly believed that business should give something back to community, as is evident from his famous statement "A business that makes nothing but money is a poor kind of business". Both Henry Ford and John Rockefeller were business leaders that deeply believed in the social responsibility of business and strove to live up to this ideal (Wulfson 2001: 136).

Corporate social responsibility (CSR) is a concept that emerged in the 1950s only, when business schools and business leaders became recognizant of the power and influence business had on people and their environment (Buchholz and Rosenthal 1998: 8). Until the 1950s most Americans trusted and respected corporate America, as it provided jobs as well as goods and services. The postwar era was characterized by a rising number of families, a booming housing industry, and a thriving car industry, all of which helped the economy prosper (Gray 1986: 18). However, during the 1950s the image of big business suffered when the American people became distrustful, skeptical, and cynical of the business community as a result of various scandals that tarnished the image of many big companies. A case in point is the defense industry, where manufacturers charged exorbitant prices on government contracts, which was at least in part responsible for the huge government deficit then. A second example of that time is executive pay, which hit new heights, while blue-collar workers had to put up with pay cuts (Gray 1986: 20).

The 1960s were marked by student protests and revolts against authority and the military-industrial establishment. A strong anti-business attitude developed especially among the younger population. The growth of high-tech industries gave rise to ecological problems, pollution and hazardous waste (DeGeorge 1987: 202). In addition to environmental concerns, people started to care about equal rights for women and minorities, occupational health and safety and consumer issues. The sweeping social change that took place in the 1960s and 1970s lastingly affected business organizations, as it kick-started the corporate-social-responsibility debate (Buchholz and Rosenthal 1998: 4). Furthermore, in the 1960s and 1970s several political and economic crises hit, including U.S. President Kennedy's assassination in 1963, the Viet Nam War, the 1970s oil embargoes and the Watergate scandal in 1975. Especially the oil embargoes undermined public trust of oil companies, as the embargoes caused fuel prices to skyrocket, while profits in the oil industry more than doubled during that time (Gray 1986: 18-19; Carroll 1989: 81). All above incidents took place at a time when the media, and in particular television, underwent enormous growth in importance and clout and the consumer movement in the U.S. gained momentum (Gray 1986: 18-19; Carroll 1989: 81). The U.S. government responded by passing numerous laws pertaining to social and ethical issues (Buchholz and Rosenthal 1998: 8). Examples include the Fair Packaging and Labeling Act of 1966, the Occupational Safety and Health Act of 1970, the Equal Employment Opportunity Act of 1972, the Resource Conservation and Recovery Act of 1976, The Clean Air Acts of 1970 and 1977 (Buchholz and Rosenthal 1998: 385; 352; 311; 452; 427).

Government and labor unions are legally entitled to take action against immoral business behavior, but proved to be inefficient and slow in responding to society's concerns (Luthans, Hodgetts and Thompson 1990: 55). Out of the need to press for ethical and socially responsible business conduct, special-interest groups have emerged to promote people's rights by focusing on issues ranging from consumerism to environmental protection (Altham 2001: 10). Consumer boycotts, favorable court rulings, and media interest have made these groups immensely powerful over the past decades (Luthans, Hodgetts and Thompson 1990: 55-56). Globalization has made for a worldwide awareness of moral issues in business, thereby enlarging the membership of special-interest groups to the world population (Webley 1998: 440). Owing to their tremendous power, they have in fact become an integral part of the system of checks and balances that exists among business, government and society (Luthans, Hodgetts and Thompson 1990: 56).

It is worth noting that the reason why corporate social responsibility has become such a prominent issue is not to be found in business per se, as it is not business behavior that has changed throughout the past 50 years but society and its values and expectations (Gray 1986: 15). Carroll (1989: 82) holds that both the business community's ethical standards and societal expectations of business behavior are constantly rising, but societal expectations rise more rapidly than actual business behavior (see Figure 1). These unequal growth rates cause a gap that gives rise to ethical problems in business. Accordingly, many business practices that are considered unethical today were tolerated decades ago. It may of course be that they were not moral issues then simply because the general public did not know about them (Carroll 1989: 81-82).

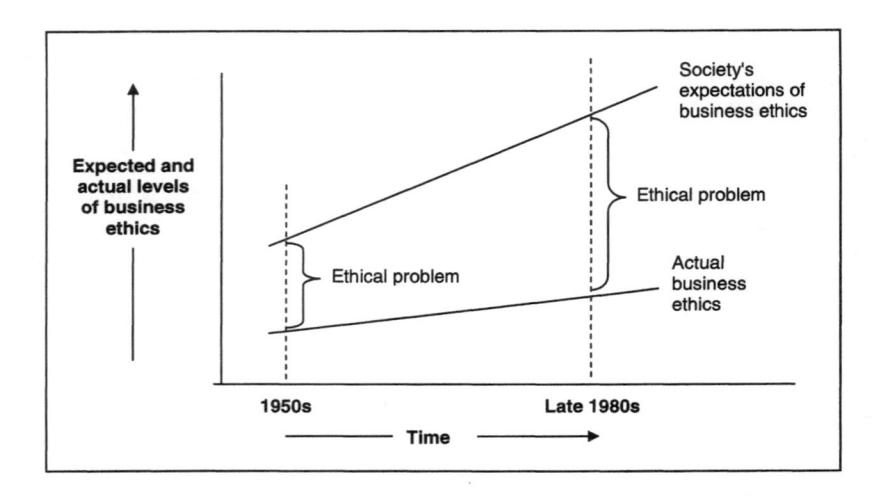

Figure 1: Societal Expectations and Business Conduct
(Source: Carroll 1989: 82)

Child labor, for example, was common practice in Western Europe a few decades ago, but is unacceptable today and also prohibited by law (Pielken 1995: 137). Another case in point is environmental protection, a public concern since the late twentieth century only. In response to environmentalism, companies have "greened" and have started to use their environmental responsibility to project images of socially responsible companies (Seeger 1997: 3). People's rising expectations towards business organizations have made companies project images of good corporate citizens by involving themselves in social issues, e.g. by donating portions of their profits to social causes (Gray 1986: 19).

3.2.2 The Rationale for Corporate Social Responsibility

As has been pointed out earlier, CSR is geared towards constituencies external to the company, e.g. customers, shareholders, suppliers, local communities and the public at large (Peach 1987: 198). There is sufficient evidence to suggest that the rationale for CSR is reputation management. For example, in 1998 the *Conference Board* conducted a survey among *Fortune 500* firms on the reasons for their involvement in community development programs. Three quarters of the respondent companies deemed enhancing their corporate images and developing trust in the company as vitally important, whereas other reasons, e.g. recruitment or attracting new customers and suppliers, were significantly less important to them (Steiner and Steiner 2000: 181-182). *British Telecom* has a management position that carries the job title "Head of ethics and reputation management" (Moon and Bonny 2001: 24). This strongly suggests that companies are aware of the fact that corporate ethics and corporate reputation are closely intertwined. Furthermore, there are communications consultants that specialize in communicating corporate ethics. A case in point is *Vogel Communications* at <http://www.ethicsworld.com>, which considers corporate ethics and corporate communication as "interlocking sets of actions" (Vogel Communications 2000).

A reputation for ethical behavior is a valuable corporate asset that may translate into higher sales. An enhanced reputation attracts customers, enhances employee morale and productivity, facilitates raising new capital and enables companies to charge premium prices (Williams and Barrett 2000: 341). Even a "bad" company may be able to build a reputation for good corporate citizenship, if it effectively manages perceptions, since reputation is a matter of perception rather than reality (Horton 1995: 131). Mitchell (1997: 27) suggests the opposite, arguing that projecting the image of an ethical player in business without delivering is bound to backfire, following the famous adage "actions speak louder than words". Companies that do not communicate their ethical stance and do not pride themselves on their ethics efforts, inevitably present themselves as companies that are unconcerned with ethics (Baker 1993: 267; 281; Mead 1998: 281; 294).

Being positioned as an ethical player — irrespective of whether this is based on fact or fiction — serves the bottom line. Verschoor (1998) examined the linkage between corporate commitment to ethics and financial performance. Previous research on this relationship had shown varied results, which Verschoor put down to the use of contentious methods that had yielded highly divergent results (Verschoor 1998: 1509). Verschoor's study indicated a positive correlation between corporate financial performance and a stated commitment to socially responsible business behavior. More specifically, the mean financial performance rank of companies that did not make any reference to their ethics policies in their annual reports was significantly lower than that of companies that emphasized their commitment to ethical behavior (Verschoor 1998: 1515).

3.2.3 Manifestations of Corporate Social Responsibility

Corporate social responsibility manifests itself in three main areas. To demonstrate responsible behavior towards the community, companies make cash or non-cash contributions to the community, draw up and publicize ethics statements, and issue social reports. The following sections explore these practices in more detail.

3.2.3.1 Corporate Philanthropy and Community Involvement

Dating back to the turn of the twentieth century, corporate philanthropy is the oldest manifestation of corporate social responsibility, although the term CSR had not been coined then (Post, Lawrence, and Weber 1999: 59). In the narrowest sense of the word, philanthropy denotes (1) "a desire to help mankind as indicated by acts of charity" and (2) "love of mankind", both of which imply a considerable level of altruism. Today, the most common usage of the word "philanthropy" — often paired with "corporate" — is simply "business giving", which smacks of PR and bears only little resemblance to the original meaning (Carroll 1989: 307).

Corporate philanthropy subsumes all corporate giving and contributions in the form of cash or non-cash items. Examples of corporate contributions include cash donations to non-profit organizations, the endowment of a chair at a university, the donation of old computers to schools (Koten 1997: 155-156), the donation of software licenses to schools (Wulfson 2001: 137), community projects, educational grants (Garbett 1988: 113), and employee volunteerism, i.e. the loaning of corporate personnel to local communities (Carroll 1989: 303). Recipients of corporate philanthropy are to be found predominantly in the fields of education, health, welfare and the arts (Carroll 1989: 313). Recipients in education typically receive endowments, research grants, fellowships and scholarships (Carroll 1989: 313-314). Companies also allocate their funds to hospitals, youth agencies, e.g. the YMCA or the Scouts, or neighborhood renewal projects (Carroll 1989: 315-316). In recent years companies have been found to give away less to health, welfare and the arts and more to education (Whitman 1999: 119). The reason for this shift may be that companies have realized that contributions to education increase the future supply of skilled personnel, from which they can benefit in later years (Carroll 1989: 314).

In the past, courts viewed corporate giving as illegal and *ultra vires* acts, i.e. acts beyond the corporations' powers. However, when U.S. Congress passed the Revenue Act of 1935, charitable contributions gained popularity, as they became tax-deductible up to 5%[4] of net profits before taxes. The legality of corporate giving remained doubtful, though, and companies feared shareholder suits based on the legal requirement that CEOs "act in a fiduciary capacity to corporate interests" (Steiner and Steiner 2000: 177). It was not until 1953 that the right of corporations to donate portions of their profits was laid down by law in the U.S. based on a court decision on the case *A.P. Smith Manufacturing Company vs. Barlow*. In this case a group of stockholders had objected to a donation the company had intended to make to Princeton University, as they felt their assets were given away. The New Jersey Supreme Court ruled that it was perfectly legal for companies to make contributions to promote social and economic welfare, and so corporate philanthropy was established by law in the U.S. (Campell, Gulas and Gruca 1999: 375; Wulfson 2001: 137; Steiner and Steiner 2000: 177).

The *Conference Board*, which seems to provide the most reliable data on philanthropy, has gathered figures on corporate giving from 1936 to 1984. According to these data, corporate giving averaged 1% of corporate pre-tax income almost throughout the entire period under review, but eventually rose to 1.6% in the early-1980s, only to decline again to 1% in the following decade (Carroll 1989: 308-309; Whitman 1999: 118). It is claimed that this rise can be put down to the Reagan Administration's marked cut in social spending in the 1980s (Carroll 1989: 309). It may or may not be a coincidence that companies

---

[4] This ceiling was raised to 10% by the Economic Recovery Tax Act of 1981 (Steiner and Steiner 2000: 177).

started to include social responsibility in their agendas at about the same time to differentiate themselves from and position themselves toward their rivals (Wulfson 2001: 141). The social and economic significance corporate philanthropy had taken on continued throughout the 1990s. Corporate giving in the United States was estimated at USD 7.4 bn in 1995 (Williams and Barrett 2000: 342) and USD 8.2 bn in 1997 (Steiner and Steiner 2000: 178). In relative terms, larger firms have been found to contribute more than smaller ones. Also, companies contribute relatively more to communities where they are headquartered. Companies that sell to consumers directly are more inclined to give than companies in the business-to-business segment (Whitman 1999: 118).

The nature of giving has changed over the past few decades, primarily because the U.S. Supreme Court made private foundations legally possible in 1960s (Whitman 1999: 119). Many big companies and private donors do not simply give away cash or non-cash items on an ad-hoc basis anymore but have established in-house foundations that handle their philanthropic activities (Campell, Gulas, and Gruca 1999: 376; Whitman 1999: 119). The establishment of corporate foundations not only facilitates the administration of contribution programs but also ensures a stable level of contributions, as foundations pool the funds companies intend to give away. So, even if the annual amount a company donates varies, the foundation is able to make consistent contributions. In the United States, foundations have legal implications that differentiate them from non-institutionalized giving, as foundations are required by law to give away 5% of their assets per annum (Wulfson 2001: 140).

The term *strategic philanthropy* evolved in the mid-1980s and denotes the strategic dimensions corporate philanthropy has taken on by doing good and serving the bottom line at the same time. It is worth noting that this idea had already emerged earlier and that only the term was coined in the mid-1980s (Carroll 1989: 318). Strategic philanthropy is defined as "an approach by which ... philanthropic endeavors of a firm are designed in a way that best fits with the firm's overall mission, goals, or objectives" (Carroll 1989: 318). The strategic dimensions are twofold. First, companies seek to ensure that philanthropy positively impacts on profitability; and second, companies attempt to align philanthropy and business goals by allocating funds to social programs that are in line with their own business.

A special form of strategic philanthropy is cause-related marketing (CRM) (Carroll 1989: 320). The idea behind the concept goes back to 1981 when credit-card company American Express pioneered strategically linking corporate giving and business deals by contributing a certain percentage of every purchase customers made with their American Express credit cards to the restoration of the New York Statue of Liberty (Wulfson 2001: 142). With CRM, companies link their contributions to sales by donating a certain percentage of every sale made on particular products to non-profit organizations or social projects. In fact, CRM represents "the tightest of linkages between a firm's profits and corporate contributions" (Carroll 1989: 320). CRM may stimulate sales, since consumers are more likely to opt for a particular brand "when they know that a needy cause will also benefit" (Campell, Gulas and Gruca 1999: 377). At the same time, an ethical issue arises, as consumers are *forced* to donate money, even if they wish not to do so (Schlegelmilch 2002). For businesses and non-profit organizations, CRM is still a very attractive form of philanthropy, as it creates a situation in which all parties benefit — the business enhances its image and increases sales, the non-profit organization receives donations and increases its public visibility, and customers feel good about their purchases (Carroll 1989: 321).

A survey of *Fortune 500* firms, conducted by the *Conference Board*, revealed a wide array of reasons why companies engage in corporate philanthropy. Among a long list of reasons cited the four most prominent reasons in descending order of popularity were: "practice good corporate citizenship", "protect and improve environment in which to live, work, and do business", "realize benefits for company employees", and "realize good public relations value" (Carroll 1989: 310-311). Campell, Gulas and Gruca (1999) also investigated the reasons for corporate giving and identified two main motivations, viz. (1) altruism and (2) business motives. First, corporate philanthropy may be driven by benevolence, stemming from "the firm's feeling of social responsibility or a sense of altruism" (Campell, Gulas and Gruca 1999: 377), in which case contributions are not intended to serve the bottom line. The second motive for corporate contributions is profit-driven, "ethical egoism", in which case contributions are expected to result in rewards or benefits for the company, which is also referred to as "enlightened self-interest" (Campell, Gulas and Gruca 1999: 376). More precisely, such business motives include:

- **Reputation enhancement:** Corporate giving serves the bottom line in that it positions the company as a good corporate citizen in the eyes of their stakeholders (Campell, Gulas and Gruca 1999: 376-377). For this to happen, companies need to talk about their good deeds publicly. However, trumpeting philanthropic activities may backfire, if consumers perceive the company's good deeds as mere profiteering (Alsop 2002).

- **Increased brand awareness:** Donating to schools, for example, raises name recognition among students. This may benefit the company in the future when these students make purchasing decisions of their own, as brand awareness may turn into brand loyalty (Wulfson 2001: 138).

- **Employee skills:** Employee volunteerism may enhance employee skills, e.g. team skills, when employees work outside the company in a new environment (Business for Social Responsibility 2002a).

- **Positive publicity:** Large donations attract the media's attention and result in publicity for the donating company, which may come at lower cost than advertising (Williams and Barrett 2000: 343).
- **Lower disposal costs:** Giving away obsolete equipment (e.g. PCs) or surplus, non-storable products (e.g. food) may reduce operating costs, as the company is able to dispose of these items free of charge (Campell, Gulas and Gruca 1999: 377).
- **Tax deductibility:** Currently, US tax law grants companies tax deductions for donations of up to 10% of their pre-tax income (Wulfson 2001: 138; 143).

3.2.3.2 Statements of Mission, Vision, and Values

Corporate America has produced mission, vision, and values statements of varying content, length and intent. A clear-cut categorization is next to impossible, as their boundaries are so blurred and

> "most of those statements turn out to be a muddled stew of values, goals, purposes, philosophies, beliefs, aspirations, norms, strategies, practices, and descriptions" (Czerniawska 1997: 185).

To provide at least some categorization, Schlegelmilch's (1998: 113-117) categorization of ethics statements into (1) mission and vision statements, (2) corporate credos, and (3) codes of ethics will be relied upon. Codes of ethics have been treated in Section 3.1.3.1 already, as they are a manifestation of business ethics mainly. Hence, ethics codes are omitted from the discussion in this section. Mission statements and corporate credos are considered manifestations of corporate social responsibility, as they are grossly unhelpful to employees and thus presumably directed at constituencies outside of the company for PR purposes.

3.2.3.2.1 Mission and Vision Statements

A mission statement seeks to set a company apart from its rivals and defines its market position. A mission also "reveals the image the company seeks to project" (Schlegelmilch 1998: 113). Lehman Brother's mission statement, for example reads as follows:

> "We are One Firm, defined by our unwavering commitment to our clients, our shareholders, and each other. Our mission is to build unrivaled partnerships with

and value for our clients, through knowledge, creativity, and dedication of our people, leading to superior returns for our shareholders" (Lehman Brothers 2002).

Mission statements used to focus on issues external to the company, particularly on the product-market domain and critical success factors (Schlegelmilch 1998: 114). Recently, companies have also begun to include internal aspects, such as company philosophy or key corporate values (see Figure 2), in their mission statements, thereby creating so-called vision statements (Schlegelmilch 1998: 114).

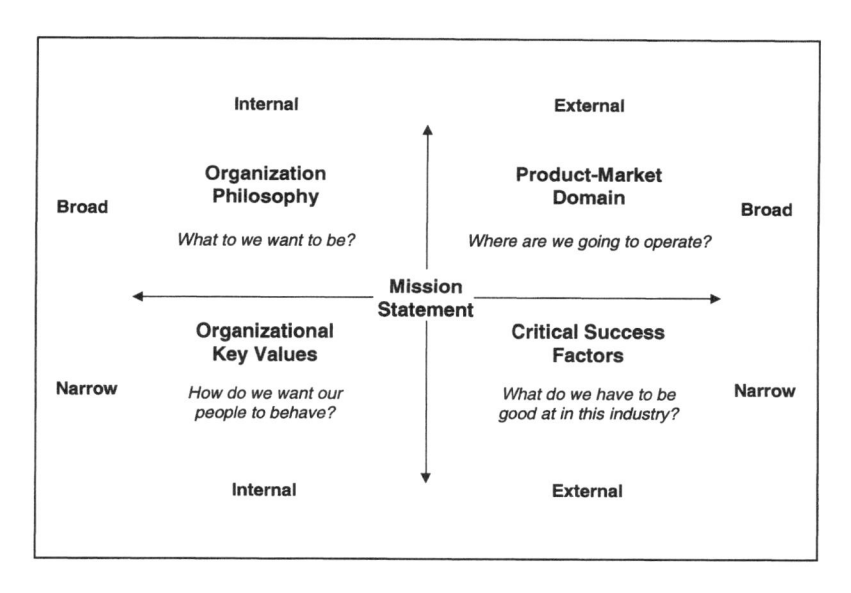

Figure 2: Contents of Mission Statements
(Source: Schlegelmilch 1998: 114)

Mission and vision statements not only differ in the direction of their foci. Additional differences between mission and vision statements were found in the literature reviewed. First, mission and vision statements differ from each other in that mission refers to the status quo, while vision refers to the future, as argued by Silvers (1995: 11) as well as Grossman and King (1993: 56). Second, mission statements answer questions such as "Who are we?", "What do we do?" and "Where are we going?" (Goodman 1998: 87; Garbett 1988: 17), thereby identifying a company's *raison d'être* (Business for Social Responsibility 2002b). A vision, meanwhile, refers to a company's long-term goals (Business for Social Responsibility 2002b), including a "a core ideology" (Czerniawska 1997: 185) and focuses "on an end result, but not necessarily on how to get there" (Silvers 1995: 10). The following sample statements illustrate the content of vision statements:

- **Bell Atlantic:**
  "We want to be our customers' first choice for communications and information services in every market we serve, domestic and international" (Bell Atlantic 2001).
- **Lexmark:**
  "We want to be known for reliability, flexibility, responsiveness, innovative products and services, and exemplary citizenship. Growth, longevity and financial success will naturally follow" (Lexmark 2001).
- **DuPont:**
  "We, the people of DuPont, dedicate ourselves daily to the work of improving life on our planet. ... We will respect nature and living things, work safely, be gracious to one another and our partners, and each day we will leave for home with consciences clear and spirits soaring" (DuPont 2001).

Overall, it can be said that mission statements and vision statements are similar in that they address both strategic issues, e.g. long-term company goals, and ethical issues. Mission and vision statements differ from ethics codes in that they do not exclusively deal with corporate ethics, but also include strategic goals unrelated to ethics. Whereas ethics codes serve as behavioral guidelines, mission and vision statements merely spell out goals. A mission or vision can theoretically be conveyed in one sentences, whereas ethics codes tend to be more specific and thus quite lengthy (Stevens 1994: 64).

3.2.3.2.2 Corporate Credos

Corporate credos spell out a company's core values and beliefs that are intended to serve as a frame of reference for decision making in the organization (Schlegelmilch 1998: 115). Credos also go by the name of values statements (Murphy 1998: 2). Such values typically include quality, service, teamwork, integrity and fairness (Kamen 1993: 10). Corporate credos are intended to guide employee conduct, yet employees of large corporations will find these statements too platitudinous and vague to be of value to them (Schlegelmilch 1998: 115; Murphy 1998: 4; "Culturing change": 65). Especially multinational corporations operating in various regions around the globe will not find such brief credos helpful, given the ethical complexities they encounter across cultures (Schlegelmilch 1998: 117). Claiming to abide by their credos internationally, makes large companies appear hypocritical, as credos cannot possibly provide sufficient guidance across cultures. Since it is highly doubtful whether such statements actually impact employee decision making, they may well be dismissed as PR documents.

3.2.3.3 Corporate Social Reporting and Auditing

Corporate social reporting is "the process of communicating the social and environmental effects of organisations' economic actions to particular interest groups" (Hooghiemstra 2000: 65). A notion synonymous with social reporting is social accounting, which denotes "the extension of accounting reports to include information about product, employee interests, community activities, and environmental impact" (Mathews 1995: 668). In recent years, social and environmental reports have become *de rigueur* for large multinationals, e.g. DuPont, IBM, or BP (Kelly 1997: 215), particularly for those operating in industries facing a predicament, e.g. oil companies, which are constantly accused of environmental pollution (Hooghiemstra 2000: 56). Patten (1992) shows that corporate social reporting in a certain industry increases, if a major incident occurs in the industry (Patten 1992 quoted in Hooghiemstra 2000: 56).

Social reports are often prepared as weapons against negative publicity, since voluntarily disclosing information on corporate social performance could cancel out the effects of negative media exposure of the company (Hooghiemstra 2000: 56) and "marginalizes would-be attackers by leaving them with nothing to uncover" ("Globalization shifts public affairs role": 1). Hooghiemstra (2000: 57-58) goes on to deem corporate social reporting a self-laudatory, image-building PR vehicle and suggests that companies use social reporting as a strategic tool in corporate reputation management. The credibility factor of voluntary social audits is high, as companies that voluntarily release social-audit reports appear as open and forthcoming (Wiesendanger 1993: 20). Frequently, companies have independent, outside auditors prepare their social reports, also referred to as social audits. Typically, they hire accounting or law firms for these probes. Not only is an outside investigation more credible, but it also enhances the corporate image with legal regulators. However, there is an inherent conflict of interest when companies *pay* outside auditors to scrutinize their business practices and to assess their social performance. The results of such an "independent" audit are possibly as biased as if the company conducted it itself (France 1996: 27; Welt and Sorell 1996: 56).

3.3 Summary of Key Points

The previous sections were intended to point out the two divergent corporate-ethics approaches that give rise to three ethics paradigms. Business ethics (BE) occurs within the company, and includes corporate phenomena such as ethics codes, ethics committees, ethics ombudspersons, ethics officers, ethics hotlines, ethics training, and ethics audits. Business-ethics efforts need to be supported by top management and a strong organizational culture to foster an ethical climate in the organization. By contrast, CSR is geared towards the company's external stakeholders with a view to changing the perceptions of its external constituencies. CSR manifests itself through philanthropy, community involvement, mission statements, corporate credos and ethical reporting. Typically, companies belong to either of these paradigms, yet there are a few companies that have demonstrated that it is possible to follow both paradigms. This distinction between BE companies, CSR companies and BE & CSR companies is fundamental to the research framework of this study.

4 The Business-Ethics Paradigm

4.1 Case 1: *BellSouth Corp.*

4.1.1 Background to the Company

BellSouth Corp. is the result of the divestiture of the American Telephone & Telegraph Co. (AT&T) in 1983. AT&T was split up into several regional holding companies, but persisted as a company. The breakup of AT&T gave birth to seven new companies, including Ameritech, Bell Atlantic, US West, Nynex, BellSouth, Pacific Telesis, and Southwestern Bell. They opened for business on January 1, 1984 (Gissen 1983: 286-287; Studabaker 1984: 70; "Culture shock is shaking Bell System": 112-115). After several mergers, acquisitions and reorganizations, BellSouth Corp. is a now holding company of a number of subsidiaries, including BellSouth Telecommunications, Southern Bell, South Central Bell (Harrison 1995: 22).

Headquartered in Atlanta, Georgia, BellSouth is a provider of communications services, employing 87,000 people worldwide. Its services include telephoning services, operator services, wireless data and communications services, broadband data communications, and Internet services. BellSouth does business primarily in the U.S. but also in Latin America, a few European countries, Israel, India, and China. It serves business and private customers as well as customers in the public sector (BellSouth 2001a, 2001b, 2001c). BellSouth has established a Federal Sales Division especially for doing business with U.S. federal agencies, both military and civil (BellSouth 2002).

In late 1987 BellSouth became involved in a government bidding scandal. The bid was for a dozen telephone switches to be used for the U.S. government's new telecommunications network worth USD 55 million. AT&T and BellSouth, although formerly one company, belonged to different bidding teams, which made them fierce competitors. Eventually, the General Services Administration (GSA) awarded substantial parts of the contract to both of them. As this and other GSA procurement contracts were allegedly not based on competitive bids and thus questionable, a federal grand jury in Washington investigated the GSA's procurement practices in 1988. The investigation turned up that Sureshar Lal Soni, a GSA engineer, had leaked confidential AT&T pricing information to BellSouth to influence the price of the bidding. In exchange for this vital information, BellSouth rewarded him with meals worth USD 400. In 1989, Mr Soni resigned from GSA and pleaded guilty to accepting gratuities from

BellSouth in exchange for valuable information he leaked to the company. He was sentenced to a fine of USD 1,000. BellSouth was not charged, but in response withdrew from the switch contract it had been awarded, admitting that the information it received might have had a bearing on its bid (Davis 1988: 1; "Former GSA worker enters guilty plea": 1).

Another scandal unfolded at Southern Bell, a BellSouth subsidiary, in 1992. To increase their bonus payments, Southern Bell salespeople signed up a total of 900,000 residential and business customers for optional telephone services they never ordered, e.g. call waiting, call forwarding and three-way calling. The Florida attorney general's office investigated the matter and found that Southern Bell had put lots of pressure on its salespeople to sell these premium services. At the same time, it generously rewarded sales agents who landed many orders, thereby encouraging salespeople to sign up customers without their consent. The nub of the problem was not misconduct by individuals but the fact that the company had not installed any mechanisms to verify customer orders to prevent such fraud. In general, the investigators believed that the company had a culture that closed its eyes to fraudulent practices. To avoid criminal prosecution, Southern Bell agreed to an out-of-court settlement offered by the Florida attorney general's office. According to the agreement of October 9, 1992, Southern Bell was to refund a little over USD $15 million to its overcharged customers and was on probation for the following three years, which included outside audits and spot checks (Luxner 1993: 8).

4.1.2 Discourse Analysis

4.1.2.1 The Ideational Function

In the course of the analysis, four main themes have emerged from the BellSouth corpus: (1) ethics and the law, (2) compliance, (3) whistle blowing and (4) corporate reputation. They are discussed in turn in the following sections.

Ethics and the Law
The page on compliance starts out with two sentences that convey the impression that BellSouth's perception of ethics does not extend beyond the letter of the law:

(1) "BellSouth is committed to maintaining its reputation as a company with the highest standards of business conduct. The corporation requires all employees ... as well as its agents, contractors, and suppliers to behave in a manner that is consistent with the standards, policies, and procedures that ensure compliance with applicable Federal, state, and local laws and regulations."

BellSouth seemingly equates legal compliance with the highest standards of business conduct. This impression is created primarily because there is no linking adjunct between the two sentences, which leaves it open whether the second sentence adds information or indicates a result, which would be achieved, for example, by using the linking adjuncts *In addition* and *Therefore*, respectively. However, in several other places of the corpus, BellSouth does distinguish between ethics and the law. The following statements illustrate this distinction:

(2) "Satisfying the letter of the law is not enough. Ours is a higher standard."

(3) "operating with the highest ethical behavior and full adherence to all applicable laws and regulations."

(4) "policies and practices that ensure we fully comply with all legal and ethical standards."

(5) "No illegal or unethical act can be justified by"

Each of these statements also contains at least one accentuating element. A comparative (*higher*) and a superlative (*highest*) stress the quality of BellSouth's ethical standards. The intensifiers *full* and *fully* underscore the notion of compliance, although the truth value of *compliance* is by its very nature not gradable. In fact, there is no midway between compliance and non-compliance, which makes the intensifiers *full* and *fully* redundant. The indefinite pronouns *all* and *no* act as quantifying determiners, expressing totality and its converse, respectively.

A noteworthy feature is the use of *high* in the corpus. Ten out of 13 times *high* is collocated with *ethics* as a qualitative adjective or with *ethical* as an adverb of degree, e.g. in the phrases *highly ethical behavior* and *highly ethical work environment*. If used as a qualitative adjective, *high* always occurs in comparative or superlative forms. For example:

Ours is a	**higher**	standard
Every action we take reflects the	**highest**	ethical standards
We are committed to the	**highest**	ethical standards
operating with the	**highest**	ethical behavior
each of us is expected to demonstrate the	**highest**	ethical behavior possible
we are personally accountable for the	**highest**	standards of behavior
reputation as a company with the	**highest**	standards of business conduct
we are performing our jobs with the	**highest**	integrity

Compliance

The page titled *Compliance* contains, as the name suggests, mostly information on BellSouth's compliance efforts. It contains a lengthy description of BellSouth's ethics initiatives, outlining who has been responsible for what since when. It has an ethics office, which is headed by the Corporate Director of Ethics and Compliance, i.e. the ethics officer, and reports directly to the CEO. BellSouth's Compliance Policy Board is equivalent to an ethics committee. The Vice-President of Corporate Responsibility and Compliance serves as ethics ombudsman. Interestingly, this office was established in 1991 — the same year the Federal Sentencing Guidelines were enacted (see Section 3.1.1). Apparently, BellSouth has no institutionalized ethics audit, but the Compliance Policy Board reports to the Audit Committee of the board of directors. Further, the page lists BellSouth's means of communicating its ethics policies to its employees. The frequent use of the agent-free passive voice on this page is striking, as it does not occur anywhere else in the corpus to such a great extent. Cases in point are *was created, is administered, are developed, is used, are furnished*, etc. Alternatively, sentences are constructed as relational processes in simple present tense, e.g. *responsibility is vested with* or *are subject to review by BellSouth Internal Audit*. Throughout the text, there is not a single *we*, which is untypical of BellSouth (see below). Only at the very end is there a five-item bullet list that spells out BellSouth's compliance principles in the first-person perspective, e.g. *To ensure we act with integrity in all we do.*

To support its employees in making decisions compliant with BellSouth's policies in ethically ambiguous situations, the company provides *Quick Self-Tests* and an online *Ethics Scenarios Game* on its Web site. The self-tests contain a number of questions employees could ask themselves when in doubt whether their behavior complies with BellSouth's policies. Such questions include, for example, *How will this look in tomorrow morning's newspaper?* The online *Ethics Scenarios Game* presents mini-cases and offers possible answers, which employees are to choose from. The game then tells employees whether they selected the correct answers and also provides them with rationales for the correct answers. The scenarios include government contracts, conflicts of interest and gratuities, which are issues BellSouth has faulted on.

BellSouth also threatens its employees with disciplinary measures, including discharge, if they violate the company's ethics policies:

(6) "*Violations of any of the standards outlined in this booklet may result in disciplinary action that could include dismissal and/or criminal prosecution. Violations may also result in severe penalties to BellSouth.*"

However, they mitigate this point by using only modal verbs, viz. *may* and *could*. The passage sounds very impersonal, as nominalizations like *violations*, *dismissal* or *prosecution* factor out the people involved in these processes. Also, the passage exhibits special prominence signaled visually by printing the font in bold italics to make it stand out from the rest of the text.

BellSouth has external ethics links to the *Ethics Officer Association*, the *Ethics Resource Center*, the *Josephson Institute of Ethics* and the *Southern Institute for Business and Professional Ethics*. These organizations give advice on implementing ethics programs and ensuring compliance in the company.

Whistle Blowing

Given that whistle-blowing is an effective way to prevent harm, it stands to reason that BellSouth encourages its employees to do so. BellSouth even points out that *failing to report suspected violations is itself a violation*. An indication that BellSouth mainly seeks to prevent harm through its ethics policies is the use of the term *violation*. Overall, it occurs 14 times in the corpus, ten times collocating with the verb *report* and the adjectives *suspected* or *possible*. These ten collocations occur in either of the following formats:

Collocation	Frequency
report a suspected violation	4
report suspected violations	3
reporting suspected violations	3
report a possible violation	1
report a possible ethical violation	1

Table 5: Collocations with *Violation*

BellSouth is careful to qualify violations as *suspected* or *possible* to ease employees' fears of reporting wrong allegations. Thus, BellSouth induces its employees to blow the whistle even if they just suspect some misconduct they cannot back with hard evidence. The fact that *report* is paired with *violation* ten times in the corpus demonstrates how important whistle-blowing is to the company.

On both the page *About Ethics* and the games page, BellSouth talks about *ethical situations* or simply *situations* rather than dilemmas or problems. Equally, *questions*, *concerns* and *gray areas* replace *problems*. These mitigations seek to present ethical problems as harmless and easy to deal with. Also, in the phrase *it is difficult for all of us to speak up when we have concerns* BellSouth not only euphemizes questions but also uses inclusive *we* to increase the acceptability of the message. Another case in point of a euphemism is the use of *gifts and hospitality* on the games page, which is intended to neutralize the negative connotation of bribery. On the page *About Ethics* BellSouth also avoids negative words and uses positive lexical items instead, e.g. *supported and protected*, *confidentially and appropriately*, *safe and confidential* and *safety net*. The notions of safety and confidentiality are supposed to ease employees' fears of reprisal when reporting a suspected violation.

BellSouth also uses negatives as a rhetoric device to encourage whistle blowing. Overall, the corpus contains 34 instances of *no/not*. There is a significant cluster of these negatives on the page *What's It All About*? in the section on the Ethics Line, BellSouth's ethics hotline. This section contains 15 instances of *no/not*, which equals almost half of all negatives in the corpus. Granted, this page is the longest page in the corpus, being three to four times longer than the others, but the clustering is still noteworthy, as it occurs in a subsection of the page only. For one, BellSouth uses *not* as way to comfort employees, e.g. as in *Don't be afraid* or *don't take it personally*. In addition, *no/not* is used to convince employees that BellSouth handles inquiries or reports made via the Ethics Line confidentially and to encourage them to use the Ethics Line:

(7) "You do not have to give your name".

(8) "If you do give your name, you can ask that it not be released."

(9) "... focuses attention on the issue — not your identity"

(10) "Ethics Office does not use CallerID and does not record phone calls."

(11) "there's no such thing as a dumb question"

(12) "No one wins when we fail to speak up"

Reputation

BellSouth believes it has a reputation as an ethical company, which it expresses in the following phrases:

(13) "a company with a reputation for honesty and integrity"

(14) "to protect the company's reputation for integrity"

(15) "BellSouth has built a reputation for operating with the highest ethical behavior and full adherence to all applicable laws and regulations"

(16) "maintaining its reputation as a company with the highest standards of business conduct"

(17) "a company known for its integrity"

The verbs *maintain*, *build* and *protect* imply that BellSouth believes it has already acquired a reputation for integrity. By its very nature, corporate reputation is not easy to assess, as it is based on the perceptions of the company's audience. BellSouth does not specify among whom it believes it has this reputation. BellSouth may well have a reputation for sound ethics among its business partners, yet it remains doubtful whether the general public or shareholders share this perception, as they probably know too little about the company's business practices. By using simply *reputation* BellSouth leaves it open whose perceptions form the basis for the company's reputation.

The company seems to believe that implementing a compliance program suffices to establish a reputation for integrity. BellSouth does not conceal its motives for implementing a comprehensive ethics program in the company:

(18) "The central objective of the compliance program is to protect and enhance the company's reputation for integrity and to reduce the potential liability associated with the application of the Federal (Organizational) Sentencing Guidelines".

It seems that BellSouth implements an ethics program solely for the purpose of creating or maintaining a reputation for integrity. At the same time, BellSouth seeks to fulfill the criteria stipulated by the Federal Sentencing Guidelines (see Section 3.1.1) to protect itself against huge fines if employee misconduct is detected.

BellSouth believes that its reputation is a heritage, although the company was founded in 1983 only:

(19) "BellSouth's reputation was built on the honesty of hundreds of thousands of people over the years ... [W]e are obligated to pass that heritage on to the women and men who follow us".

BellSouth's goal is to preserve this heritage, as the company is aware that reputation is a fragile asset (*we recognize that we can diminish that reputation in one single instant*). The company seeks to make employees aware of the fact that its reputation could be shattered as a result of their misconduct. Therefore, BellSouth urges its employees to call the Ethics Line when in doubt and it repeatedly points out that the company's reputation is largely shaped by employee conduct:

(20) "BellSouth's reputation comes from the quality of every single employee's conduct."

(21) "the reputation ... of our company depends on the decisions each of us makes"

(22) "The reputation of our company depends on the service we provide and on the decisions we make every day."

The varied expressions BellSouth uses to refer to its employees (*employee, each of us, we*) are also remarkable. The emphatic use of *every* or *each* in all three statements seeks to stress that every action and decision is potentially harmful to the company's reputation.

BellSouth equates reputation with trust and wants its readers to believe that its stakeholders completely trust the company, as if there had never been any case of distrust, which is unlikely in view of the major fraud BellSouth has committed.

(23) "One of our greatest competitive assets is our reputation — the TRUST our customers, our vendors and suppliers, and our communities place in us".

(24) "We are committed to the highest ethical standards because we want people to know they can count on us".

Using the categorical present tense in *place*, BellSouth treats trust as an actual state rather than a desired one, thereby suggesting that this trust has existed in the past and is likely to exist in the future as well. Although *can* in the phrase *they can count on us* expresses deontic modality, it does not express this modality here, as the phrasal verb *to count on* is typically preceded by a modal verb, according to *Collins Cobuild English Language Dictionary* (1987). Thus, *they can count on us* conveys the same meaning as the categorical present tense above, viz. establishing the company's trustworthiness as an undeniable fact.

On the page *Community Outreach*, BellSouth states the rationale for its philanthropic activities: *BellSouth sponsors community events and programs that enhance our visibility and brand*. Evidently, BellSouth engages in corporate giving also solely for the purpose of enhancing its reputation.

4.1.2.2 The Interpersonal Function

BellSouth
Table 6 contains a frequency analysis of words BellSouth uses to refer to itself. These include personal pronouns, possessive pronouns, nouns and the company name.

	Subject	Object	Genitive	Adjective[5]	TOTAL
we / us / our	91	31	n.a.	94	**216**
BellSouth	12	15	15	18	**60**
company	0	11	4	3	**18**
corporation	1	2	1	-	**4**
it / its	-	-	n.a.	6	**6**

Table 6: Breakdown of References to BellSouth

BellSouth seems to prefer the use of personal and possessive pronouns to the company name. First-person pronouns and possessive adjectives occur more than twice as often as nouns or the third-person pronoun *it*. *We/us/our* is used both inclusively and exclusively. Inclusive *we* means that BellSouth speaks for itself and on behalf of its readers. Cases in point include *the decisions we make every day* and *each of us*. Also, *As we launch into e>space* [sic!], *let us work together* in CEO Duane Ackerman's letter is an example of inclusive *we*. Exclusive *we* can be classified into (a) "We, the company", (b) "We, the employees" and (c) "We, the ethics office". Examples of these three categories include:

(a) The statement *We strive for excellence in everything we do including ... a great place to work for our employees* in the Value Statement must be made by "We, the company", as only a company has employees. Similarly, Duane Ackerman's letter contains phrases like *We are using Internet technology to e>tize [sic!] our business ... to offer new powers ... to our employees*. Here, too, *we* stands for the company as an institution because of the phrase *our employees*.

---

[5] Following *Collins Cobuild English Usage* (1992: xvi), *our* is treated as a possessive adjective, although it is sometimes considered a genitive (cf. Greenbaum and Quirk 1990: 109).

(b) The assertion *We respect each other* in the Value Statement is obviously made by BellSouth's employees. Likewise, *we act as responsible employees and managers* on the compliance page and *BellSouth's interests will dictate our decisions* are obviously uttered by employees. It is worth noting that *we* speaking on behalf of the employees must address another audience, e.g. customers or the general public.

(c) *We will research the issue and try and get an answer back to you* on the *Ask Ethics* page is clearly a statement made by "We, the ethics office", directed at employees.

Employees

As expected of a company in the business-ethics paradigm, BellSouth's main addressees of the Web pages are its employees. BellSouth's employees are referred to as a *team*, e.g. as in the Value Statement: *We work together as one BellSouth team*. Likewise, the salutation of Duane Ackerman's letter reads *Dear BellSouth Team Member*. Despite the team spirit BellSouth conveys here, it distinguishes between employees and managers in other places, for example in the phrase *we act as responsible employees and managers* on the compliance page. The corpus also contains the phrases *A special note to those who supervise* and *As a manager, you ...*, which also make this classification evident.

A letter from CEO Duane Ackerman on corporate ethics signals the CEO's commitment to corporate ethics. The letter is signed simply *Duane*. Using merely his first name, BellSouth's CEO pretends to bond with his employees. He presents himself as an ordinary human equal to all other employees and does not highlight his position as CEO of the company. The first-name basis conveys solidarity and makes him appear more accessible rather than some distant figure at the top.

All direct audience addresses in the form of *you* or *your* relate exclusively to employees. The corpus contains 72 instances of *you* and 42 instances of *your*, whereas *employee(s)* is used only 32 times as subject, object, genitive or adjective. The personal address occurs typically on pages that serve the sole purpose of helping and guiding employees in some way, e.g. pages like *Ask Ethics*, *Seven Keys*, *What's it All About?* and the games and scenarios pages. These pages not only include employees in the discourse through second-person pronouns and possessive pronouns, but also use imperatives, e.g. *Think about*, *Please read*, *please choose*, *Remember* and the like. Despite their imperative mood, these statements do not come across as commands but rather as an offer for help, primarily because of the polite tone that is established lexically, e.g. *If you want, if you prefer, may help you,* and *please.*

You and *I* is also used inclusively in the clause *Since you and I inherited a company with a reputation for honesty and integrity* in the Code of Conduct. As there is no identifiable single-person writer, *you and I* is a substitute for *we* and is intended to give the content an informal, down-to-earth touch.

BellSouth also mixes second-person personal pronouns (*you*) and possessive adjectives (*your*) and *employee(s)* within the same page, or even paragraph. The page *About Ethics*, for example, first talks about employees, e.g. *to create an environment where BellSouth employees feel supported* and then switches to the second person:

(25) "**The Role of the Employee is to:**
- Make ethics a part of your everyday job.
- Be a role model.
- Help others to make the right decisions.
- Ask, if you don't know the answer!"

The pages featuring the quick self-tests include statements made and questions asked from the first-person point of view, simulating an inner monologue:

(26) "Since I know this is wrong, I shouldn't do it!"

(27) "Since I'm not sure, I should ASK someone!"

(28) "If I do it, will I feel bad?"

(29) "Will I sleep soundly tonight?"

(30) "Would I tell my children to react in the same way?"

Such personal questions are expected to evoke strong emotions on the part of the employees. The tangible nature of these questions makes it easier for employees to answer them, as opposed to more abstract questions like *Will my actions stand the test of time?* or *Does it comply with our VALUES?*. The latter question seems extremely difficult to answer in view of the vagueness of BellSouth's corporate values.

BellSouth also considers people more important than policies in decision-making. The following statements illustrate this point:

(31) "it's important to each of us to feel good about decisions we make"

(32) "common sense and professional judgment should be used"

Statement 31 occurs three times in the corpus in various places. The feel-good factor mentioned in statement 31 and *common sense* and *judgment* mentioned in statement 31 make employees believe that BellSouth trusts them and wants them to make decisions based on their own feelings.

At no point does BellSouth insinuate that employees are incapable of making the right decisions or are in need of decision-making guidance. The company presents the games and self-tests as an optional decision-making aid:

(33) "Use these quick self-tests to help you think about your individual situation."

(34) "Play the game and you might learn something new!"

(35) "some questions that may help you think through certain situations"

(36) "questions and statement to consider before making a decision"

The modals *may* and *might* as well as the verbs *help* and *consider* convey the voluntary nature of these games and self-tests. BellSouth is aware that decisions are guided by the decision-makers' own values and feelings.

Although BellSouth pretends to trust the decision-making capabilities of its employees, the text often adopts a patronizing tone, which actually suggests the opposite. This lack of trust is realized by the imperative *Remember*, which occurs nine times in the corpus. Four of these occurrences are intended to encourage employees to ask when in doubt, with *ask* even being capitalized to emphasize it:

(37) "Remember, the important thing is to ASK."

(38) "Remember, if you don't know the answer, ASK!"

(39) "Remember, the best thing you can do when you face an ethical situation is to ASK for help."

(40) "Remember, it's always correct to call the Office of Ethics and Compliance ... if you don't know how to handle a situation."

The patronizing tone is equally prominent in the following statements, where BellSouth appeals to its employees' conscience to deter them from acting unethically.

(41) "Remember, it's important to each of us to feel good about decisions we make" (see above)

(42) "Remember that we always have options"

(43) "Remember, people can often infer more from what you don't say than what you do say about ethics."

(44) "Remember, each of us is expected to demonstrate the highest ethical behavior possible"

(45) "Remember that failing to report suspected violations is itself a violation" (see above)

Stakeholders

The word *stakeholder* occurs only once in the corpus: *The Office of Ethics and Compliance is available to all employees and stakeholders to help answer questions*. Evidently, *stakeholders* is taken to mean external constituencies only, excluding employees. Based on this distinction, employees were discussed separately from stakeholders. The corpus contains several enumerations of the company's stakeholder groups. The following four statements encompass all stakeholders mentioned:

(46) "our responsibilities to our customers, our owners, our vendors and suppliers, our families, the communities where we live and work, and to each other".

(47) "We each have an obligation to practice good business ethics-to ourselves, to each other, to our customers, to our shareholders, and to everyone we do business with".

(48) "The corporation requires all employees at every level of the business, as well as its agents, contractors, and suppliers to behave in a manner …".

(49) "the decisions we make every day … , whether we are interacting with our customers, our suppliers, our competitors or each other".

On the whole, BellSouth mentions the following stakeholder groups:

- Shareholders / Owners
- Agents and Contractors
- Vendors
- Competitors
- Families
- Customers
- Suppliers
- Communities

Stockholders are referred to as *shareholders* in the value statement, but called *owners* in the code of conduct. The term *owners* clearly empowers the position of shareholders, as they are considered part of the company rather than mere providers of funds. Contractors and agents are mentioned only once each on the page on compliance, where BellSouth lists all groups required to adhere to BellSouth's policies and standards. Vendors, mentioned five times, always occur as part of the phrase *vendors and suppliers* and can thus be subsumed within suppliers. Competitors are brought up only twice: First, when reputation is considered a *competitive asset*; and second, when BellSouth states that its reputation is dependent *on the way we are interacting with ... our competitors*. BellSouth does not specify this interaction and, above all, does not commit itself to fair competition. Further, BellSouth considers the families of all employees stakeholders and voices its responsibilities to them in the corporate code of conduct. A section titled *Our Families Can Count on Us* reads as follows:

(50) "We want our families to be proud that we work for a company known for its integrity and for us as individuals. We seek a healthy balance between our work and our family life".

Considering that a code of conduct typically stipulates guidelines for behavior, this paragraph appears a bit out-of-place, especially because it does not spell out any responsibility or commitment. Also, the terms *seek* and *balance* are rather vague and make possible varied interpretations.

Customers

Both the Value Statement and the Code of Conduct contain sections focusing on customers. While the section *Our customers* in the Value Statement merely asserts that BellSouth aims at meeting customer needs, BellSouth commits itself to providing excellent service to customers under the value of *Excellence*. The value of *Integrity* points to honesty in interactions with customers. The Code of Conduct also emphasizes BellSouth's commitment to honesty and trustworthiness in customer dealings:

(51) **"Our Customers Can Count on Us**

We believe our first responsibility is to the people who count on us for their telecommunications needs ... We will deal with customers straightforwardly and honestly. They will know they can depend not only on our products and services, but on our word and character".

BellSouth further commits itself to *fair treatment* of customers and recognizes it has *an obligation to practice good business ethics* to its customers. BellSouth points out that its reputation is shaped by its interactions with its stakeholders, including customers. The phrase *our reputation — the TRUST our customers ... place in us* is laden with self-confidence and presupposes this trust. This appears rather exaggerated and over-optimistic in view of the fraudulent practices BellSouth pleaded guilty to in 1992.

Suppliers

BellSouth's relationship with its suppliers centers around three keywords: compliance, fairness and trust. BellSouth does not impose any ethical standards on its suppliers and, in fact, does not expect anything that goes beyond the provisions of the law. It merely expects it suppliers to abstain from illegal practices:

> (52) "The corporation requires all ... suppliers to behave in a manner that is consistent with the standards, policies, and procedures that ensure compliance with applicable Federal, state, and local laws and regulations".

Explicitly mentioning legal compliance in this context suggests that this is not always standard practice and can thus not be taken for granted. Otherwise, it would not have to be stipulated.

BellSouth commits itself to treating its suppliers in a fair manner, as it states twice. First, in Duane Ackerman's letter *fair treatment* of suppliers is considered a *core issue*. Second, the code of conduct contains the clause *Vendors and suppliers must know we will be fair*. BellSouth even presupposes their trust in the phrase *Our vendors and suppliers can count on us*.

Communities

The general public is referred to as *communities* in the discourse. In the very first paragraph of the code of conduct, BellSouth assumes responsibility towards the communities where it operates: *our responsibilities to ... the communities where we live and work*. This assertion also shows that BellSouth's notion of communities denotes cities and towns rather than people. For example, *Our communities* is one of the values in BellSouth's Value Statement, according to which BellSouth seeks to *make our communities better places to live, work and grow*. The vagueness of *better* is specified in BellSouth's Code of Conduct. The clause on communities reads:

> (53) "**Our Communities Can Count on Us**
> Beyond the quality, day-to-day service they expect from us in telecommunications, the cities and towns where we operate can also count on us for help in civic, charitable, and other community activities."

This assertion in the Code of Conduct evidences that BellSouth also intends to give to its communities, which appears to be a rather unusual statement in a code of conduct. BellSouth's giving is, however, mainly self-serving. On the page *Community Outreach*, it frankly states that its contributions are intended *to improve the well-being and vitality of the communities we serve while aligning with the interests and opportunities of BellSouth.* This explains why *BellSouth's community outreach emphasizes education* and the BellSouth Foundation also funds only education. That way, BellSouth seeks to raise children's interest in technology in order to benefit from them as skilled workforce or technology-savvy customers. BellSouth also has an employee volunteer program, called the *BellSouth Pioneers*, which encourages employees to participate in local community programs.

4.1.2.3 The Textual Function

The corpus for the analysis contains almost all ethics-related pages found on BellSouth's Web site. These pages are found in the subsections *Ethics & Compliance*, and *Community*, which are not directly accessible from BellSouth's home page but only via the menu item *about us* on the top-level menu bar that spans across the top of every page. Upon entering the subsection *Ethics & Compliance*, a vertical menu bar appears on the left side of the screen, listing the contents of the subsection *Ethics & Compliance*. This menu bar is constantly visible when users navigate BellSouth's ethics-related pages.

Most of BellSouth's ethics-related pages were formerly distributed in the form of a printed brochure titled *Commitment Booklet*. BellSouth has not dismantled the original structure of the booklet, as the ethics menu still functions as a table of contents of this electronic booklet. CEO Duane Ackerman's introduction and a conclusion are still part of the electronic booklet, too. This makes for the cohesion of the pages that were formerly part of the booklet. The ethics menu also contains hyperlinks to other ethics pages including the games and scenario pages, the *Ask Ethics* page and the page describing the corporate ethics office. BellSouth has only one crosslink in the business-ethics part of the corpus (viz. *Customers click here ...*) and three crosslinks on the community-outreach page. Evidently, the ethics menu is the main cohesive device BellSouth uses to link its pages. In addition, BellSouth has submenus on top of some pages that link to paragraphs on the same page.

4.2 Case 2: *Lockheed Martin Corp.*

4.2.1 Background to the Company

4.2.1.1 Company Profile

The Lockheed Martin Corporation is a fairly new company, founded as a result of a merger between Lockheed Corp. and Martin Marietta in March 1995 in an effort to consolidate the U.S. defense industry in the 1990s. Overall, Lockheed Martin has acquired or merged with all or parts of 17 companies (Hartung 2000; Lockheed Martin 2000b). Headquartered in Bethesda, Maryland, Lockheed Martin has operations in 56 countries and employs 126,000 people worldwide. Lockheed Martin is an industrial conglomerate active in fields such as aeronautics, space systems, defense electronics, technology support to government agencies, and commercial IT services. (Lockheed Martin 2000a; 2000b; 2000c; 2001). As the world's largest manufacturer of weapons, Lockheed Martin depends on contracts from U.S. government agencies, particularly the Pentagon, and foreign governments (Hartung 2000). As of 2000, 50% of Lockheed Martin's sales stem from the U.S. Department of defense, 22% from the NASA and other U.S. government agencies, 7% from U.S.-based commercial customers, and 21% from international business (Lockheed Martin 2000a).

4.2.1.2 Overcharges, Illegal Payments and Arms Export

As the U.S. defense budget has been cut continuously over the past decades, U.S. defense contractors like Lockheed Martin increasingly rely on foreign contracts. The need to secure foreign contracts has caused several players in the U.S. defense industry, including Lockheed Martin, Northrop Grumman and Boeing, to engage in corrupt practices to survive (Pasztor 1995: B3).

In the early 1970s, Lockheed lost contracts with major European airlines, including Alitalia, Lufthansa, and Sabena. Therefore, it had to look for business elsewhere and turned to Japan. To sell its TriStar jets to Japan's All Nippon Airways, it used a Japanese middleman, who successfully negotiated the deal with the Japanese government. In 1976 it came to light that Lockheed had paid a total of USD 12 million to high-ranking Japanese officials, which amounted to less than 3% of the contract value, though. Lockheed had not suggested these payments, but had made them upon request of its Japanese middleman. These payments did not violate U.S. laws then, as the U.S. Foreign Corrupt Practices

Act was not enacted until 1977. However, these payments were illegal under Japanese law and so the Japanese middleman and Japanese officials were convicted, which had serious implications for Japanese politics. Lockheed was not convicted, but acquired the image of a corrupt company (Kotchian 1977: 7; "Ruling ends": 9; "Conviction upheld": 1).

In 1982, Lockheed sold C-5 cargo planes to the U.S. Air Force. Four years later, auditors from Pentagon's Defense Contract Audit Agency charged that Lockheed withheld information on cost savings and overcharged the Air Force by about USD 500 million on these cargo planes. Allegedly, Lockheed had adopted a new wage-negotiating strategy a few months before entering into contract negotiations with the Air Force. This strategy produced labor costs lower than the Air Force had assumed when it entered into contract negotiations. Under the Truth-in-Negotiations Act, Lockheed would have been required to inform the Air Force during the contract negotiations about the new wage-negotiations strategy and the resultant cost savings (Carrington 1986: 1).

A grand jury in Atlanta indicted Lockheed in 1994 on charges of violating the 1977 Foreign Corrupt Practices Act. According to the indictment, Lockheed had paid consulting fees to a consultant in Egypt in 1989, who was also a member of the Egyptian parliament then. The consultant had facilitated the sale of three Lockheed aircraft to Egypt. At first, Lockheed denied the allegations and even pointed to its "excellent record of integrity" (Harris and Ricks 1994: A12). In January 1995, however, Lockheed Martin pleaded guilty to the charges and had to pay USD 10 million in settlements according to the plea agreement. The company declined to comment on the matter publicly (Pasztor 1995: B3; Pasztor and Cole 1995: B6).

In 1994, Lockheed sold satellite technology to Asia Satellite Telecommunications in China. According to the U.S. Department of State, the satellite technology Lockheed sold to Asia Satellite could be applied to missile development. Therefore, the U.S. government charged Lockheed Martin with sharing critical technological knowledge with China, which is a violation of the U.S. Arms Export Control Act. In June 2000, Lockheed Martin agreed to pay USD 13 million in settlements to the U.S. government (Hartung and Ciarrocca 2000; "Lockheed Martin agrees to pay": 1; U.S. Department of State 2000).

At about the same time, it was discovered that two Lockheed Martin subsidiaries had overcharged the U.S. Navy on a procurement contract by USD 1.8 to 3.8 million. In an out-of-court settlement over Lockheed Martin's pricing practices in May 2000, Lockheed Martin agreed to pay the U.S. government USD 5 million (Hartung and Ciarrocca 2000).

4.2.1.3 The Defense Industry Initiative on Business Ethics and Conduct

Reported instances of fraud in the U.S. defense business in the 1980s diminished public confidence in the defense industry. A 1986 report by the President's Blue Ribbon Commission on Defense Management pointed out that the U.S. defense industry was in need of higher ethical business standards to safeguard its public image. U.S. defense contractors decided to join forces, founding the Defense Industry Initiative on Business Ethics and Conduct (DII) to raise ethical standards in the industry by committing themselves to the DII Principles (The Defense Industry Initiative 2000: 4).

In practical terms, the DII Principles require all signatories to implement a code of ethics, to conduct ethics-training programs, to set up mechanisms (e.g. hotlines) for employees to voice ethical concerns, to review their practices annually, and to share their knowledge and experiences with other DII signatories (The Defense Industry Initiative 2000: 4). The DII recognizes that ethics is different at every company and thus allows companies a lot of leeway when it comes to implementing the DII Principles (The Defense Industry Initiative 2000: 12). The DII Principles address issues such as business courtesies, kickbacks, confidential information, conflicts of interest, bidding, negotiating, charges to government, political contributions and the like (The Defense Industry Initiative 2000: 14-28).

4.2.1.4 Lockheed Martin's Ethics Program in the Media

The above incidents have prompted Lockheed Martin to implement a comprehensive ethics program. Its well thought-out approach to business ethics has made its ethics program a model for other companies in the industry (cf. Greengard 1997a: 51; Carey 1998: 57-58; Keller 1997: 19; "The view from Taft": n.p.). Lockheed Martin has ethics offices at all 70 business units worldwide. Its ethics hotline receives more than 4,000 calls a year (Greengard 1997a: 51). Ethical misconduct is rigorously sanctioned at Lockheed Martin, as is evident from the fact that 217 employees were fired for ethics violations from 1995 to 1999 (McCarthy 1999: B1).

To circumvent employee resentment and skepticism toward ethics training, Lockheed Martin has opted for the unconventional route of capturing its employee's attention — it makes them play board games (Carey 1998: 57; Keller 1997: 19). The board game, titled *The Ethics Challenge*, was designed by executives and an external consulting company. In the first six months after its introduction in 1997, all 175,000 Lockheed Martin employees got to play the game as part of their annual ethics-training requirements. The game features characters from Scott Adams' comic strip Dilbert™ (Carey 1998: 57-58). The Dilbert™ characters are also in the accompanying videos and posters ("The view from Taft": n.p.). The rules of the game are described below:

> "The game presents a maze of potential ethics challenges that a team of Lockheed employees must navigate. One person — generally a manager or supervisor — acts as the game's leader, while as many as seven players form a team. The leader and each team have a book of ethical scenarios that corresponds to a stock of case file cards. The leader chooses a card, and the teams refer to the corresponding case in their books. The teams have five minutes to discuss the situation and propose a solution" ("The view from Taft": n.p.).

The training tool is supposed to teach Lockheed Martin's employees about ethical decision-making (Carey 1998: 57-58). The board game turned out to be hugely popular among employees, not least because of Dilbert™. He is someone who people — especially office workers — can relate to easily ("The view from Taft": n.p.). Another factor is that the game offers real-world scenarios in an amusing way. It balances its serious message with humor, which is very effective in competing for employee attention (Carey 1998: 58). After the tremendous success of the board game among its own employees, Lockheed Martin shared the game with more than 1,500 companies, universities and schools (Carey 1998: 58).

In 1999, Lockheed Martin introduced Web-based training on ethics and legal compliance in addition to its board game. Originally, this interactive training was produced for CD-ROMs, but Web-based training offered clear advantages over CD-ROMs. Not only are Web-based training modules easier to access, but the Web-based system also records how many training sessions each employee completes. The training sessions focus on issues such as sexual harassment, insider trading, kickbacks and gifts (McCarthy 1999: B1).

4.2.2 Discourse Analysis

4.2.2.1 The Ideational Function

Identifying themes that cut across pages is hardly possible with the Lockheed Martin corpus, as it contains nine largely unrelated pages. Compliance is the only theme that appears on various pages. This section also regards Lockheed Martin's Value Statement and its Ethical Principles as themes. Although these are not themes in the sense that they appear again and again throughout the corpus, they are considered themes because together they take up just under

40% of the corpus. This is partly attributable to the fact that the Ethical Principles occur twice in the corpus, but also shows that Lockheed Martin's WWW information on corporate ethics is not very comprehensive.

The Value Statement
The Value Statement sets forth the six values Lockheed Martin espouses: *ethics, excellence, "can-do", integrity, people* and *teamwork*. It is worth noting that ethics and integrity are two separate values. Under integrity Lockheed Martin includes *truthfulness, trust, dignity* and *respect*, which reflects the common notion of integrity. However, Lockheed Martin's understanding of *ethics* appears unusual: *We will be well-informed in the regulations, rules, and compliance issues that apply to our businesses around the world.* With this understanding of ethics, Lockheed Martin unequivocally positions itself in the business-ethics paradigm.

While Lockheed Martin uses exclusively the committal future tense (i.e. *We will*) in the paragraph on ethics, it uses the categorical simple present tense throughout the remaining text, e.g. *We excel, We demonstrate, We utilize*, etc. This choice of tense suggests that Lockheed Martin does not believe that the company actually lives up to its values and therefore carefully phrased it as aspirations rather than the categorical truth. The use of prominence devices in the Value Statement is also remarkable. They include indefinite pronouns expressing totality (*all, every, everyone*), adjectives with emotive overtones (*innovative, inspired, challenging, enhanced, positive, superior*), superlatives (*highest, best*), and adverbs expressing forcefulness (*aggressively, continually, enthusiastically*).

Ethical Principles
A document entitled *Ethical Principals* [sic!] outlines Lockheed Martin's ethics policy. The misspelling in the headline undermines the credibility of the claims made on the page to some extent, as it indicates some degree of carelessness in dealing with the issue. Lockheed Martin's Ethical Principles encompass *honesty, integrity, responsibility, trust, respect* and *citizenship*. Interestingly, these principles include integrity, although ethics and integrity were separate items on the values statement. Similarly, trust and respect are separate principles, although they were subsumed under integrity in the value statement. The careless use of ethical concepts and terms indicates how little importance Lockheed Martin attributes to them.

Under integrity, Lockheed Martin commits itself to delivering on promises, raising *issues* and *admit*[ting] *error*. Subsuming these activities under the heading of integrity suggests that Lockheed Martin does not have a very clear understanding of integrity. Integrity is a principle separate from honesty, although it largely overlaps with the latter. The principle of integrity includes the phrase *To say precisely what we mean, and to deliver what and when we promise*, while honesty includes the assertion *To have the courage to speak our truth, and to be absolutely forthright in all cases*. Similarly, there is no apparent difference between *to raise and address difficult issues that may affect safety, performance, or legal responsibility* and *to call attention to any workplace violation of law, safe design and engineering standards, ethical codes*, the latter of which is included in the principle of responsibility. Again, the issues Lockheed Martin intends to raise center on legal compliance.

The principle of responsibility reads as follows:

(1) "To speak out without fear of reprisal to call attention to any workplace violation of law, safe design and engineering standards, ethical codes, community standards, sexual harassment, equality, diversity, health and related issues."

The order in which the issues are enumerated implies that Lockheed Martin gives higher priority to compliance than to social issues. The company sees its prime responsibilities in abiding by laws, standards and codes, but also recognizes its responsibility towards its employees by mentioning sexual harassment, equality, diversity and health. The use of the ambiguous term *community standards* suggests that Lockheed Martin is referring to standards imposed by municipalities rather than societal expectations of company conduct.

The principle of trust contains three different commitments, all of which concern Lockheed Martin's customers: *our position as stewards of our customers' businesses, supporting our customer enterprises* and *to raise issues if customer practices* ... Lockheed Martin does not make it explicit who is to trust whom and how far trust relates to these commitments. The heading *trust* seems thus inappropriate.

Lockheed Martin's ethical principles also include citizenship, under which Lockheed Martin seeks *to obey all the laws of any country in which we do business*, but also *to give back to the communities*. Here, too, Lockheed Martin's main concern is legal compliance, and obviously its understanding of citizenship does not extend beyond the law. Giving is obviously of minor importance to the company, as it is mentioned after compliance.

Lockheed Martin does not completely shy away from using negative language on its ethical-principles page. To refer to ethical misconduct the company uses words and phrases like *error* and *workplace violation*, but also more neutral terms such as *difficult issues, issues*, or *in all cases*. *To admit error* seems to be a superfluous claim, as once some wrongdoing is discovered it need not be admitted anymore. *Issue* is highly ambiguous in this context, especially when it collocates with *raise*, as in *to raise and address difficult issues* and *to raise issues if. To call attention to any workplace violation* is equally vague, as raising issues or calling attention to an issue does not necessarily imply that the company intends to eliminate these problems.

Compliance
A page focusing on supplier relationships voices Lockheed Martin's intention to select suppliers in a fair and objective manner and urges suppliers to comply with Lockheed Martin's ethics standards. The word *compliance* is, however, not used at all. Instead, Lockheed Martin uses phrases like *to follow established routines and procedures, to respect the limitations, by company policy, guidelines that pertain to our working relationship with you, meet our standards* and *are not permitted*. All these phrases diminish the power of the term *compliance*.

As has been pointed out above, legal compliance is also an issue in both the Value Statement and the statement of Lockheed Martin's Ethical Principles. While the Ethical Principles contain phrases such as *to obey all laws* and *to call attention to workplace violation of law* [and] *ethical codes*, the Value Statement contains the only occurrence of the word *compliance*: *We will be well-informed in the regulations, rules, and compliance issues that apply to our businesses around the world*. Also Lockheed Martin's Q&A ethics page takes up the issue of compliance indirectly in one of the questions: *How does the Corporate Office of Ethics and Business Conduct support high ethical standards at Lockheed Martin?* This question implies that the company has high ethical standards and that the ethics office sees to it that the company complies with them. The 17 external hyperlinks listed on the page *Other Ethics Sites* include links to the *Ethics Officer Association*, the *Ethics Resource Center*, the *Defense Industry Initiative*, the U.S. Department of the Interior, the Office of Government Ethics, the *Josephson Institute of Ethics*, and *Transparency International*. These organizations are potentially helpful in resolving compliance issues. The above examples confirm the impression that Lockheed Martin's ethical discourse centers on compliance, as is typical of a company in the business-ethics paradigm.

4.2.2.2 The Interpersonal Function

Lockheed Martin
Lockheed Martin uses both the first-person perspective and the neutral third-person perspective to refer to itself. A quantitative analysis reveals that first-person pronouns outnumber the use of *Lockheed Martin* and *the corporation* by far, as is illustrated in the breakdown in Table 7.

	Subject	Object	Genitive	Adjective	TOTAL
we / us / our	34	6	n.a.	38	78
Lockheed Martin	5	7	1	9	22
corporation	4	-	4	-	8
company	-	-	-	1	1
it	1	-	n.a.	2	3

Table 7: Breakdown of References to Lockheed Martin

No general pattern is discernible as to where the use of *we/us* is preferred to the use of the company name. A few remarkable text features can be pointed out, though. *Lockheed Martin* occurs on all pages in the corpus apart from the statement of Ethical Principles. It is worth noting that nine of the 22 instances of *Lockheed Martin* occur on the philanthropy page (see below for discussion). There are 17 occurrences of *we* in the Value Statement, which makes up 50% of all instances of *we*. Interestingly, the Ethical Principles, which are related to the Value Statement in terms of content and register, contain only three instances of *we*, as all sentences are subject-free, starting with an infinitive.

We/us/our is always used exclusively. This is typically evident from the content, but also made explicit a few times, for example in *us as a Corporation, we as a team*, and *we ... as responsible employees of Lockheed Martin*. These examples also suggest that *we/us/our* do not always refer to the same speakers. In the first example, *we* is the company as an institution, while in the latter two examples *we* speaks on behalf of Lockheed Martin's employees.

Stakeholders
The company enumerates its audiences twice on the page outlining its ethical principles:

(2) "To have the courage to speak our truth, and to be absolutely forthright in all cases, with our customers, co-workers, suppliers, communities, and shareholders."

(3) "To value the differences as well as similarities in all of our customers, co-workers, suppliers, communities, and shareholders."

The sequence in which they are named suggests that customers are — not surprisingly — the company's most important stakeholder group. Lockheed Martin ascribes more importance to suppliers and communities than to its shareholders, although shareholders are as vital to a public corporation as customers. Shareholders probably do not play a significant role, as roughly 50% of the stock is owned by trust companies, which are also trustees for some of Lockheed Martin's employee-benefit plans (Lockheed Martin 2002: 17-18). According to the Ethical Principles, *minority candidates* are a group Lockheed Martin pays special attention to in its hiring decisions. The rationale behind supporting minority groups reads as follows: *so that the Corporation reflects national diversity*. This is not the rationale one would expect for such an ethical principle, as minority hiring is laid down in the U.S. Equal Employment Opportunity Act anyway (De Cenzo and Robbins 1994: 60) and Lockheed Martin's workforce is thus required to reflect national diversity to a certain extent. Espousing minority hiring as an ethical principle thus seems superfluous, unless this principle is driven by the aspiration to support a disadvantaged group.

Employees
The main addressees of Lockheed Martin's Web pages are the companies' employees. This is evident from the fact that all instances of second-person pronouns in the corpus address company employees rather than customers. These pages directly address their audience using second-person pronouns and imperatives:

(4) "If you have any ethics questions, these documents are available to help you. If you have further questions, please call 1-800-LM-ETHIC."

(5) "Choose the language of your choice"

The Q&A page on corporate ethics seeks to give guidance to employees *who may have ethical issues or inquiries*. By using the modal verb *may* Lockheed

Martin mitigates the fact that employees encounter ethical problems at work and presents it as a mere possibility. This mitigation makes employees feel less guilty about using the HelpLine, i.e. Lockheed Martin's ethics hotline. Also, problems are euphemized as *issues or inquiries* to mitigate the negative connotation of problems or difficulties. The company personalizes the content of the Q&A page by putting themselves in the shoes of its employees, sometimes even transferring the questions to the first-person perspective:

(6) "How do I contact the Corporate Ethics HelpLine?"

(7) "When I call the Ethics HelpLine to report observed misconduct, what information will I be asked to provide?"

(8) "What is your advice to .... ?"

Using first-person and second-person pronouns, the company enters into a direct dialogue with its employees and involves them in the subject matter. This gives the message a down-to-earth touch and guarantees that employees feel concerned by the message. This unifying tone also takes away employees' fear of calling the ethics hotline, primarily because some of the questions are in fact presuppositions of employees' fears. For example:

(9) "Is there caller ID on the 800-LM-ETHICS phone lines?"

(10) "Are HelpLine calls taped?"

(11) "Can I remain anonymous and still keep track of what is happening on an ethics case opened as a result of my contact?"

By clicking on these questions, users are provided with Lockheed Martin's answer in a pop-up window. These answers reassure employees that they will remain anonymous when they contact the hotline.

Suppliers
Suppliers are addressed in a far more distant tone than Lockheed Martin employees. The page directed at suppliers conveys this distance through the use of passive voice (e.g. *suppliers are urged to*), nominalization (*appearance, treatment of suppliers, in the procurement of*) and the absence of second-person pronouns. Not only does this depersonalize the text, but it also makes the text sound like a legal document. The following paragraph is an appropriate illustration of Lockheed Martin legalese:

(12) "Lockheed Martin employees are not permitted to accept cash of any amount or any thing of value that has a retail or exchange value of $20 or more from individuals, companies, or representatives of

companies having or seeking business relationships with Lockheed Martin. However, our employees may accept meals, refreshments, or entertainment of nominal value on an infrequent basis in connection with normal business discussion."

In the very first paragraph on the supplier page, Lockheed Martin constructs positional meaning in the following phrases: *to treat all suppliers uniformly and fairly* and *to objectively and impartially weigh all facts in making an award decision*. The adverbs of manner in these phrases convey Lockheed Martin's evaluation of its supplier selection procedure, which it wants to see as fair and free of preferential treatment. However, the use of *we endeavor to, it is our goal to* and *we strive to* reduces the certainty of these statements, as Lockheed Martin does not guarantee that it is actually able to achieve these envisioned states. Thus, this paragraph also realizes negative positional meaning regarding Lockheed Martin's attitude toward the enactment of its own goals.

Another striking feature is the use of euphemisms in the second paragraph to make the assertions sound harmless and less threatening. For example, *gifts and other favors* are used to neutralize bribes. *An uncomfortable situation* substitutes for difficulties or problems. *Are urged to* simply means "must", and *avoid* and *may not* replace "must not".

The supplier page also exhibits an original letter, signed by CEO Vance Coffman, which was sent to all Lockheed Martin suppliers. Both the letter posted and the remaining text on the Web page seek to impose Lockheed Martin's values and principles on its suppliers (e.g. *are urged to, not permitted, may*). The speech function category of the supplier page is clearly a command. Between the lines, Lockheed Martin threatens to terminate the business relationship, if suppliers do not comply with Lockheed Martin standards. The company does not make this threat explicit, though, but implies it in the following statement in the CEO letter: *We are counting on you to do the same* [meet our standards]. This suggests that Lockheed Martin intends to discontinue business relations with suppliers who fail to comply with its standards.

Customers

Lockheed Martin's customers, and above all U.S. government agencies, are the secondary addressees of its ethics pages, as they need to be convinced that Lockheed Martin is a company with sound ethics. The ethical-principles page is the only page that refers to customers explicitly. First, customers are included in the enumeration of Lockheed Martin's stakeholders (see above). Furthermore, Lockheed Martin considers itself *stewards of our customers' businesses*, which implies that Lockheed Martin believes it has the power and capacity to do so.

Lockheed Martin even goes so far as to expect its customers to pursue the same ethics policies as itself: *to raise issues if customer practices are not in alignment with our ethics practices*. Although this suggests that Lockheed Martin takes ethics seriously, the significance of this statement is diluted when one considers that Lockheed Martin mainly sells to U.S. government agencies. Questioning their ethics is pointless and would not change anything, and so this claim does not seem very credible. At the same time, Lockheed Martin claims *to value the **differences** ... in all of our customers* (emphasis added) on the ethical-principles page. This appears hypocritical, considering that Lockheed Martin does not accept deviations of its customers' ethics policies from its own policy. Apparently, Lockheed Martin values differences, but does not tolerate them.

Community

Lockheed Martin refers to the general public as *the communities*. The pages directed at the general public are those in the section *Community Relations*. The introductory page does not include the audience in any way and barely includes Lockheed Martin in the assertions made. The subheading reads *Lockheed Martin Brings the Spirit of Community to the World*, which is the only reference to Lockheed Martin on this page. The page consists of three rather similar statements, including this one:

(13) "In Baltimore, teachers from around the country explore new active, collaborative, and project-centered practices that bring math and science to life for kids."

Apart from the fact that this statement as well as the other two statements do not refer to Lockheed Martin at all, it shows how much importance Lockheed Martin assigns to teaching children science.

The page on philanthropy in the *Community Relations* subsection is especially peculiar, as one cannot fail to notice that Lockheed Martin does not use a single *we* and only one *our* on that page. Rather, it uses *Lockheed Martin*, *The Lockheed Martin Corporation* or *It*. The absence of personal pronouns makes the page lack warmth and friendliness. That way, Lockheed Martin does not relate to its audience very convincingly. The matter-of-fact way the company deals with corporate philanthropy is also reflected in the frequent use of the passive voice, e.g. as in *are administered by*, *contributions are made primarily to*, *are now combined into* and *is based on*. Similarly, nominalizations such as *contributions*, *distribution*, *development* and *integration* remove the agent, viz. Lockheed Martin, from the scenery. By depersonalizing the text, Lockheed Martin distances itself from the activity and marginalizes it. Although corporate philanthropy is by its very nature an emotive issue, Lockheed Martin's text sounds distant and cold. Not only does this convey the impression that philanthropy is of minor concern to the company, but Lockheed Martin also manages to present philanthropy as if it were merely an administrative procedure:

(14) "The total available annually for distribution is based on the previous year's sales and earnings, and related factors such as performance and business priorities."

Particularly the phrase *available annually for distribution* reveals how uninvolved Lockheed Martin is with the issue. Also, pointing to financials in connection with corporate giving suggests that the motive behind philanthropy is not pure altruism. Rather, contributions are treated as tax-deductible expenses. Similarly, Lockheed Martin frankly admits that it seeks to align its contributions to its own business goals:

(15) "The Lockheed Martin Corporation is committed to a program of philanthropy that supports the Corporation's strategic business goals".

Nowhere does the company explain why it donates money at all. Rather, it outlines how it calculates the annual level of contributions and what projects qualify for donations. Lockheed Martin states that *K-16 Math and Science Education ... [is] the primary focus of Lockheed Martin philanthropy*. The fact that the company donates to education mostly suggests that it does not give to the community as a way to demonstrate social responsibility but rather to increase the future supply of engineers. This impression is also created on the introductory page in the *Community Relations* subsection (see above). Lockheed Martin also donates money to *Local activities that directly benefit Lockheed Martin employees and quality of life in the community*, but neither specifies these activities nor cites examples.

4.2.2.3 The Textual Function

Only the pages outlining Lockheed Martin's ethical principles and corporate values and the page on philanthropy exhibit peculiar thematic developments. They will be discussed in turn before examining the cohesion of the Web pages.

Themes

The ethical-principles page spells out Lockheed Martin's six core principles in the format of the following example:

(16) "**Trust**
To recognize our position as stewards of our customers' businesses. To place the best of our thinking, energies and abilities into supporting customer enterprises. To be willing to raise issues if customer practices are not in alignment with our ethics policies."

The page consists exclusively of isolated, infinite phrases starting with the infinitive of a verb or even with a split infinitive. These statements are largely agent-free. Only in a few rare cases is *we* or the possessive pronoun *our* used. Hence, the theme of these clauses is the action rather than the agent, which is reinforced by the use of adverbs a few times, e.g. *to be absolutely forthright, to say precisely what we mean, to forthrightly admit error.* Cohesion within the page is achieved by organizing every paragraph identically — the name of the principle as a heading, followed by an explanation of the principle. Although there are no verbal cohesive devices such as linking adverbs or references, the text is still cohesive owing to its syntactic parallelism.

Unlike the ethical-principles page, the corporate-values page does thematize the agent. It consists of complete sentences, the theme of which is predominantly *We* or — to put even greater emphasis on the agent — *Each of us*. As can be seen from the example below, the corporate values statement outlines the corporate values in a manner analogous to that of the page on ethical principles:

(17) "**ETHICS**
We will be well-informed in the regulations, rules, and compliance issues that apply to our businesses around the world. We will apply this knowledge to our conduct as responsible employees of Lockheed Martin, and will adhere to the highest standards of ethical conduct in all that we do."

The heading (viz. the name of the value) is followed by an explanation of how the value is enacted in Lockheed Martin's day-to-day business. Here, too, the absence of cohesive language material does not reduce the text's cohesion. Linking adverbs and the like are simply not necessary, since the text is of a declarative nature rather than a narrative. Therefore, individual sentences need not necessarily relate to each other.

The page on corporate philanthropy contains a total of eight complete sentences, the first four of which thematize Lockheed Martin. The sentences start with *The Lockheed Martin Corporation*, *Lockheed Martin*, *It* and *The Corporation's core businesses* and primarily profile the company. The theme of the remaining four sentences is the administration of corporate philanthropy. The sentences start with *The philanthropic activities*, *Philanthropic activities*, *Philanthropic contributions* and *The total* and each contains a verb in passive voice. The text is markedly incoherent, especially because the eight sentences are divided into five one-sentence or two-sentence paragraphs. Also, sentence adjuncts and references are non-existent, apart from *It* in the third sentence, referring to Lockheed Martin.

Cohesion
Lockheed Martin has separate subsections for different audiences. The home page takes users to sections directed at investors (*Investor Relations*), prospective employees (*Careers*), minority candidates (*Diversity*) and suppliers (*Suppliers*). Employees and the public at large will find information relevant to them in the section *About us*, which has subsections titled *Ethics* and *Community Relations*. The flowchart in Figure 3 gives an overview of Lockheed Martin's ethics Web pages and ethics menus, and shows where they can be found on the Web site.

All business-ethics pages found are to be found in the subsection *Ethics*, while the pages on community relations and on philanthropy are in the subsection *Community Relations*. The chart in Figure 3 also shows that Lockheed Martin has no crosslinks between documents, but uses exclusively menus to connect its Web pages. The *Code of Ethics and Business Conduct* included in Figure 3, which Lockheed Martin also refers to as *code of conduct*, is available for download as Acrobat™ file in fourteen languages, but was not included in the corpus on grounds of file format.

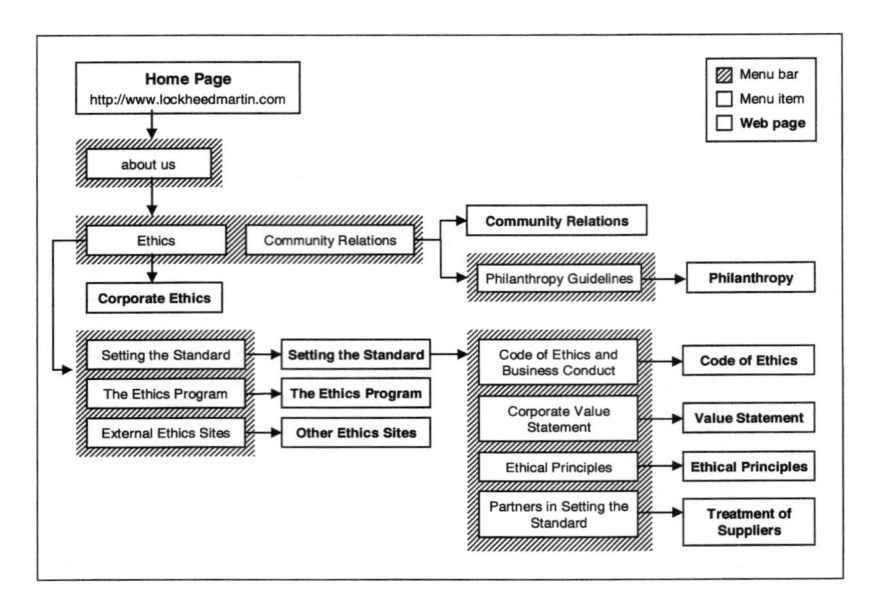

Figure 3: Cohesion among Lockheed Martin's Web Pages

Images are sparsely used on the Web site. If at all, they always occur as small photographs in the top-right corner and depict the same motif. They all highlight the use of sophisticated technology but always include employees as well to humanize technology. Notably, the majority of these people are male.

4.3 Intra-Paradigm Analysis

This section sets out to demonstrate that both BellSouth and Lockheed Martin are ideal representatives of the business-ethics paradigm. The following pieces of evidence are intended to support this claim:

- **Compliance:** Since preventing harm is the main objective of companies in the business-ethics paradigm, they pay special attention to compliance. The discourse analyses show that compliance is the key theme in both company discourses. Both companies mention compliance with laws and regulations as an objective. BellSouth even explicitly refers to the Federal Sentencing Guidelines, which Lockheed Martin does not do. Further, both companies encourage employees to call the ethics hotline when in doubt. BellSouth even requires its employees to blow the whistle on suspected misconduct they observe.

- **Institutionalization:** Both companies have institutionalized ethics into their organizations to a great extent. They have comprehensive ethics programs in place, comprising most of the features characteristic of the business-ethics paradigm, viz. ethics codes, ethics officers, ethics hotlines and ethics committees. Cases in point are Lockheed Martin's Corporate Office of Ethics and Business Conduct and its HelpLine, and BellSouth's Office of Ethics and Compliance and its Ethics Line.

- **Ethics Associations:** As was pointed out in the introduction to Chapter 3, companies in the business-ethics paradigm are typically members of the *Ethics Officer Association*, and so are BellSouth and Lockheed Martin. They both provide hyperlinks to the *Ethics Officer Association* — BellSouth on the page *Resource Links* and Lockheed Martin on the page *External Ethics Sites*. In addition, both companies provide links to the *Ethics Resource Center* in Washington and the *Josephson Institute of Ethics* in California, both of which are prominent NGOs advising companies on compliance programs.

- **Internal focus:** The main addressees of their Web pages are the companies' employees. This is not only evident from the fact that all instances of *you* address company employees, but also from the support of employees in ethics-related matters. BellSouth has online self-tests and a scenarios game, while Lockheed Martin has the Dilbert™ board game. However, while BellSouth has all this publicly available on the WWW, Lockheed Martin does not do so, which suggests that BellSouth's uses ethics for PR. This is also evident from the fact that BellSouth's Web pages publish information that are of no interest to the general public, e.g. the disciplinary consequences of employee misconduct, while Lockheed Martin does neither on its Web site.

- **Philanthropy:** Corporate giving is an issue in both corporations, yet they do not talk about it at great length. Both have foundations administer corporate giving, viz. the BellSouth Foundation and the Lockheed Martin Corporation Foundation. BellSouth and Lockheed Martin make it explicit that they donate chiefly to education. BellSouth lists education as the first of three areas that its community outreach encompasses. Lockheed Martin clearly states that education is the *primary focus* of its giving activities. The fact that both donate to education mostly suggests that they do so in order to raise children's interest in technology and possibly even increase the future supply of engineers and computer scientists.
- **Web technology:** BellSouth's online ethics games and Lockheed Martin's Q&A page with pop-up answers are the only interactive devices on their ethics Web pages. Hypermedia technology is not used anywhere else on their ethics sites. According to media reports (see Section 4.2.1.4), Lockheed Martin has intranet-based ethics training, so it obviously makes use of hypermedia to a larger extent but does not make it publicly available.

5 The Corporate-Social-Responsibility Paradigm

5.1 Case 3: *Ben & Jerry's Homemade, Inc.*

5.1.1. Background to the Company

5.1.1.1 Company Profile

In the late 1970s Ben Cohen and Jerry Greenfield enrolled in a correspondence course in making ice cream. In 1978 they opened their first ice cream parlor, named Ben & Jerry's Homemade, in a renovated gas station in Burlington, Vermont (Rigby 1998: 55). Soon they started packing ice cream in pints and sold it to grocery stores and restaurants. As business prospered, Ben and Jerry's started franchising in 1981. In the same year, when Ben & Jerry's outlets were still confined to Vermont only, Ben & Jerry's ice cream was already recognized as the best in the world by *Time* magazine. In 1984, the company went public as Ben & Jerry's Homemade, Inc., but offered stock exclusively to Vermont residents at first. The idea behind limiting the stock offer to local residents was that the community should benefit from the company's financial success. Two years later, Ben & Jerry's also offered its stock nation-wide (Ferrell and Gable 1997: 276). In 1988 Ben and Jerry's ventured abroad for the first time, setting up shop in Canada and Israel. In the following years Ben and Jerry's expanded to several European and Asian countries as well (Ben & Jerry's 2000). Company founders Ben Cohen and Jerry Greenfield remained at the helm till 1995 and are now involved in the Ben & Jerry's Foundation only (Ben & Jerry's 2001). After just over 20 years in business, Ben & Jerry's generated sales of USD 237 million in 1999 (Ben & Jerry 1999). More current financial information is not publicly available, as Ben & Jerry's became a wholly-owned subsidiary of Unilever in 2000.

Although neither Ben Cohen nor Jerry Greenfield is a native of Vermont (Taylor 1997: 374), their business is deeply rooted in Vermont, as is evident from the brand-name suffix *Vermont's Finest All Natural Ice Cream*. The company's paramount symbol is a black-and-white cow, referred to as the "holy cow" (Jackson 2001), which fits the brand name, given the ubiquity of black-and-white cows in Vermont. Furthermore, the cow is symbol of fresh milk, which underlines the naturalness of the ice cream.

A variety of factors have helped the company establish a "quirky image that differentiated itself substantially from those of its competitors" (Arnold 2001: 17). First, Ben & Jerry's unorthodox ice cream flavors with "wacky" names (Arnold 2001: 17) (e.g. Chunky Monkey and Cherry Garcia) and funky, colorful packaging, e.g. tie-dye containers (Ferrell and Gable 1997: 276), make the products stand out. Also, Ben & Jerry's founders Ben Cohen and Jerry Greenfield have succeeded in establishing themselves as "brand icons" (Arnold 2001: 17). In the United States, the high-profile company does not even need to advertise, since its founders Cohen and Greenfield "are such well-known personalities" ("Ben & Jerry's to raise its UK profile": 12) that they have managed to build their brand merely through public relations (Arnold 2001: 17). Together, Ben Cohen and Jerry Greenfield are more than just two individuals who founded a company. Owing to their long friendship they are referred to as "the pair" (cf. Rigby 1998: 55; Taylor 1997: 374) or the "twosome" (Rigby 1998: 56) in the press. The two remnants of the hippie era (Smith 2000: 54) are reported to wear tie-dye socks, "sloppy T-shirts ... and worn jeans" (Rigby 1998: 54). Ben Cohen and Jerry Greenfield reinforce the company's "wholesome, small-town origins" (Arnold 2001: 17) and stand for "modern hippiedom, adult fun, letting go and rediscovering the child in you" (Arnold 2001: 17). Their "Sixties flower-child philosophy" (Taylor 1997: 374) and "down-home hippie folksiness" (Rigby 1998: 55) has shaped Ben & Jerry's corporate culture and corporate identity. The two founders also manage to instill this laid-back hippie atmosphere into their annual general meeting of stockholders, who are for the most part individuals from Vermont. These AGMs are reportedly "well attended by the locals in a carnival-type atmosphere" (Rigby 1998: 56).

Another factor conducive to Ben & Jerry's immense success is its unorthodox marketing campaigns. The company promotes its products not by conventional ways of TV commercials or newspaper advertisements, but rather stages newsworthy events of value to local communities. The ensuing media coverage is essentially free advertising (Ferrell and Gable 1997: 277). For example, Ben Cohen and Jerry Greenfield traveled across the United States with their Cowmobile, a solar-powered, modified mobile home, and distributed free scoops of Ben & Jerry's ice cream. This bus project was also intended to raise money for charity (Eismann 1992: 25; Ben & Jerry's 2001).

5.1.1.2 Caring Capitalism

Corporate philanthropy is also a driving force behind Ben & Jerry's success, as Ben & Jerry's has acquired an image of a company with a "social conscience and [a] sense of humor" (Marconi 1996: 184). Ben Cohen and Jerry Greenfield have bestowed an ethically oriented culture on their company, which sets it apart from most rivals (Mazur 2001: 26). Ben & Jerry's coined the term Caring Capitalism, which rests on the notion that a company that manufactures a high-quality product and cares for its community can, at the same time, be financially successful. And for Ben & Jerry's this has proven right (Fombrun 1996: 129). According to the Director of Social Mission and Development at Ben & Jerry's, the company does not have a formal code of ethics, but relies only on its brief Statement of Mission to guide the company's business conduct (Bankowski 1997: 26).

A major element of Ben & Jerry's Caring Capitalism is the well-being of their employees. In the company's early days, compensation policy held that no employee, including Ben Cohen and Jerry Greenfield, could make more than two times the salary of the lowest-paid employee (Laberis 1999: 20). Ben & Jerry's compensation ratio was changed to 5:1 later on and was further relaxed to 7:1 in 1990. Nevertheless, key executive positions remained vacant for months because of low compensation (Wiesendanger 1993: 20). In 1994, when the company was searching for a new CEO to replace Ben Cohen and Jerry Greenfield, it reluctantly discarded the ratio plan, as it was unable to attract high-caliber executives with this restraining compensation scheme (Laabs 1995: 12; "The ice-man goeth": 70). Critics have argued that the compensation ratio only worked when Ben Cohen and Jerry Greenfield were at the helm, as they made a fortune on their stock holdings so that compensation was next to irrelevant to them (Laberis 1999: 20). In addition to fair executive compensation, Caring Capitalism also includes a variety of unorthodox employee benefits, such as casual attire at work or the possibility to take leave of absences from work to do voluntary work in the community. The Joy Gang, a group of employees seeking to promote the idea of fun at work, regularly organizes party-like events. This idea goes back to Jerry Greenfield, whose motto is "If it's not fun why do it?" (Laabs 1992: 51). The company also has a futon room for employees to take a nap, which is intended to raise productivity at work (Condon 1992: n.p.).

The second major focus group of Ben & Jerry's Caring Capitalism is the community and society at large. In various campaigns the company has taken a stance on issues of public concern. Examples of Ben & Jerry's social activism include a campaign to promote voter registration in 1998, a protest against a nuclear power plan in New Hampshire in 1990, and a campaign in 1992 to support the Children's Defense Fund in making U.S. Congress aware of children's needs (Ben & Jerry's 2001). Ben & Jerry's PartnerShop project is another reflection of Caring Capitalism. The project started in July 1992 when Ben & Jerry's opened a franchise in Harlem, New York, which was run by residents of a homeless shelter in Harlem. The idea was to get homeless men off the streets by providing housing facilities and employing them in the Harlem franchise (Eismann 1992: 24; Fombrun 1996: 340; 354-355). In summer 2001, Ben & Jerry's launched a national contest in the U.S. titled *Citizen Cool* to find twelve everyday heroes in twelve big cities throughout the United States. These heroes were supposed to have effected positive change in their neighborhoods. The top three heroes starred in a 30-minute documentary on citizenship, which was shown in schools and at independent film festivals, opening in December 2001. The *Citizen Cool* contest was promoted on local radio stations, via direct mail, and on Ben & Jerry's Web site. Essentially, the contest was just a marketing campaign for the launch of Ben & Jerry's new flavor Concession Obsession (Rasmusson 2001: 14; Reyes 2001: 7).

Ben & Jerry's gives to the community primarily through its foundation. The Ben & Jerry's Foundation was established in 1985 and receives 7.5% of corporate pre-tax profits to fund community projects and non-profit organizations that seek to alleviate social problems (Ben & Jerry's 2001; Eismann 1992: 25). In addition, Ben & Jerry's gives away 40% of earnings from its Rainforest Crunch ice cream to help save the rainforest. In 1988 Ben & Jerry's initiated a campaign named "1% For Peace", which aims at allocating 1% of the national defense budget to peace-promoting initiatives. Company tours of the company premises in Waterbury — one of the main tourist attractions in Vermont — also yield money for social causes (Eismann 1992: 25).

In recognition of its socially responsible business conduct Ben & Jerry's received the Corporate Giving Award from the Council on Economic Priorities in 1988 and the Lawrence A. Wien Prize from Columbia University in 1989. Also, the New York University Stern School Reputation Index has ranked Ben & Jerry's number five overall and number one in the social responsibility category, as it points out in its company history on its Web site (Ben & Jerry's 2001).

Arguably, Caring Capitalism is merely cause-related marketing or clever point-of-purchase politics (Eismann 1992: 24). To make its social efforts more credible, Ben & Jerry's conducts social audits and publishes their results on its Web site. For years, the company's annual report has included both a financial report and a social report. The social audit, conducted by outside experts, assesses the company's social performance in areas such as employee compensation and benefits, occupational safety, environmental affairs, community involvement, and customer service (Wiesendanger 1993: 20). However, being positioned as a socially responsible company has its downside, too, particularly because such companies have "two bottom lines to work to" (Rigby 1998: 55). In their book *Ben & Jerry's Double Dip*, Cohen and Greenfield (1997: 149) point out that the negative aspect of their business strategy is "the phenomenon of elevated expectations" (Cohen and Greenfield 1997: 149). Their point is the following:

"When you set yourself up as a model, when you say you're trying to do things in a different and a better way, you set yourself up for criticism. No one expects Chevron to do much for society. But people expect a lot from Ben & Jerry's. ... When we don't achieve our aspirations, we're criticized for being hypocritical. It comes with the territory" (Cohen and Greenfield 1997: 149).

A case in point concerning such hypocrisy is when Perry Odak, who was previously employed by a US manufacturer of guns, became CEO despite the fact that Ben Cohen and Jerry Greenfield were known as advocates of gun control. What Jerry Greenfield deemed "an ironic situation" (Rigby 1998: 55) was pure hypocrisy to the media (Taylor 1997: 374).

5.1.1.3 Reputation Threats

5.1.1.3.1 The Takeover by Unilever

A major event in Ben & Jerry's history was its takeover by Unilever in 2000. When rumors of a possible takeover appeared in January 2000, concerned customers demonstrated outside Ben & Jerry's New York scoop shops, warning the company against selling out. Consumers feared that Ben & Jerry's would not only lose its independence but would also have to abandon its commitment to Caring Capitalism. In economic terms, the takeover made perfect sense, though, as Ben & Jerry's needed a powerful partner to realize its expansion plans. Eventually, Unilever took over Ben & Jerry's for USD 326 million in April 2000, which resulted in a big premium on Ben & Jerry's share price ("Ben & Jerry's: Will 'caring capitalism' yield to creamy profits?" 2000; "Unilever scoops up Ben & Jerry's" 2000).

When in Fall 2000 Unilever appointed Frenchman Yves Couette as CEO of Ben & Jerry's to succeed Perry Odak, Ben Cohen and Jerry Greenfield threatened to quit the company, as they had preferred an incumbent Ben & Jerry's executive to become CEO (Smith 2000: 54). Die-hard fans of Ben & Jerry's set up a Web site dedicated to the two company founders at <http://www.savebenjerry.com>, which is not online any more, though. The Web site sought to persuade Ben Cohen and Jerry Greenfield to remain with the company, as otherwise the company's spirit would get lost (Hofman 2001: 68). The clash of corporate cultures is also evident from the resignation of Ben and Jerry's UK head of marketing Ian Hill in May 2001. He stepped down because of disagreements with Unilever, primarily about the company's strategic direction (Arnold 2001: 17). As of April 2001 Ben Cohen and Jerry Greenfield are no longer part of the management team but devote their time to social activities, in particular to the Ben & Jerry's Foundation (Hofman 2001: 68; Mazur 2001: 26-27). The company history on Ben & Jerry's Web site ends in 1999 and does not make any reference to the Unilever takeover (Ben & Jerry's 2001), apart from one brief note on its financials page.

The press also voiced harsh criticism regarding the takeover. For example, *The Wall Street Journal* lamented:

> "Yet another icon of counterculture idealism takes the money and runs in this golden age of markets and mergers. The ice-cream maker Ben & Jerry's Homemade Inc., that utopian experiment in peace, love and capitalism, is selling itself to a multinational consumer-products behemoth whose name sounds like a machine tool — Unilever" (Brancaccio 2000: A34).

The takeover did, however, not completely destroy Ben & Jerry's ethically-oriented corporate culture, as was feared. The takeover agreement included a clause according to which Unilever was not to change Ben & Jerry's social mission (Mazur 2001: 26-27). Unilever committed itself to maintaining Ben & Jerry's philanthropic efforts by continuing to give 7.5% of operating profits to charity ("Business: Fat and thin": 63-64; "Unilever scoops up Ben & Jerry's" 2000).

5.1.1.3.2 Dioxin and the Eco-Pint Scandal

Another scandal hit Ben & Jerry's in April 1999. Ben & Jerry's had switched its ice-cream packaging from bleached paperboard to clay-coated unbleached paperboard and called these ice-cream pints Eco-Pints. As bleaching discharges hazardous wastewater, including chemicals such as dioxin, such a manufacturing process was unacceptable to the company ("Environmentally conscious carton" 1999: 48). Ben & Jerry's distributed in-store brochures pointing out the dangers of dioxin, including cancer and genetic defects ("Scoops of hypocrisy" 2000). It still prides itself on having introduced "the ice-cream industry's first pint container made from unbleached paperboard" on its Web site (Ben & Jerry's 2001). The unbleached pint container is, as the company puts it,

> "a major breakthrough key to one of the company's environmental mission goals: reducing the company's use of all paper products bleached white with a chemical process that is one of the country's leading causes of toxic water pollution" (Ben & Jerry's 2001).

In March 2000 the Competitive Enterprise Institute and Citizens for the Integrity of Science, two Washington-based think tanks, discovered that Ben & Jerry's ice cream contained a lot more dioxin than its packaging ever could (Franz 2000: 76). The two think tanks then filed an advertising complaint with the Federal Trade Commission, charging that the new environmentally friendly ice-cream carton misled customers, as it failed to inform them that the ice cream itself contained dioxin as well (Franz 2000: 76). The company denied that it had been "trying to deceive the public by not pointing out that dioxin is found in most food products" (Franz 2000: 76). As a result of this turmoil, Ben & Jerry's revised its brochures ("Scoops of hypocrisy" 2000).

5.1.1.3.3 The Rainforest-Crunch Scandal

Ben & Jerry's Rainforest Crunch ice cream — made of Brazil nuts — was launched as part of a well-meant cause-related-marketing initiative that turned out to be a big fiasco. Ben & Jerry's idea was that Amazon natives could make a living from harvesting Brazil nuts instead of selling off land rights to miners and foresters. This was intended to prevent the Amazonian rainforests from being further deforested. When Rainforest Crunch hit the market in 1990, its label clearly stated that "buying the ice cream helps preserve the Amazon's endangered rain forests". The product was instantly successful and Ben & Jerry's did not only benefit from its sales but also from the invaluable free publicity Rainforest Crunch attracted (Entine 1995).

However, the rainforest project backfired when the media reported that the nuts used to produce Rainforest Crunch did not stem from natives' harvests. Originally, Ben & Jerry's had intended to buy Brazil nuts from the native Amazonian Xapuri cooperative. However, when demand rocketed, the cooperative was not able to supply the quality and quantity required (Entine 1995). Ben & Jerry's was then forced to buy nuts from the commercial market and the Xapuri cooperative stopped supplying altogether. While the company had launched a thriving product, the promised benefits for the Amazonians had failed to materialize. Critics argued that the income native Amazonians generated by selling land rights could never have been matched by selling nuts. Today, Rainforest Crunch is still one of Ben & Jerry's flagship products, yet its label no longer includes a reference to supporting indigenous Amazonian people, but still talks about sustainable harvesting in the rainforest (Entine 1995).

5.1.2 Discourse Analysis

5.1.2.1 The Ideational Function

A *WordSmith* word-frequency list of the Ben & Jerry's corpus has revealed that the most frequent terms in the Ben & Jerry's corpus center around production (*milk, cows, cream, dairy, Vermont*), society (*social, community*) and philanthropy (*grant, foundation*). Another term among the most frequent words is *dioxin*, which Ben & Jerry's dedicates a whole page to. The current section will examine these four subjects plus Ben & Jerry's Statement of Mission.

Vermont Dairy Products

The company was founded in Vermont and is still headquartered there. Ben & Jerry's repeatedly points out that its products are made from Vermont dairy products. Since it is so deeply rooted there it included *Vermont* not only in its brand name but also chose the Vermont cow as its brand icon. Ben and Jerry's uses visual elements to emphasize this point, placing numerous images of the Vermont cow on its Web pages.

Ben & Jerry also emphasizes the naturalness, freshness and high quality of its products, frequently by using superlatives. The following phrases illustrate how Ben & Jerry's describes its products:

(1) "To make, distribute and sell the finest quality all natural ice cream ... made from Vermont dairy products"

(2) "we favor natural foods produced locally at family farms"

(3) "made from fresh Vermont milk and cream"

(4) "Ben & Jerry's products meet or exceed all standards of food safety everywhere they are sold"

The superlatives contained in the above statements suggest that Ben & Jerry's ice cream is seemingly better than competitive products, yet the company does not bring up competitors once in the whole corpus. Ben & Jerry's product names also reflect this superiority, e.g. as in *World's Best Vanilla* and *Vermont's Finest All Natural Ice Cream*. The superlatives referring to Ben & Jerry's products are the only superlatives in the whole corpus.

Vermont does not only come up as the origin of Ben & Jerry's dairy ingredients but also as the recipient of Ben & Jerry's philanthropy. Ben & Jerry's has employee community-action teams (CATs) *at five Vermont sites*, who *distribute small grants to community groups within the state of Vermont*.

Social Focus
The corpus contains 25 instances of *social* and two instances of *societal*. The latter collocate with *change* and *problems*. Twelve instances of *social* also collocate with *change, problems, issues* and *action*. For example:
- (5) "We support projects which are models for social change"
- (6) "grants to not-for-profit, grassroots organizations ... which facilitate progressive social change"
- (7) "Take A Stand – Political & Social Action"
- (8) "increase public awareness around social issues"

Ben & Jerry's provides financial support only to projects capable of eliminating social problems and effecting social change. Ben & Jerry's also points out that it does not fund education, research, scholarships, or individuals in need. Hence, Ben & Jerry's philanthropy is directed at society as a whole rather than its individual members. *Social* is also the title of one of the three parts of the mission statement. The term *social responsibility* does not occur in the corpus at all. *Responsibility* occurs only once on the dioxin page in the sentence *We have also expressed our belief that business has a responsibility to improve the quality of life in our communities*, which closely matches the concept of social responsibility. Ben & Jerry's also publishes three *Social Audit* reports from the years 1999, 2000 and 2001 as well as *CERES*[6] *Reports* from the years 1999 and 2000.

The Statement of Mission
Created in 1988, Ben & Jerry's Statement of Mission (see Exhibit 3) is the core of its corporate ethics. It is the only ethics statement the company has and, as the company claims, guides all its decisions. This three-part mission statement outlines Ben & Jerry's product mission, economic mission and social mission. The product mission states the *raison d'être* of the company — producing and selling ice cream. The economic mission of making a profit is actually a prerequisite for survival rather than a *mission*. The social mission focuses on society as a whole, but does not specifically highlight employee benefits, which are actually a central part of Ben & Jerry's Caring Capitalism.

---

[6] CERES is the Coalition for Environmentally Responsible Economics, a U.S. coalition of environmental advocacy groups. Companies that have signed the CERES Principles commit themselves to continuous environmental improvement. <http://www.ceres.org>

> **STATEMENT OF MISSION**
>
> **BEN & JERRY'S IS DEDICATED TO** the creation & demonstration of a new corporate concept of linked prosperity. Our mission consists of three interrelated parts.
>
> **UNDERLYING THE MISSION** is the determination to seek new and creative ways of addressing all three parts, while holding a deep respect for individuals inside and outside the company, and for the communities of which they are a part.
>
> **Product**
> To make, distribute and sell the finest quality all natural ice cream and related products in a wide variety of innovative flavors made from Vermont dairy products.
>
> **Economic**
> To operate the Company on a sound financial basis of profitable growth, increasing value for our shareholders, and creating career opportunities and financial rewards for our employees.
>
> **Social**
> To operate the Company in a way that actively recognizes the central role that business plays in the structure of society by initiating innovative ways to improve the quality of life of a broad community - local, national, and international.
>
> Underlying the mission of Ben & Jerry's is the determination to seek new & creative ways of addressing all three parts, while holding a deep respect for individuals inside and outside the Company and for the communities of which they are a part.

Exhibit 3: Ben & Jerry's Statement of Mission

There is no apparent reason for repeating the second paragraph in the end, given that the mission statement is not a very long document anyway. Also, the minor modifications made to the repetition do not appear plausible. Interestingly, Ben & Jerry's does not use the pronoun *we* at all and includes only three instances of *our*, collocated with *mission*, *employees* and *shareholders*. Instead of *we*, it uses *the Company, the company,* or *Ben & Jerry's*. In most places the text does not contain agents at all. Also, the nominalizations *creation*, *demonstration* and *determination* make the text sound impersonal and formal. The mission statement does thus not convey the same nonchalant tone as on other pages.

What the media call *Caring Capitalism* is referred to as *a new corporate concept of linked prosperity* in Ben & Jerry's Statement of Mission. *Linked* here obviously refers to linking profits and social activism, which is equally reflected in the term *Caring Capitalism*. It is worth noting that Ben & Jerry's does not commit itself to donating 7.5% of its pre-tax profits in the mission statement.

Philanthropy

Ben & Jerry's commits itself to giving away 7.5% of its pretax profits either through the Ben & Jerry's Foundation or in the form of employee volunteerism and corporate grants. Ben & Jerry's does not overemphasize this 7.5% commitment, as only the page *Everything you ever wanted to know about Ben & Jerry's* includes this commitment, while the pages dedicated to philanthropy do not make this claim.

Ben & Jerry's donates its ice cream in the course of its product donations program. Ben & Jerry's cites the corporate motto "If it's not fun, why do it?" in connection with ice-cream donations on the page *Product Donations*, asserting that *giving away free ice cream is about as fun as it gets*. Ben & Jerry's seems to strongly involve employees in its philanthropic activities. The company supports employee volunteerism in the form of *employee Community Action Teams*. Further, employees are allowed to participate in decision-making in the Ben & Jerry's Foundation. The concept of philanthropy is realized in the text by nouns like *philanthropy*, *grant*, *grantmaking* and *donation* and the verbs *to fund* and *to give away*. When referring to its monetary donations, Ben & Jerry's prefers the verb *to fund* and the noun *grant* to describe the giving procedure, whereas it uses exclusively *donation* to refer to product donations.

The page outlining Ben & Jerry's giving guidelines appears rather impersonal in tone, primarily because the process of grantmaking is the focus of the text rather than the participants in this process. This is evident from the 34 instances of agent-free passive voice. The following two examples serve to illustrate how the passive functions to exclude agents from the grantmaking process:

(9) "Letters of Interest may be submitted at any time and are reviewed on an ongoing basis. However, they may take up to eight (8) weeks to be reviewed"

(10) "Application materials will be sent along with the invitation letter. Full proposals will be reviewed three times a year"

Ben & Jerry's makes grants only to organizations with 501(c)3 status[7]. It uses negatives to add a strict tone to its giving guidelines. The page outlining Ben & Jerry's funding guidelines contains 16 instances of *no/not*. Ben & Jerry's points to the large number of applications as a reason for these stringent guidelines: *Due to the great volume of grant requests we receive, we regret that we will be unable to review requests that do not conform to these guidelines.* Examples of such guidelines include:

(11) "a readable font size (no less than 10 pt.) and one inch margins"

(12) "We do not accept FedEx or express delivery packages"

(13) "We do not accept faxed or e-mailed Letters of Interest"

(14) "No full grant proposals will be reviewed without ..."

(15) "Please do not send additional backup materials, videos or cassettes with your Letter of Interest as they will not be reviewed and cannot be returned"

(16) "We cannot expedite a funding decision"

Furthermore, Ben & Jerry's repeatedly rules out the funding of certain projects, more often than it states the criteria for projects eligible for funding. This may be put down to the fact that it receives a lot of applications for funding of projects that do not qualify. Therefore, it seeks to deter potential applicants from submitting requests that are not eligible for funding:

(17) "We do not offer grants to support basic or direct social service programs"

(18) "these types of programs do not fall within the scope of the Ben & Jerry's Foundation"

(19) "The Ben & Jerry's Foundation does not offer grants to support ... "

(20) "The Ben & Jerry's Foundation does not fund: ..."

Generally, Ben & Jerry's does not try to avoid the use of *not* by euphemizing negative phrases. The phrase *we will be unable to* is the only one that seeks to mitigate a negative situation, as it clearly means *will not*. However, the page outlining the funding guidelines also contains a significant cluster of modal verbs, which are next to non-existent on the other pages in the corpus. These modal verbs are used to stipulate funding criteria without using negatives. They express a strong or modest obligation:

---

[7] Article 501(c)3 of the United States Federal Internal Revenue Code (IRC) lays down the criteria according to which non-profit organizations can become tax-exempt organizations (Casey 2000).

(21) "Projects must: ..."
(22) "Letters of Interest ... must be submitted ..."
(23) "Grant applicants need to ..."
(24) "Applicants should: ..."
(25) "This letter should be attached to the Cover Page"
(26) "Letters should employ a readable font size"

To make the text sound more polite, Ben & Jerry's uses *wish* instead of *want*: *the proposal deadline for which you wish to be considered* and *if you wish to be considered for*. The polite tone of the page is also reinforced by the use of *Thank you* (twice) and *please* (eight times).

In the course of its *PartnerShop* program, Ben & Jerry's teams up with non-profit organizations to form *social enterprises*. The partnership formed between Ben & Jerry's is visually emphasized by a picture of shaking hands. The idea of these *PartnerShops* is to provide unemployed, socially disadvantaged people with jobs, who Ben & Jerry's refers to euphemistically as *people who may face barriers to employment*. The donation Ben & Jerry's makes to this project is that it waives the franchise fee for the operators or the *PartnerShops*.

Dioxin
On the page dealing with the issue of dioxin, Ben & Jerry's responds to the dioxin scandal that hit the company in 1999/2000 (see Section 5.1.1.3.2). Ben & Jerry's uses *The true facts* as the heading of the page and repeats this phrase in the text: *we try to give you, our customer, the true facts*. Although facts are by definition true, Ben & Jerry's presupposes that customers have been given wrong information. The very first sentence reads *As most of you know, Ben & Jerry's cares about its customers and it cares about the environment*, which presents Ben & Jerry's caring as a well-known fact.

The main message of the page is that Ben & Jerry's ice cream does not contain dioxin to a health-endangering extent and meets all food-safety standards. Ben & Jerry's engages in special pleading by putting forward very one-sided arguments. For examples, it blames Junkscience.com for the whole controversy, but fails to mention the Washington think tanks that brought up the issue originally. According to Ben & Jerry's, Junkscience.com *attempted to challenge and ridicule attempts by the U.S. Environmental Protection Agency to raise concerns about dioxin*. It seems that Ben & Jerry's mentions the EPA to lend its argument third-party credibility by appealing to authority and presents Junkscience.com as an opponent of the U.S. government. The defensive tone established throughout the page is further reinforced by the statement *Junkscience.com itself acknowledges that eating the ice cream is safe*, in which Ben & Jerry's again blames Junkscience.com for stirring up an unnecessary controversy simply to harm Ben & Jerry's. Ben & Jerry's considers itself a victim of Junkscience.com by claiming that it was *singled out* by Junkscience.com to make a *political statement* rather than raise *a food safety issue*. Although Ben & Jerry's acknowledges that dioxins are a *global problem*, it plays down the threats posed by dioxin in its ice cream by claiming that other foodstuffs also contain dioxins: *Dioxins exist across the entire food chain, and are present in all dairy and meat products, in fish and also in mother's milk.* The company also talks about *trace amounts of dioxin* in its ice cream, which makes dioxins in Ben & Jerry's ice cream appear less threatening.

5.1.2.2 The Interpersonal Function

Ben & Jerry's
Table 8 provides an overview of the uses of pronouns and nouns referring to Ben & Jerry's.

	Subject	Object	Genitive	Adjective	TOTAL
we / us / our	71	16	n.a.	44	**131**
Ben & Jerry's	14	12	n.a.	13	**39**
company	3	4	-	1	**8**
it / its	-	-	n.a.	3	**3**

Table 8: Breakdown of References to Ben & Jerry's

In general, first-person pronouns occur three times as often *Ben & Jerry's* in the corpus. *We* even occurs five times as often as *Ben & Jerry's*. Personal pronouns come in the form of inclusive or exclusive pronouns. Examples of inclusive *we* include:

(27) "With enough demand from all of us, food stores and dairy manufacturers will have to listen"

(28) "Simple reason tells us that ..."

(29) "harmful chemicals that may enter our environment"

Exclusive *we* either speaks on behalf of all employees, on behalf of management or the company, and on behalf of the Ben & Jerry's Foundation. Examples of the employee perspective include *At Ben & Jerry's we believe that*, *At Ben & Jerry's, we favor*, or *We at Ben & Jerry's agree*. The management perspective occurs in statements like *We have filed suit in Chicago*, *We plan to actively challenge the laws that*, or *we'll continue to use whatever legal means necessary*.

The language Ben & Jerry's uses on its Web site is quite varied in terms of register. It seems that static pages, e.g. giving guidelines or the mission statement, are written in formal, non-descript English, whereas pages focusing on current events project Ben & Jerry's "cool" and "hip" image, using very colloquial language. An example of this was found on the opening page of February 2, 2002. One sentence read:

(30) "And though you'll want to get right to the bottom of this sweet & cheeky treat, it'd be more tasteful to wait 'til you get home (or wherever you hang your hat)" (Ben & Jerry's 2002).

The text on the *Product Donations Information* page illustrates the same point:

(31) "As we like to say around here, "If it's not fun, why do it?" and you gotta admit, giving away free ice cream is about as fun as it gets. We're sorry to say that you happened to catch us in the process of streamlining our donations process — fewer forms and stuff like that. ... If you have any questions in the meantime, won't you please bop us a note ?
Best,
The donations folks at Ben & Jerry's"

Striking elements in these extracts are the replacement of *and* with & (e.g. *sweet & cheeky*), contractions like *you'll, 'til, it'd, gotta, We're* and *won't*, and colloquialisms like *hang your hat, stuff, bop, Best* and *folks*, all of which express Ben & Jerry's nonchalance.

Audience Address
Audiences are fairly well included in the discourse. The pages contain 40 instances of *you* and 21 instances of *your*, which makes a total of 61 personal addresses. An interesting pattern emerges as to where *you/your* is used. These personal addresses occur primarily on the pages *Take a Stand*, *We're starting a food fight*, and the pages on child labor in the chocolate industry and dioxin. On these pages, the personal address is used mainly as a rhetoric device to increase

111

the acceptability of the message and to convince the audience that Ben & Jerry's shares their concerns, thereby unifying Ben & Jerry's and its audience. Examples include:

(32) "Like you, we too would urge an immediate solution for the problem of child trafficking."

(33) "We want to try to give you, our customers, the true facts."

(34) "We've always wanted to tell you that ..."

(35) "What can you do about rBGH?"

(36) "We're fighting for your right to know what's in your food. And we're asking you to join us."

You is also used generically as a replacement of *one*, which reflects Ben & Jerry's colloquial tone, e.g. as in: *you can't treat a dairy cow with a drug whose effects are possibly wideranging.*

The page outlining Ben & Jerry's giving guidelines obviously addresses potential grant applicants. The opening line of the page on foundation guidelines is *Dear Friends*, which creates a certain level of closeness and familiarity between the company and the grant applicants, although their relationship is just about to start. Labeling them as *friends*, Ben & Jerry's gives the funding procedure a human touch. By giving to *friends*, Ben & Jerry's suggests that it wants to help because it cares about the applicants. The page includes a total of 16 *you/your* and gives prospective applicants instructions on how to apply for funding.

The subheading of the page *Company Info* reads *Everything You Ever Wanted To Know About Ben & Jerry's*, assigning the role of interested reader to the audience. Also, *everything* and *ever* create the impression that the reader is presented with comprehensive information. Paradoxically, the page is extremely short, containing 365 words. It consists of three main sections, the third of which is basically a repetition of the first section, in some places even word-perfect.

Stakeholders

Ben & Jerry's ethics Web pages put little emphasis on these stakeholders that are vital to the company, viz. customers, employees, shareholders and suppliers. This can be put down to the fact that its ethics approach focuses on society as whole, as is typical of a company in the CSR paradigm.

Customers

In the Statement of Mission, customers are only mentioned implicitly in the commitment to high-quality products. The fact that the product and not the customers is the focal point of the commitment shows how little ethical attention Ben & Jerry's pays to its customers. This is also evident from the fact that customers are mentioned only twice in the whole corpus, on the page on dioxin. The dioxin page is intended to counter the customers' fears regarding dioxin in Ben & Jerry's ice cream. Ben & Jerry's claims it *cares about its customers* and addresses them directly, e.g. in the phrase *to give you, our customers, the true facts*. Similarly, Ben & Jerry's commitment to food safety reads:

(37) "Ben & Jerry's products meet or exceed all standards of food safety everywhere they are sold ... That has been our commitment to you, and we stand behind it."

Employees

According to the mission statement, Ben & Jerry's seeks to provide *career opportunities* and *financial rewards* for its employees. Apart from this loose commitment, there is no further specification of this commitment anywhere in the corpus. Although the business press has reported widely on Ben & Jerry's employee benefits (see Section 5.1.1.2), the company does not pride itself on them at all. In all other places where employees are referred to in the corpus, they are the agents of philanthropy rather than recipients, e.g. on the page on the Ben & Jerry's Foundation, in which employees actively participate as board members.

Shareholders

As opposed to customers, shareholders are mentioned in the three-part mission statement. The company commits itself to *increasing value for our shareholders* as part of its economic mission. The term *value* is a bit vague in a financial context, and obviously does not refer to dividend payments, which are indirectly hurt by Ben & Jerry's commitment to giving away 7.5% of its pretax earnings. Evidently, the mission statement has not been updated since the takeover in 2000, when Ben & Jerry's became a *wholly-owned subsidiary of Unilever*, as Ben & Jerry's claims on its financial page. It does thus not have shareholders, as it is not publicly traded anymore.

Suppliers

Seemingly, Ben & Jerry's imposes ethical standards on its suppliers only to the extent that it does not approve of the use of growth hormones. On the page dedicated to recombinant Bovine Growth Hormones (rBGH), Ben & Jerry's repeatedly pledges to buy dairy products only from suppliers who do not use rBGH, because it believes the use of hormones in the dairy industry creates a *synthetic, chemically-intensive, factory-produced food supply*. Ben & Jerry's even claims it pays a premium to those farmers who refrain from using the growth hormone and intends to fight for the right to put an anti-rBGH label on its products, which it is not allowed in all U.S. states.

Anticipating the audience's suspicion of cows being treated with rBGH, Ben & Jerry's uses the negatives *no/not* as rhetoric devices to make its statements more forceful. The corpus includes 36 instances of *not* and seven instances of *no*, which makes up a total of 43 negatives. 18 of these occur on the rBGH page, seeking to emphasize that Ben & Jerry's suppliers do not use rBGH. The following list includes a few examples:

(38) "the family farmers who provide our milk and cream do not treat their cows with recombinant bovine growth hormone (rBGH)"

(39) "The family farmers who supply our milk and cream pledge not to treat their cows with rBGH"

(40) "we don't use milk or cream from cows treated with rBGH"

(41) "we're committed to using only milk and cream from cows that have not been treated with rBGH"

(42) "We will continue to offer a premium to co-op member farms that do not use rBGH"

However, there are also two phrases which use *free* to emphasize that suppliers do not use the rBGH hormone, as in *purchasing an rBGH-free dairy supply* and *we use only milk and cream from rBGH-free cows*.

Community

Apart from Ben & Jerry's mission statement, which guides the company's decisions, all ethics pages are externally oriented, directed at the public at large or customers. These pages focus on either philanthropy or social activism, both of which are intended to effect social change. Ben & Jerry's wants the community to *profit by the way Ben & Jerry's does business*. Apart from this statement and the social mission of the mission statement, Ben & Jerry's mentions communities only as recipients of philanthropy, e.g. employee volunteerism in the form of *Community Action Teams* in Vermont. Also, Ben & Jerry's postal address reads *30 Community Drive*, which strongly suggests that Ben & Jerry's changed the street name to emphasize its social agenda.

5.1.2.3 The Textual Function

Ben & Jerry's home page is essentially a large Macromedia Flash™ movie and requires users to make a choice among the United States, the United Kingdom, the Netherlands, France, and Japan to enter one of the customized country sites. Upon entering the United-States subsite, one is taken to a page containing a horizontal menu bar, a vertical menu bar, and an opening page advertising Ben & Jerry's latest flavors. Neither the vertical nor the horizontal menu bar has a clearly-marked section on corporate ethics. In fact, pages on ethics are rather dispersed in Ben & Jerry's Web site. Figure 4 provides an overview of all ethics-related pages on Ben & Jerry's Web site that were included in the analysis. The flowchart also illustrates the lack of structure the Web site exhibits. The first vertical menu bar includes a total of 21 items, four of which link to pages related to corporate ethics. The company's Statement of Mission — its core ethics document — is not accessible from the home page, but only via the menu item *Company Info*. Upon clicking *Company Info*, the menu items of the vertical menu bar change, producing a different menu bar, which contains a link to Ben & Jerry's Statement of Mission. This menu structure makes the site difficult to navigate.

Ben & Jerry's has a total of nine crosslinks either to ethics pages or to other pages of the Web site, e.g. *Financial Info*. It has also nine external links on its ethics pages, e.g. to UNICEF, Amnesty International, the Food and Drug Administration and the Vermont Senator.

There are no straight lines on Ben & Jerry's Web site, which gives the whole page a comic-style look. The Web pages are overdecorated with little graphic images of cows and ice-cream cones that appear to have been placed on the pages rather randomly, as they typically do not relate to the content of the pages, but only to the company's image of fun.

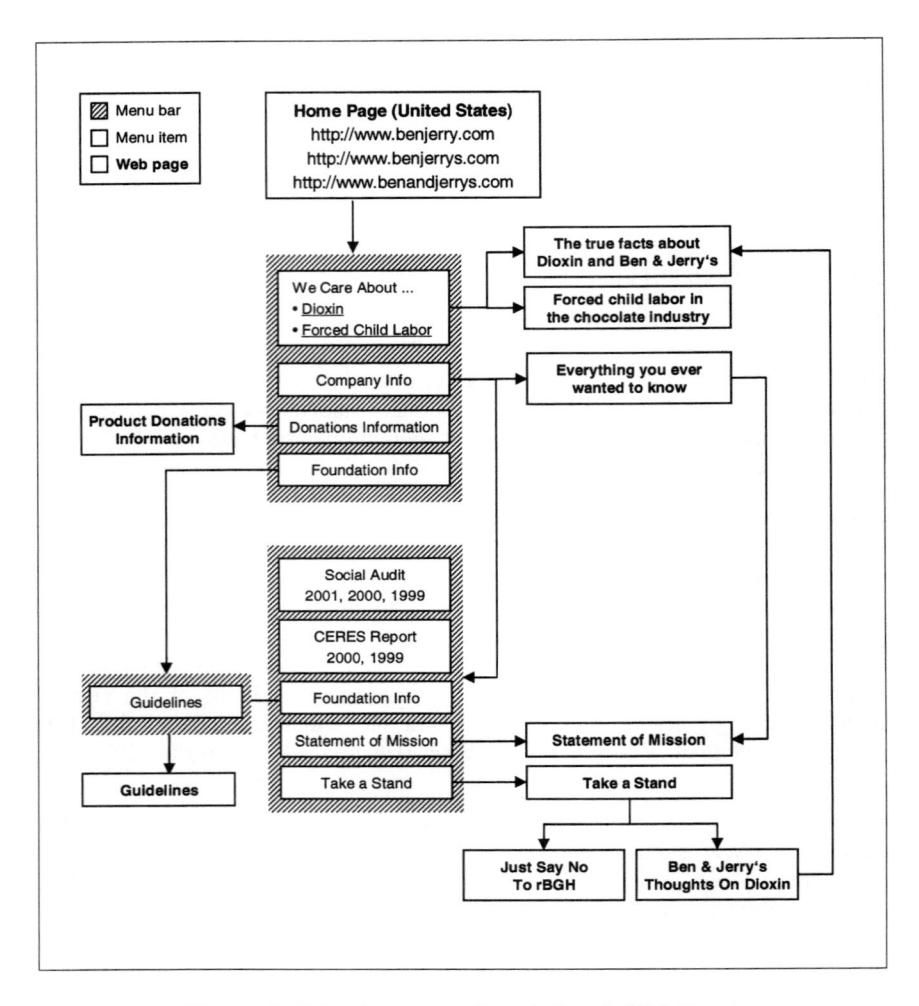

Figure 4: Cohesion among Ben & Jerry's Web Pages

With every page sporting a different look, Ben & Jerry's Web site lacks visual consistency and artful design. For Ben & Jerry's there seems to be no such thing as company colors. The site is richly colored and sports virtually all shades on the color chart. The background color of the text is always white, yet the text is framed by colors ranging from yellow to dark blue. The font face alternates between the Windows fonts "Comic" and "Times New Roman". The "Comic" font is a rather unusual choice for a screen presentation, but it mirrors the font used on Ben & Jerry's packaging and printed material most closely.

5.2 Case 4: *McDonald's Corp.*

5.2.1 Background to the Company

5.2.1.1 Company Profile

McDonald's origin goes back to 1940 when brothers Richard and Maurice McDonald founded a carhop restaurant in San Bernardino, California. By 1948 they had become dissatisfied with the existing concept of drive-in carhop restaurants and converted their restaurant into a self-service counter-service restaurant, founding the world's first McDonald's restaurant (McDonald's USA 2001a; Hamstra 1998: 74). They replaced "flirty female wait staff" with an all-male crew, and chinaware and glasses with paper service ware, which eliminated costs for broken plates and glasses (Hamstra 1998: 74). Their menu was limited to a few basic, standardized items: burgers, fries, shakes, and sodas. The processes in producing these menu items required only minimum effort. These efficiencies cut down waiting time but did not make possible much variety in the menu (Romeo 1998: 6). Nevertheless, the limited menu, coupled with low prices, made their restaurant concept novel (Pepin 1998: 177; Rigby 1997: 70).

When Raymond Albert Kroc, a mixer salesman (Pepin 1998: 176), did business with the McDonald brothers in 1954, he was so thrilled by their concept that he bought exclusive franchising rights from the McDonald brothers in the same year and never changed their fundamental concept (McDonald's USA 2001a; Pepin 1998: 177). In 1955 Ray Kroc opened his first McDonald's restaurant in Des Plaines, Illinois — now a museum — and subsequently founded a company that evolved into McDonald's Corp. (McDonald's USA 2001a). When in 1961 the McDonald brothers also sold ownership rights to their concept and their brand to Ray Kroc for USD 2.7m, they forfeited a multibillion-dollar fortune (Hamstra 1998: 74). Reportedly, the McDonald brothers, who had failed to see the economic potential for their restaurant concept, were bitter about not receiving just credit for their revolutionary concept (Hamstra 1998: 74). Ray Kroc may not be the creator of the modern fast-food restaurants, but he is still considered one of America's greatest entrepreneurs (Pepin 1998: 178). In 1990, *Life* magazine named him as one of the "100 Most Important Americans of the 20th Century" (McDonald's 2001e). Ray Kroc's success can be put down to three factors: First, he had realized that Americans do not dine, but eat, which made him enter the fast-food business in the first place (Pepin 1998: 176). Second, when he got to know the McDonald's concept, he recognized its possibilities and seized the opportunity to turn it into profitable business

(Hamstra 1998: 74). Ray Kroc did not only grasp a promising concept, but he was also able to "implement it in the best possible way" (Pepin 1998: 178). Lastly, his obsession with quality, service and cleanliness made McDonald's a pleasant restaurant experience for customers (Pepin 1998: 176). Ray Kroc, who had served as chairman of the board from 1955 until his retirement in 1977 (McDonald's 2001d), died in 1984 (McDonald's 2001a).

McDonald's has always been a franchising company and even today 70% of all outlets are owned by franchisees (McDonald's 2001f). In the United States, the share of restaurants owned by individuals is even 85% (McDonald's USA 2001a). An important strategic move conducive to McDonald's economic success was entering the real estate business when the company started to franchise outlets. McDonald's leased sites and subleased them to franchisees, who also had to pay a security deposit. These deposits were used to buy additional land, which added to McDonald's wealth (Naim 2001: 36). In 1965, McDonald's went public on the New York Stock Exchange and has been included in the Dow Jones Industrial Average since 1985 (McDonald's 2001a).

In 1967, McDonald's ventured abroad for the first time, opening restaurants in Canada and Puerto Rico (McDonald's 2001e). In 1971 it opened restaurants outside North America, setting up shop in Japan, Australia, and Europe. McDonald's foreign operations had expanded to 43 countries by 1985 (McDonald's 2001e). A major event in the company history was setting up shop in Moscow, Russia in 1990 (Hume 1990: 16). Today, McDonald's Corp. is a global corporation with more than 28,000 outlets in 121 countries and claims to be largest foodservice retailer in the world (McDonald's USA 2001b; 2002b) with 1.5 million employees (McDonald's 2001c) serving 45 million customers a day worldwide (Naim 2001: 29). Table 9 illustrates McDonald's growth in terms of restaurants.

Year	Number of restaurants
1955	2
1960	200
1970	1,500
1980	6,000
1990	11,500
1996	20,000
2001	30,000

Table 9: Restaurant Growth at McDonald's from 1955 to 2001
(Source: McDonald's 2001e; 2002b)

McDonald's underwent tremendous growth until the 1990s. In the mid-1990s, however, McDonald's faced a major crisis as a result of various incidents, including poor stock performance, menu promotions that flopped, negative publicity, customers dissatisfied with quality, and declining sales (Puzo 1997: 10). In the years 2000 and 2001 serious problems emerged again. People's fears over BSE and foot-and-mouth disease caused McDonald's sales in Europe to fall 6% in 2001. The strong dollar, the economic slowdown in Asia, and weak sales in the U.S. put an additional squeeze on the company. McDonald's was forced to take profit-boosting measures, e.g. slashing jobs and cutting back its restaurant growth (Van Houten 2001: 12-13; "McDonald's hit by mad-cow fears", 2001; "Foot-and-mouth hits McDonald's", 2001).

McDonald's has always had a reputation for strong social involvement. In the 1950s, long before McDonald's was in need of an image campaign and long before corporate philanthropy was a strategic tool, the company became involved in the community. In 1957, Ray Kroc himself delivered "free hamburgers to Salvation Army workers in Chicago at Christmas" (McDonald's 2001e) and also dressed up as Santa Claus at Christmas to collect money for the Salvation Army in downtown San Diego ("McDonald's heiress": 16). Also Ray Kroc's widow made it into the papers with generous donations of several million US dollars, e.g. to flood victims in North Dakota in 1997 and to the University of San Diego in 1998. Subsequently, *Fortune* magazine ranked her 36th among the top philanthropists in the United States (Allen 1998: 33). In 1998 Ray Kroc's widow also donated USD 80 million to the Salvation Army to set up a community center in San Diego ("McDonald's heiress": 16). A more recent gesture of philanthropy by McDonald's was delivering free Chicken McNuggets to rescue workers at New York's World Trade Center after the terror attacks of September 11, 2001 (Alsop 2002).

McDonald's social involvement was reinforced when it opened the first of its numerous Ronald McDonald Houses in Philadelphia in 1974 (McDonald's 2001e). The idea was to accommodate parents of seriously ill children while the children are hospitalized, so that parents and children can spend more time together throughout the treatment (McDonald's 2001a). In 2002, there were 212 Ronald McDonald Houses worldwide (McDonald's 2001b). Overall, McDonald's has made USD 300 million in contributions to its Ronald McDonald Houses (Naim 2001: 29). Accordingly, *Fortune* magazine ranked McDonald's number one in social responsibility in their 2000 survey (Naim 2001: 29; McDonald's 2001e).

5.2.1.2 McDonald's Corporate Symbols and Icons

McDonald's corporate identity is principally shaped by its logo, the Golden Arches, and its mascot, Ronald McDonald. Basically, the Golden Arches are a modernistic 'M', graphically represented by a pair of bright yellow arches. They became the company's logo in 1961, after they had already been the main theme of McDonald's first radio jingle aired in 1960, which was "Look for the Golden Arches" (McDonald's 2001e). Typically, the Golden Arches are found on a bright red background.

Another famous symbol of McDonald's is its mascot Ronald McDonald, a "pasty-faced clown, famous for sporting luminous plus-fours and stripy stockings" (Duffy 2002). Ronald McDonald was created in 1963 and helped draw families into McDonald's restaurants due to his popularity among kids (Pepin 1998: 177; McDonald's 2001a). When McDonald's started to air TV ads in 1965, featuring Ronald McDonald, the clown was better known than the U.S. President among kids (Pepin 1998: 177). McDonald's also named its charitable institution — the Ronald McDonald Houses — after the clown. In 1996 Ronald McDonald got a makeover and was transformed into slimmer "90s type of guy" (Peterson 1996: 43). A 1997 study on preferences of children on brands found that 100% of US children surveyed were familiar with Ronald McDonald. The majority of children also rated McDonald's their favorite restaurant ("Bring me the rating of Ronald McDonald": 26). In 1998, McDonald's not only launched a line of home videos featuring Ronald McDonald but also introduced a new character named Iam Hungry (Kramer 1998: 1).

In France McDonald's replaced its mascot Ronald McDonald with Asterix the Gaul in January 2002, coinciding with the opening of the movie Asterix and Cleopatra. In all other 120 countries where McDonald's does business, Ronald McDonald's is still the company's mascot, with the exception of Japan where the clown is not called Ronald McDonald but Donald McDonald for phonetic reasons. With this move in France, McDonald's intended to soothe anti-American-culture feelings among the French population, which McDonald's has always perceived as an obstacle to succeeding in France. Ronald McDonald's replacement clearly indicates that McDonald's has abandoned its one-size-fits-all marketing approach for a think-global-act-local strategy ("McDonald's takes on Asterix", 2001; Duffy 2002).

5.2.1.3 McDonald's Reputation Threats

Back in the 1950s McDonald's became known for its motto "Quality, Service, and Cleanliness", which are values that McDonald's still upholds today (McDonald's 2001e). However, particularly after Ray Kroc's death, image problems emerged. To many, McDonald's has become a symbol of "society's throwaway mentality" (Eisenhart 1990: 25), U.S. economic hegemony, global cultural homogenization, junk food, and genetically engineered food (Naim 2001: 26; Pepin 1998: 177). In a 2001 interview, McDonald's incumbent CEO Jack Greenberg takes a stance on the onslaught of criticism the company has received during the past decades, which he deems "misconceptions" and blunt "lies" (Naim 2001: 27). The following sections focus on issues that have harmed McDonald's reputation and also explore how McDonald's has handled these issues.

5.2.1.3.1 The McLibel Case

In the mid-1990s the UK lawsuit *McDonald's vs. Morris and Steel*, better known as McLibel, brought with it the biggest PR disaster in McDonald's history (Guttenplan 1996: 13). McDonald's sued Dave Morris and Helen Steel, two British environmental activists, for distributing leaflets entitled "What's wrong with McDonald's?" (Corning 1999: 38). These leaflets attacked various aspects of McDonald's business, accusing the company of exploiting its staff, of deliberately targeting its ads at young children, of destroying rainforests, and of producing low-vitamin, high-fat, and high-salt food. Further charges included inhumane slaughtering methods and packaging that caused pollution (Corning 1999: 38; Guttenplan 1996: 13; Rapoport 1995: 15; Jardine 1999: 16). The McLibel trial began before a London court in June 1994 and had become the longest civil case in British history by December 1995 ("McLibel support campaign": 1). Legal proceedings were eventually completed in June 1997 when McDonald's won the case and was awarded £60,000 by way of damages (Atkins 1997: 33).

The reason why the trial took place in the United Kingdom is not solely that the defendants were British. Rather,

> "it is ... the difference between American and British law that explains why McDonald's is suing in Britain for criticisms the company admits 'are in the public domain in America' " (Guttenplan 1996: 13).

Interestingly, under British law, defamatory statements are considered false and the defendant has to prove that the contested statements are true (Atkins 1997: 33). Under US law, however, McDonald's would not have been able to sue, as the burden of proof would have been on the plaintiff. Hence, McDonald's would not only have had to prove that the leaflets were libelous but also that "the statements were made with reckless disregard of their falsehood" (Guttenplan 1996: 13).

The charges pressed against McDonald's could have been equally pressed against any other company in the fast-food industry. The defendants and their supporters argued that they had singled out McDonald's as the focal point of their attacks, since they would expect a leading industry giant to set an example for other players in the industry (Jardine 1999: 16). Apparently, a global brand such as McDonald's is more prone to attacks from environmental pressure groups and consumer activists as a consequence of its ubiquity and marketing success. Jardine (1999) points out that McDonald's

> "can boast widespread availability, value for money, a highly recognisable and consistent product the world over, and high standards of service. It spends $2bn on advertising and millions on PR to project a trustworthy, family-friendly image. But perversely, it is these very qualities which have made it a victim of its own success" (Jardine 1999: 16).

After the trial, criticism was voiced that McDonald's used its economic clout to silence its critics before the court. The company responded by claiming it took legal action only to bring out the truth and not to claim damages (Atkins 1997: 35). Suing was clearly a tactic that backfired, as it made McDonald's look paranoid. What is more, the court trial highlighted aspects of corporate behavior the public would not have been aware of otherwise, e.g. animal exploitation or advertising targeted at young children. The ensuing PR disaster eroded the company's reputation substantially and the fact that McDonald's won the case was irrelevant then (Jardine 1999: 16).

McDonald's clearly overreacted by stubbornly filing a lawsuit for libel against two individuals. They could have come up with more creative ways of handling the PR crisis outside the courtroom, e.g. by inviting independent auditors. That way, the company would have effected a win-win situation, with McDonald's safeguarding its reputation and the two individuals learning the truth about the company. Instead, McDonald's opted for a solution that hurt both parties. The defendants lost the case and were to pay damages and McDonald's lost its reputational standing.

5.2.1.3.2 Junk Food

The 1980s saw growing demand for low-calorie fast food among the American people. McDonald's came under a lot of criticism over the poor nutritional value of its burgers, fries and shakes. This has also been the focal point of attack in anti-McDonald's ads. Adbusters, an anti-advertising Web site run by a Vancouver-based global network of artists and activists (Adbusters 2002c), created spoof ads, drawing attention to McDonald's health-endangering food (see Figure 5).

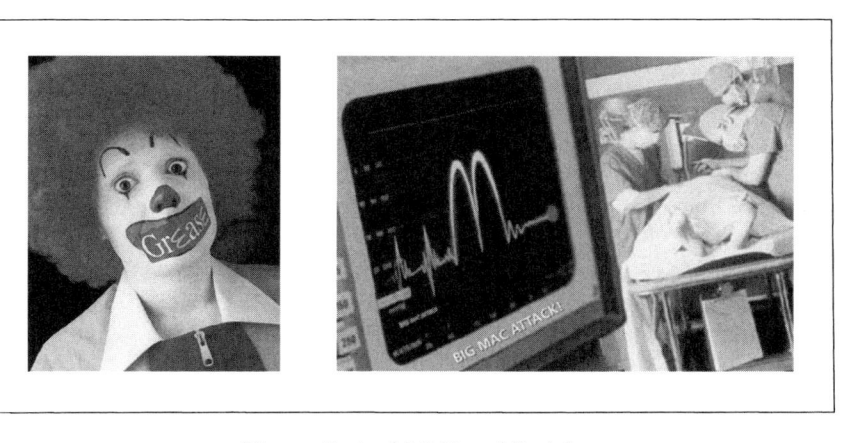

Figure 5: Anti-McDonald's Ads
(Source: Adbusters 2002a & 2002b)

To counter this criticism and to appeal to nutrition-conscious consumers, McDonald's developed a low-fat beef burger — the McLean Deluxe (Mendelson 1996: 43; Shellenbarger 1991: B1; Stone 1997: n.p.). A seaweed derivative was used to replace the fat naturally contained in beef (Stone 1997: n.p.). In addition, McDonald's also began to use vegetable oil instead of high-cholesterol adipose for its French fries in 1990 and also released the nutritional content of its menu items (Shellenbarger 1991: B1). The 320-calorie McLean burger, advertised as "91% fat free, 100% delicious" (Hume 1993: 3-4), did well in US test markets, but failed to catch on nationally after its official roll-out in 1991 (Shellenbarger 1991: B1; Stone 1997: n.p.). By 1993 it was clear that the McLean burger did not appeal to customers, as it generated only an estimated 2% of total sales annually (Hume 1993: 3-4). Albeit a good idea, the low-fat burger simply did not taste good. Therefore, in 1996, McDonald's removed the McLean burger from the menu, thereby abandoning its attempt to sell healthy food (Mendelson 1996: 43).

Although McDonald's officially switched from beef tallow to vegetable oil as the cooking medium for its French fries in the United States in 1990, it turned out later that it had still injected beef flavoring into its fries since then. Vegetarians, and especially the Hindu community, for whom beef is extremely repellent, felt that McDonald's had willfully misled and deceived them for a decade. In May 2001, three lawsuits were filed against McDonald's in a Seattle court, alleging that McDonald's disguised the existence of beef flavoring in its French fries. One lawsuit, filed by three vegetarians, two of whom were Hindus, even sought class-action status on behalf of an estimated 16 million vegetarians and non-vegetarians. Arguably, McDonald's did not willfully deceive its vegetarian customers, but only downplayed the practice of adding beef extract. At any rate, McDonald's did take the matter seriously and updated the nutrition information posted on its Web site (Dailey 2001: 12; "McDonald's to give more information about its ingredients": C13; Evans 2001). McDonald's also apologized on its Web page for not disclosing complete nutritional information about its French fries:

> "McDonald's sincerely apologizes to Hindus, vegetarians and others for failing to provide the kind of information they needed to make informed dietary decisions at our U.S. restaurants. ... We regret we did not provide these customers with complete information, and we sincerely apologize for any hardship that these miscommunications have caused among Hindus, vegetarians and others" (McDonald's 2002a).

Another recent stakeholder concern is beef safety. Increasingly, people are concerned about both BSE and genetically-modified (GM) animal feed, which is used "to increase the muscle bulk of animals or improve their milk yield" ("McDonald's dumps GM-fed meat", 2000). To ease people's fears, McDonald's promised its customers to purchase only meat that had not been reared on genetically-modified feed ("McDonald's dumps GM-fed meat", 2000).

5.2.1.3.3 McJobs

The prefix "Mc" not only refers to the company McDonald's but also "evokes something that is American cultural hegemony. 'Mc' cheapens ideas, it reduces them", as Naim (2001: 29) claims, e.g. in "McJobs". "McJob" actually originates from McDonald's itself, which coined the term in 1983 when promoting its affirmative action program for disabled employees. By the late 1980s the term "McJob" had taken on a broader meaning, denoting low-paid, short-term service jobs, particularly in the fast-food industry (Altculture 2001; Walsh 1998a: 11). The term McJob has become part of everyday vocabulary and is now even included in *The American Heritage Dictionary of the English Language*, according to which McJob is a slang term referring to

> "a job, usually in the retail or service sector, that is low paying, often temporary, and offers minimal or no benefits or opportunity for promotion" (American Heritage Dictionary 2000).

Over the years, the whole fast-food industry has acquired a "McJob" image, since the repetitive nature of the jobs requires only minimal skills and leaves no room for creativity. Due to the standardization of processes workers have become "de-skilled", which makes them interchangeable and provides them with little to no job satisfaction. This might be the reason why staff turnover in the U.S. fast-food industry is higher than in any other industry, amounting to 300% a year. Since the jobs demand next to no skills and thus only little training, this extraordinarily high turnover is not even very expensive for the companies (Ritzer 2000: 137; Schlosser 2001: 72-73).

Still, McDonald's and Burger Kind sought to counter this McJob image by raising wages and introducing employee-training programs. Shortly before minimum-wage legislation was introduced in the United Kingdom in 1999, both McDonald's and Burger King raised their wages as it had become clear that both had been paying well below the minimum wage to be introduced (Walsh 1998a: 11). In 1998 McDonald's launched an initiative to make the company an "employer of opportunity" and to make itself more popular among present and prospective employees. The company sought to get rid of its reputation for low-paid, dead-end jobs by banking on its workforce diversity and by introducing training schemes in partnership with colleges (Walsh 1998b: 16).

5.2.1.3.4 Waste Production

Being criticized for producing massive mountains of garbage, McDonald's launched McRecycle USA in 1990, a program aimed at reducing waste by purchasing recycled materials (Hume 1991: 32). The company committed itself to spending a minimum of USD 100 million on recycled products annually, e.g. for its newspapers and hamburger cartons (Eisenhart 1990: 25), and subsequently phased out the previously used polystyrene hamburger boxes

(Hume 1991: 32). McDonald's commitment to waste reduction was considered a conscious move "to enhance its environmentally responsible image by taking a leadership role in the recycling movement" (Eisenhart 1990: 25), especially because McDonald's sought help from PR agencies to project a green image of the company and to enhance the visibility of McRecycle USA in the media (Hume 1991: 32).

By 1993 McDonald's had already spent a total of USD 600 million on recycled materials and the company prided itself on having spent twice the amount it had originally planned to spend in the three-year period ("McDonald's spends big on recycling": 124). Arguably, the initial purchasing target was deliberately set lower than expected in order to capitalize on the accomplishment of exceeding it.

5.2.1.3.5 Labor Issues in China

In 1998, McDonald's came under media scrutiny when a toy company in Shenzhen, mainland China, was found to produce toys for McDonald's Happy Meals under poor occupational health and safety conditions. The factory was owned by a Hong Kong subcontractor. The paint that workers used to spray the plastic toys released toxic emissions that caused dizziness, headaches, nausea and skin rash. McDonald's responded to these allegations by sending independent auditors to the factory. Eventually, air quality was improved and allegedly met the standards mandated by the U.S. Occupational Safety and Health Administration. As the workers had also largely failed to wear protective masks at work, McDonald's made wearing masks mandatory (Saywell 1998: 46).

On August 27, 2000 the *South China Morning Post* reported that McDonald's sold toys with its meals in Hong Kong that were manufactured at a sweatshop in Shenzhen, mainland China. The sweatshop had child laborers package the toys for less than USD 3 per day and put them up in cramped dormitories. Apparently, the children had lied about their age and had used false identification cards in order to get employed, as the legal working age in China is 16 (Chinoy 2000; Associated Press 2000a; Associated Press 2000b). The Hong Kong office of McDonald's then said they would take the issue seriously and promised to have an independent audit team investigate the matter (Chinoy 2000). The investigation did not turn up any evidence of child labor, but revealed that the factory paid poor wages and infringed working-time regulations. Allegedly, all under-age workers were locked away during the investigation ("McDonald's cuts ties with Chinese factory": 2000). According to the Associated Press (2000b), however, the child workers had already been dismissed a few days after the news had broken. Either way, McDonald's felt there was sufficient evidence that the factory had failed to comply with McDonald's code of conduct and therefore discontinued doing business with this Chinese factory ("McDonald's cuts ties with Chinese factory": 2000).

5.2.1.3.6 Anti-McDonald's Web Sites

There are two major anti-McDonald's Web sites on the Internet, seeking to harm McDonald's reputation.

McDonaldization.com

McDonaldization.com went online in February 2000. Its mission is "to educate about the perils of the McDonaldization process" (McDonaldization 2001a). The term McDonaldization goes back to George Ritzer, author of the book *The McDonaldization of Society*[8], according to whom McDonaldization is

> "the process by which the principles of the fast-food restaurant are coming to dominate more and more sectors of American society as well as the rest of the world" (McDonaldization 2001c).

These principles include efficiency, calculability (i.e. quantity over quality), predictability (i.e. the uniformity of products), and control (i.e. the substitution of non-human labor for human labor) (McDonaldization 2001b). As of January 2002 the Web site is not particularly rich in content, but seems to be more interested in selling books on McDonald's, via its link to Amazon.com.

McSpotlight.org

McSpotlight is a Web site created in 1996 by the McInformation Network, an international group of volunteers (McSpotlight 2001c; McSpotlight 2001d). The McInformation Network "is dedicated to compiling and disseminating factual, accurate, up-to-date information" (McSpotlight 2001c) on McDonald's business practices. The group provides a meticulous coverage of the McLibel trial on its Web site, which suggests strong ties with the McLibel support group, but the McInformation Network deems itself "autonomous to, but supportive of"

---

[8] Ritzer, G. (1995): *The McDonaldization of Society*. Pine Forge Press.

(McSpotlight 2001c) the McLibel defendants and their supporters. To boot, the group's charges are strikingly similar to those of the McLibel defendants. The *raison-d'être* for the McSpotlight Web site reads as follows:

> "McDonald's spends over $2 billion a year broadcasting their glossy image to the world. This is a small space for alternatives to be heard" (McSpotlight 2001b).

The group strongly objects to the spreading of multinationals "into every corner of the globe" (McSpotlight 2001a) and has singled out McDonald's primarily because of the company's steamroller approach to expansion. It considers McDonald's "a particularly arrogant, shiny and self-important example of a system which values profits at the expense of anything else" (McSpotlight 2001a). McSpotlight covers a range of issues on which McDonald's is said to have faulted, including nutrition, advertising, the environment and employment (McSpotlight 2001a). First, they charge that McDonald's promotes an unbalanced, unhealthy diet that is high in fat and may cause diabetes, heart diseases and cancer. McSpotlight criticizes not only the fact that the company calls its products nutritious, but also that it sponsors sports events and opens restaurants in hospitals. Further allegations include advertising targeted at children, the disregard of animal rights, and massive waste production. In addition, McDonald's is indirectly blamed for the destruction of tropical rainforests, as these are allegedly chopped down to make space for cattle ranching. Employment is another matter of concern at McSpotlight. They believe that McJobs are not only inhumane but also force independent restaurants out of business, as their labor costs are significantly higher than McDonald's (McSpotlight 2001a). McSpotlight (2001a) further claims that McDonald's uses its financial clout to silence its critics — the media in particular — by suing them and so McDonald's poses a threat to free speech.

Overall, it seems safe to say that the accusations uttered by McSpotlight lack substance, e.g. as in phrases like "Nutritionists ... argue that", "Some people say", "Many people say" (McSpotlight 2001a). What is more, most allegations are carefully phrased as questions, presumably to avoid legal action, e.g. "Can a multinational company operating on McDonald's scale **not** contribute to global warming...?" (McSpotlight 2001a; original emphasis). Surprisingly, McDonald's spent a fortune on the McLibel trial but has not yet silenced the McSpotlight Web site, although the Web site's claims are equivalent to those against which the company filed a lawsuit for libel (Reed 1999: 18). Apparently, McDonald's has learned its lesson from the McLibel case and shies away from taking legal action against its critics.

5.2.2 Discourse Analysis

5.2.2.1 The Ideational Function

The three main themes in McDonald's ethical discourse include social responsibility, philanthropy, environmental responsibility, and animal welfare and food safety, which are discussed below.

Social Responsibility

The main page on social responsibility, entitled *A Heritage of Social Responsibility*, quotes company founder Ray Kroc, who believed that the company has *an obligation to give back to the communities that give us so much*. Much apparently refers to sales and human resources, as there is nothing else that a community could give to a company. There is also a statement by incumbent CEO Jack Greenberg, who claims that *we are a socially responsible company*. The page further includes the following three-sentence paragraph:

> (1) "McDonald's is an organization founded on a heritage of giving back to the communities in which we live and work. Being a good citizen has been inherent in the fabric of the company since its inception. Leadership and doing the right thing has been the legacy of McDonald's throughout our 45-year history."

The slow information rate in this paragraph is hard to overlook. Essentially, each sentence expresses the same idea — that McDonald's has always been a socially responsible company. Considering that the page heading expresses just that in five words (*A Heritage of Social Responsibility*), the whole paragraph is more or less redundant. McDonald's hides this redundancy through lexical variation, by using *giving back*, *good citizen* and *the right thing* instead of *social responsibility* and *since its inception*, *legacy* and *45-year history* instead of *heritage*.

McDonald's *commitment to social responsibility* encompasses animal welfare, education, environment, people, quality and safety, and the Ronald McDonald House Charities (RMHC). The main social-responsibility page of McDonald's Web Site includes hyperlinks to separate pages dedicated to these six commitments as well as to a page titled *Recent Recognition*. This page lists a number of honors and magazine rankings McDonald's has received owing to its socially responsible business conduct. These awards are obviously intended to support McDonald's responsibility claims. Although McDonald's never uses the term *reputation* as such, it mentions brand enhancement in connection with social responsibility on the page *Recent Recognition*: *we also work to ... enhance McDonald's brand by being a leader in social responsibility.*

Obviously, social responsibility is a means to an end for McDonald's and appears to be driven by self-interest rather than altruism.

Philanthropy

McDonald's lexicon to refer to philanthropy does not exclude typical terms like *philanthropy* or *giving*. In one place it says that it *provides free goods and services*, but uses primarily *support* in the rest of the text.

(2) "McDonald's supports Ronald McDonald House Charities (RMHC)"

(3) "Funding and volunteer support"

(4) "McDonald's customers support RMHC"

McDonald's engages in corporate philanthropy through its foundation — the Ronald McDonald House Charities (RMHC). The foundation has its own Web site at <http://www.rmhc.org> and so the page on RMHC on the corporate Web site does not describe the RMHC at great length. McDonald's funds Ronald McDonald Houses and similar organizations around the world. In addition to financial support, the Houses are supported through employee volunteerism and donations from customers (*McDonald's customers support RMHC generously*). Encouraging customers to donate money can hardly be considered corporate philanthropy, as the contributions do not come from McDonald's. But still, this approach is superior to cause-related marketing, as McDonald's does not force its customers to donate money, as would be the case with cause-related marketing.

Environmental Responsibility

The notion of responsibility reappears solely on the page on McDonald's commitment to the environment, where the company acknowledges that its business conduct has a bearing on the lives of millions of people:

(5) "McDonald's believes it has a special responsibility to protect our environment for future generations."

However, the company makes only two firm commitments on this page. First, it pledges to reduce and prevent waste, which is required by law in many countries or states anyway. The commitment to waste reduction appears to be a response to the charges that have been brought against the company regarding waste production (see Section 5.2.1.3.4). Second, McDonald's commits itself to the conservation of natural resources and the minimization of energy consumption and counters the charge that it destroys rainforests to make space for cattle grazing. Its commitment reads: *We will not permit the destruction of rain forests for our beef supply. This policy is strictly enforced and closely monitored.* The use of the two adverbs of manner (*strictly* and *closely*) and the negative *not* make for the forcefulness of the statement. To underline its commitment to environmental protection, McDonald's also points out that it has appointed an environmental affairs officer.

Further, McDonald's commits itself to promoting environmental values, which it regards as an obligation:

(6) "[W]e believe we have an obligation to promote sound environmental practices by providing educational materials in our restaurants and working with teachers in the schools."

McDonald's seems to use environmental education as a disguise for raising brand awareness among children by providing them with educational pamphlets. The company's educational practices are particularly questionable, as it does not confine them to the premises of its restaurants but extends them to schools as well. Evidently, it seeks to convince children of its environmentally sound business conduct, thereby influencing the perceptions of a relatively uncritical consumer group.

Animal Welfare and Food Safety

McDonald's has been criticized for inhumane treatment of animals, especially by the McLibel supporters. McDonald's counters this criticism by committing itself to *animal welfare*. The term *animal welfare* is an exaggerating enhancement, given that animals are a commodity in the food industry. This enhancement is also achieved by a picture of cows grazing peacefully on a green meadow.

McDonald's uses the euphemism *animal welfare* 16 times on this page. Alternatively, it uses the more neutral *treatment/treating* six times and *animal handling* once. The overuse of *animal welfare* is a rhetoric enhancement that seeks to add warmth to the fact that animals are first reared in factory farms and eventually killed, although McDonald's does use the negative word *slaughtered* once. Therefore, *animal welfare* appears to be an oxymoron if used by a company that sells mostly hamburgers. McDonald's still seeks to ease consumers' concerns about the well-being of the animals that provide the meat for the burgers. The following phrases stem from McDonald's commitment to animal welfare and illustrate how the company couples *animal treatment* or near-synonyms of it with positively colored words:

(7) "McDonald's cares about the treatment of animals"

(8) "our responsibility .... includes working with our suppliers to ensure good animal handling"

(9) "McDonald's believes that the humane treatment of animals is an integral part of our world class supplier system"

(10) "McDonald's believes treating animals with care and respect is ..."

(11) "McDonald's supports that animals should be free from cruelty, abuse and neglect"

(12) "... embracing the proper treatment of animals"

(13) "McDonald's believes in the ethical treatment of animals"

(14) "animals should be raised, transported and slaughtered in an environment free from cruelty, abuse and neglect"

Words like *care and respect*, *good*, *humane*, *proper* and *ethical* add a positive tone to the issue of animal treatment, yet the hypocrisy is hard to overlook, as it is hard to imagine how animals could be killed ethically. Killing clearly is an inevitable process in the fast-food industry, but coupling it with *ethical* (Example 13) or *humane* (Example 9) appears to be a contradiction in terms.

McDonald's claims that it does not own and raise the animals but merely buys *food products* from suppliers. It does not use the word *meat* at all. Still, these *food products* are quite obviously meat, as McDonald's mentions *beef, pork and poultry products* and *slaughtered* later on in the text. By stressing that the animals do not belong to McDonald's, the company shifts the blame for the emergence of the issue of inhumane animal treatment to its suppliers. However, it acknowledges that it — as the purchaser of such products — has a responsibility for animal treatment as well (Examples 15 and 16) and even considers itself a responsible purchaser (Example 17):

(15) "our responsibility as a purchaser of food products includes working with our suppliers to ensure good animal handling practices"

(16) "McDonald's recognizes our responsibility as a major purchaser of animal products"

(17) "McDonald's ... will ensure our purchasing strategy is aligned with our commitment to animal welfare issues acting as a responsible purchaser."

McDonald's fails to specify these responsibilities, but pledges to buy only from suppliers who *maintain the highest standards*.

The animal-welfare page lists seven *Guiding Principles*, all of which are very vague, platitudinous and contain redundancies. For example, McDonald's commitment to food safety reads as follows:

(18) "Safety: First and foremost, McDonald's will provide its customers with safe food products. Food safety is McDonald's number one priority. Food safety at McDonald's Corporation is central to company operations and supply chain management. To this end, food safety is integrated into all facets of our business from raw material production to our customer service operations."

These four sentences express largely the same idea, viz. McDonald's commitment to food safety, with each sentence adding new information. They fail to specify what is meant by food safety and leave it open how McDonald's seeks to fulfill its commitment. The findings of Section 5.2.1.3.2 suggest that food safety is likely to mean beef from cattle that have not been fed with GM feed and tested for BSE and foot-and-mouth disease.

McDonald's commitment to animal welfare contains seven instances of *continu-* out of 14 instances in the whole corpus. They occur either in the collocation *continuous improvement* or in the following phrases:

(19) "We will continue to dedicate resources to monitor and coordinate activities associated with improving animal welfare"

(20) "McDonald's works continuously with our suppliers to audit animal welfare practices"

(21) "We will continually educate ourselves and our suppliers relative to animal welfare issues"

(22) "McDonald's Corporation will continually look for ways to improve our standards and work toward achieving the above stated standards"

This cluster of *continu-* suggests that McDonald's system leaves plenty of room for improvement, which is in particular evident from the collocations of *continu-* with *improve(ment)*. Especially example 22 (*work toward achieving*) evidences that McDonald's has not reached its animal-welfare goals yet. At the same time, *continu-* embraces the past, the present and the future in one word, stressing that McDonald's has done these things and will do them in the future as well.

5.2.2.2 The Interpersonal Function

McDonald's

McDonald's self-references occur predominantly in the first person, as Table 10 shows.

	Subject	Object	Genitive	Adjective	TOTAL
we / us / our	69	5	n.a.	105	**179**
McDonald's	30	15	n.a.	24	**69**
company	1	2	-	-	**3**
it / its	1	-	n.a.	5	**6**

Table 10: Breakdown of References to McDonald's

The only two instance of inclusive *we* are in the phrases *McDonald's is committed to the education of our youth* and *McDonald's believes it has a special responsibility to protect our environment*. All other instances of *we/us/our* speak on behalf of the company or its employees and are thus instances of exclusive *we*.

The mix of *we/our* and *McDonald's* within a page and even within a sentence occurs quite frequently. These sentences with mixed viewpoints typically start with *McDonald's* as the theme of the sentence and continue with *we/our*. Apart from the page on McDonald's commitment to RMHC, which does not use first-person pronouns, all pages contain a mix of first-person and third-person viewpoints. The following passages illustrate how viewpoints change back and forth between the first person and the third person:

> (23) "McDonald's cares about the treatment of animals so we are continuing to take a leadership role in improving conditions and operations at our suppliers' facilities. Although McDonald's does not typically own, raise or transport animals, we do recognize that our responsibility as a purchaser of food products includes working with our suppliers to ensure good animal handling practices. McDonald's believes that the humane treatment of animals is an integral part of our world class supplier system."

These shifts in viewpoint appear a bit irritating, as they create the impression that McDonald's and *we* are two separate entities. Possibly, McDonald's seeks to emphasize the difference between "We, the people of McDonald's" and the company as an institution.

McDonald's presents itself as a leader in all fields, ranging from business in general to social responsibility, environmental matters, quality and safety, education and animal welfare. Examples of the 16 instances of *lead-* include:

(24) "Leadership and doing the right thing has been the legacy of McDonald's throughout our 45-year history."

(25) " ... being a leader in social responsibility"

(26) "We realize that in today's world, a business leader must be an environmental leader as well. ... We will lead, both in word and in deed."

(27) "Over the years, McDonald's has been a leader in setting and strictly enforcing high quality and safety standards."

(28) "McDonald's is committed to the education of our youth. We all take this leadership role very seriously."

(29) "We take a leadership role in education matters"

(30) "McDonald's cares about the treatment of animals so we are continuing to take a leadership role in improving conditions and operations at our suppliers' facilities."

(31) "McDonald's will lead our industry working with our suppliers and industry experts to advance animal welfare practices and technology."

Lead- conveys positional meaning in that it expresses McDonald's evaluation of itself vis-à-vis its competitors, constructing an identity of superiority for the company.

Competitors

Competitors are brought up only once on the page on animal welfare where McDonald's commits itself to *sharing best practices with our competitors*. Apart from that, McDonald's avoids the notion of competitors, presumably to divert attention away from its fierce competition with Burger King in the U.S. It talks about *competitive pay* and pay *at or above local market*, but in all other places sticks to superlatives and other expressions of superiority to convey the impression that its standards are higher than those of other players in the industry. Examples include:

(32) "the world's best quick service restaurant experience"

(33) "We are aligned with world-class suppliers that share our high standards"

(34) "Our employment practices stand head and shoulders above employment laws"

(35) "setting and strictly enforcing high quality and safety standards — often exceeding those established by industry and governments"

Stakeholders

The page on the environment is the only that enumerates McDonald's stakeholders:

(36) "we are committed to timely, honest and forthright communications with our customers, shareholders, suppliers and employees. ... By maintaining a productive, ongoing dialogue with all of these stakeholders, we will learn from them."

In this statement, McDonald's establishes the relationship with its stakeholders groups as one of open communication and mutual learning. The relationships McDonald's builds with customers, suppliers and employees are discussed below in more detail. Shareholders are mentioned only once more, when McDonald's commits itself to sharing its progress in *animal welfare* with its customers and shareholders.

Employees

McDonald's Web pages compel readers to believe that people are of vital importance to the company. McDonald's has no such things as a mission or a value statement, but it has formalized its values in the form of its *People Promise* and its *People Vision*. The *People Vision* reads: *To Be the Best Employer in Each Community Around the World*. This is quite a bold statement, particularly because of its superlative language, viz. *best*, *each*, *Around the World*. Also, *best* leaves room for varied interpretations, as McDonald's does not specify any criteria for evaluating *best*. The *People Promise* is also peculiar:

(37) "**Our People Promise:**

To the 1.5 million people who work at McDonald's in 119 countries around the world, and to all future employees, we want you to know that

We Value You, Your Growth and Your Contributions."

These four instances of the personal address are the only second-person pronouns in the whole corpus. Here, they underline how much McDonald's cares about its employees, quite obviously to counter its McJob image. The company seeks to convince the audience that its jobs are not dead-end jobs but offer growth opportunities and career prospects. McDonald's also visually underlines its employee commitment by using pictures showing employees of ethnic diversity who seemingly enjoy their work. This emotional appeal is obviously intended to convince the audience that McDonald's is a good employer, suggesting that McDonald's delivers on its *People Promise* and its *People Vision*.

McDonald's obviously chose people over employees for the titles of these two statements to humanize the employer-employee relationship. McDonald's tends to use *people* instead of *employees* quite frequently, e.g. as in *people principles*, *people practices* and *our people*. The corpus contains 26 instances of *people* and 26 instances of *employee(s)*. These figures strongly suggest that McDonald's seeks to make it clear that it regards its employees as people rather than human resources, hence the frequent use of *people*. The idea of being a *people company* is made explicit in the following statement:

(38) "We're not just a hamburger company serving people;
we're a people company serving hamburgers."

McDonald's dedicates a whole page to education, which focuses mainly on McDonald's teenage employees, though, and has nothing to do with education per se. The fact that education is among McDonald's top six commitments suggests that a significant portion of McDonald's employees are high-school students. To enhance the fact that young people have to juggle school and work, McDonald's presents this employment as a training opportunity:

(39) "We train our employees to be better students and citizens. Our training programs help develop students' skills and highlight the importance of responsibility, self-discipline and ethics."

McDonald's obviously feels obliged to justify why it employs students at all, when stating *Employment at McDonald's provides many students with financial resources that enable them to continue their education*. This suggests that they would not be able to go to school, if they did not work at McDonald's, and so McDonald's performs a good deed by employing them. In reality, it is far more likely that McDonald's employs teenage workers on a part-time basis, as they are relatively cheaper than adult full-time employees. The page also states that "We ... encourage them to consider a career with us", which is appears to be an empty platitude in view of the high turnover rate and the limited options for promotion in the fast-food industry.

McDonald's does not treat these teenage workers as adults, as it also brings up their parents and teachers and seeks to form *partnerships* with them:

(40) "We ... work in partnership with parents and educators to ensure that our school-age employees see education and schoolwork as their top priorities."

(41) "McDonald's promotes a dialogue between parents, educators and students and is committed to building partnerships that address and promote education issues."

These partnerships seemingly aim at achieving a balance between school and work, which McDonald's highlights as an unequivocal commitment. It also spells out this commitment, when claiming *Employees' schedules are designed to be mindful of their school responsibilities.* Or: *When faced with a choice between education and an employment commitment, education will always come first.* Apart from the fact that this sentence is ungrammatical, as it is not education but the student that faces the choice, it also expresses McDonald's commitment to education.

Suppliers

McDonald's suppliers are referred to in the corpus almost as often as its employees (22 vs. 26 times), which suggests that supplier relationships are a central issue in the company's ethical discourse. McDonald's is aware that the general public cares about issues that arise in the sphere of its suppliers, e.g. the treatment of animals or environmental degradation. Therefore, McDonald's stipulates certain conditions regarding animal welfare, employment policies and environmental protection that suppliers have to adhere to. McDonald's also emphasizes that it audits its suppliers' operations to make sure they comply with these standards. To highlight the importance of quality, McDonald's honors excellence among its suppliers with a quality award.

McDonald's claims to procure from *world-class suppliers that share our high standards* and that *maintain the highest standards and share McDonald's commitment.* The verb *share* creates the impression that suppliers apply these standards without having been instructed to do so. Nowhere does McDonald's insinuate that it imposes standards on its suppliers. It is careful to use mitigations or expressions with positive connotations instead:

(42) "We expect our suppliers to follow the same philosophy"

(43) "Compliance with these policies will receive consideration with other business criteria in evaluating both current and potential McDonald's suppliers"

(44) "We intend to continue to work in partnership with our suppliers"

(45) "we work closely with our suppliers"

(46) "our responsibility … includes working with our suppliers"

(47) "Partnership: McDonald's works continuously with our suppliers to …"

(48) "McDonald's will lead our industry working with our suppliers and industry experts"

Stressing cooperation with suppliers, McDonald's constructs a relationship based on partnership rather than dependency to cancel out the unequal power relations between the company and its suppliers.

McDonald's also has a code of conduct for suppliers, which prohibits prison labor, child labor and discrimination, and sets rules pertaining to working hours and compensation. McDonald's monitors supplier compliance with this code in the form of *external third-party audits*. The company named its audit report *McDonald's Corporation Shareholders' Report on Supplier Social Compliance*, which suggests that this report is actually a response to a shareholder resolution. The reason why the code plays a relatively small role in McDonald's ethical discourse is that it is not relevant to most suppliers. An analysis of the country statistics that McDonald's provides (McDonald's 2002b) reveals that over 86% of restaurants are in industrialized countries with stringent employment legislation. These countries include the USA, Canada, most European countries, Japan, Australia, and New Zealand. Since McDonald's buys food supplies from local suppliers, child labor or prison labor is unlikely to occur at suppliers' facilities in these countries anyway. Thus, the code has only little relevance to McDonald's core business, as it only applies to 14% of its operations. The code's first two provisions focus on forced labor and child labor, which strongly suggests that the code is merely a response to McDonald's labor issue in China in 2000. Although McDonald's claimed to have a code (see Section 5.2.1.3.5), it is doubtful whether it had this very code in place then.

Franchisees and Owner/Operators
As mentioned in the company profile, McDonald's does not operate most of its restaurants itself but franchises them to *independent* owners. The company refers to them as either *franchisees* or *owner/operators*. McDonald's utters

ethical commitments to employees on behalf of its franchisees, which suggests that they are not really that independent when it comes to personnel management:

(49) "The Company, our franchisees and affiliates are each committed to creating an environment that values and respects employees."

(50) "McDonald's and its independent owner/operators have made a commitment to our employees that we strive to achieve with our actions every day."

(51) "McDonald's Corporation and McDonald's Owner/Operators are similarly committed to ensuring that the McDonald's job experience complements and supports employees' educational goals."

These commitments are, however, so vaguely put that they can hardly be put into practices anyway.

Customers

McDonald's promises its customers safe, high-quality food products, which it deems *the most important items on our menu* and assures them that they *can have confidence in McDonald's*. McDonald's suggests that its restaurants provide more than just food by using the word *experience* in this context and by collocating it with enhancing adjectives:

(52) "Restaurants are adequately staffed to allow for a good customer experience"

(53) "to create exceptional restaurant experiences"

(54) "our goal of being the world's best quick service restaurant experience"

CEO Jack Greenberg refers to customers in his statement *Our customers are proud to have us in the neighborhood because we are a socially responsible company*. The categorical present tense (*are*) establishes his utterance as unequivocally true, although neither the claim in the main clause nor the claim in the subordinate clause is verifiable. The words *proud* and *socially responsible* load the assertion with emotion, seeking to construct an ethical identity. Also, the sentence connector *because* provides an interesting rationale for the customers' alleged pride, as it suggests that customers perceive the company as socially responsible.

Children

McDonald's present itself as a company concerned about the well-being of children. For one, this is evident from the Ronald McDonald House Charities, through which McDonald's confines its corporate giving activities to the *health and well-being of children*. Further, McDonald's seeks to assure parents that McDonald's Happy Meal toys and the playgrounds (*PlayPlaces*) at McDonald's restaurants are safe. The page on quality and safety contains a short paragraph on safety for children:

> (55) "**Safe fun for children**
> Parents can be confident that our Happy Meal toys and PlayPlaces are safe. For years, we have been using state-of-the-art technology to scientifically analyze the safety of toys and other promotional items for the McDonald's System. We also have been working with the world's leading manufacturers and installers of fun and safe playground equipment and renowned safety consultants so that playtime at McDonald's meets our strict specifications."

McDonald's foregrounds safety lexically by using *safe/safety* in every sentence. Further, it uses adverbs and adjectives that assign special prominence to the notion of safety, e.g. *state-of-the-art*, *scientifically*, *world's leading*, *renowned* and *strict*. McDonald's seeks to reassure parents that it does everything possible to make sure that their children are in safe hands at McDonald's.

Communities

McDonald's understanding of *communities* denotes towns rather than people. For example, phrases like *to Be the Best Employer in Each Community Around the World* and *the communities in which we live and work* regard communities as a place. McDonald's believes it has an *obligation* to give back to the communities, although it seemingly does not give equally to all communities where it operates. It states on its page on RMHC that it has 206 Ronald McDonald Houses in 33 countries, but does not specify what it gives to the communities in the remaining 87 countries. This suggests that community giving is regionally focused.

McDonald's pretends to care about the communities by stating *we also work to strengthen relationships with our communities*. At the same time, McDonald's presupposes strong ties with communities in the following example:

> (56) "Given our close relationship with local communities around the world, we believe we have an obligation to promote sound environmental practices."

One might easily fail to see the logic of this sentence, as environmental protection should actually be independent of the closeness of community relations. But McDonald's presents close relations as the rationale for environmental protection. Additionally, McDonald's also uses the following woolly words to express its environmental responsibilities towards future generations:

(57) "McDonald's believes it has a special responsibility to protect our environment for future generations. This responsibility is derived from our unique relationship with millions of consumers worldwide. ... Hence our determination is ... to take actions beyond what is expected if they hold the prospect of leaving future generations an environmentally sound world."

As discussed above (Section 5.2.2.1), McDonald's environmental commitments do not extend beyond resource minimization and waste recycling. Nevertheless, the effusive language in the above statement constructs an exclusive relationship between McDonald's and the communities. This is achieved through attitudinal lexis (*special, unique*) as well as the prominence devices *millions* and *worldwide*. Also, the agent-free passive *is expected* does not substantiate whose expectations McDonald's actions exceed.

5.2.2.3 The Textual Function

McDonald's home page contains three links related to corporate ethics: *Social Responsibility*, *RMHC* and *People Promise*. Every link on the home page opens the relevant page plus a top-level, horizontal menu bar containing the same links as the home page. The link *Social Responsibility* points to the introductory page on corporate ethics and opens a vertical menu bar comprising McDonald's ethics menu. As the flowchart in Figure 6 illustrates, McDonald's ethics section is well-structured. Overall, McDonald's has 19 crosslinks, most of which do, however, point to pages that are not included in the corpus for reasons of space or relevance. The main seven pages on corporate ethics are similarly structured, using bullets as signposts and following the same design. Images are rarely used and show either McDonald's restaurants, happy employees or grazing cattle.

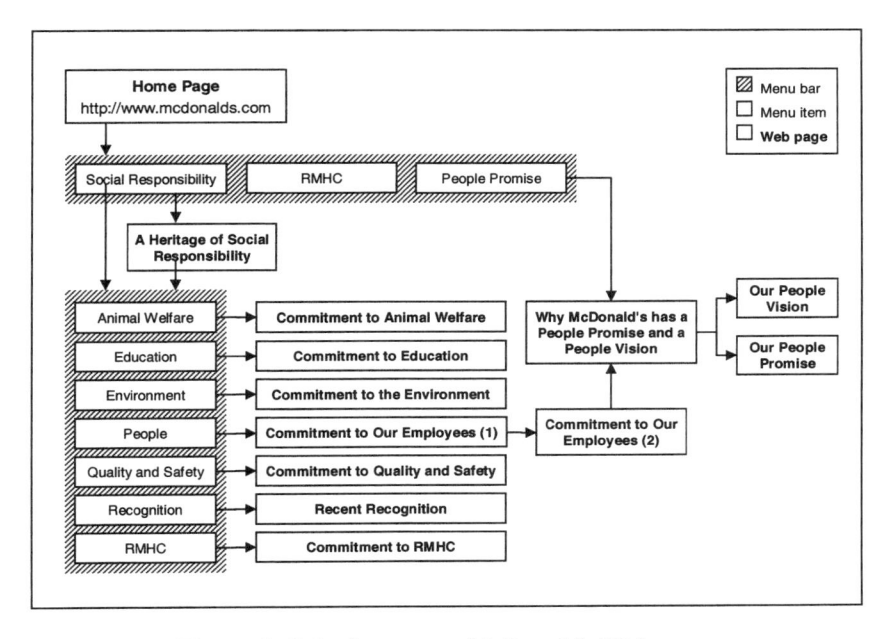

Figure 6: Cohesion among McDonald's Web pages

5.3 Intra-Paradigm Analysis

- **Ethics statements:** Ben & Jerry's Statement of Mission and McDonald's People Promise and People Vision are ethics statements reflecting the social-responsibility paradigm. All three are brief, unspecific, and outline the corporate mission and/or vision. These statements focus on goals and have thus only limited applicability to day-to-day decisions.
- **Code of conduct:** Ben & Jerry's does not have a code of conduct but believes that its Statement of Mission suffices to guide employee decision-making. McDonald's does not have a code of conduct for employees either, but it has a brief code for its suppliers. Even if McDonald's has a code of conduct for suppliers, this does not mean it belongs to the BE or the BE & CSR paradigm, as the weight it puts on the implementation of its code is miniscule. This merely confirms that ethics codes are found across paradigms.
- **Philanthropy:** Both companies have private foundations that administer their corporate giving activities. The Ben & Jerry's Foundation and the Ronald McDonald House Charities have separate pages on the companies' Web sites. The RMHC even have their own Web address at <http://www.rmhc.org>. Both companies provide comprehensive information on how to apply for a grant, on the projects that qualify for grants, and on the projects that have been funded recently. The two foundations differ in their target groups, as the Ben & Jerry's Foundation funds projects that effect social change, while the RMHC help severely ill children and their parents. Ben & Jerry's also commits itself to donating 7.5% of its pre-tax earnings. In addition to monetary donations, both companies donate products as well.
- **Social reporting:** Ben & Jerry's released social-audit reports in 1999, 2000 and 2001, and CERES reports in 1999 and 2000. It has not released any CERES reports since 2000, when it was taken over by Unilever. This suggests that the takeover had an effect on the company's social performance, although Unilever claimed it would maintain Ben & Jerry's ethics policies. These reports contain general information on social-responsibility activities at Ben & Jerry's, whereas its Web pages are mostly dedicated to specific issues, e.g. dioxin, rBGH and child labor in the chocolate industry. McDonald's social-compliance report focuses on supplier compliance rather than McDonald's ethical performance. McDonald's issued a real social-responsibility report in 2002. This report is now available online, but was not when I compiled the corpus. As has been pointed out in Section 3.2.3.3, social reports are a relatively new phenomenon, which is

also evident from the fact that Ben & Jerry's issued its first social report in 1999 only.
- **Stakeholders:** The community is the main stakeholder group of both companies. Ben & Jerry's focuses on specific social issues, e.g. rBGH or dioxin, while McDonald's social concerns are of a more general nature, e.g. animal welfare and the environment. McDonald's also claims to care about employee well-being, which Ben & Jerry's does not do.
- **Organizational structure:** Ben and Jerry's has appointed a Director of Social Mission, who corresponds to the ethics officer in the business-ethics paradigm. This director has overall responsibility for the company's social affairs. McDonald's mentions its Environmental Affairs Officer, but does not reveal whether it also has an officer with comprehensive responsibility for social affairs.
- **Ethics Associations:** Ben & Jerry's and McDonald's are members of Business for Social Responsibility, and Ben & Jerry's was even one of the founding members. Surprisingly, both companies do not mention this on their ethics Web pages.

6 The BE & CSR Paradigm

6.1 Case 5: *Nike, Inc.*

6.1.1 Background to the Company

6.1.1.1 Company Profile

In 1962 Phil Knight and his former university athletics coach Bill Bowerman founded Blue Ribbon Sports (BRS), a U.S. distributor of running shoes from Japan. They opened their first retail outlet in 1966, when sales started to take off. In 1971, eventually, they developed a shoe line of their own but still had the shoes manufactured in Japan. They named the shoe line Nike, after the Greek goddess of victory. In 1978 the company Blue Ribbon Sports was renamed Nike. In the ensuing years, Nike underwent tremendous growth and went public in 1980. Today, Nike does business in 120 countries and employs 22,000 people worldwide. The company sells mainly shoes and apparel but also sunglasses and watches. The company is headquartered in Beaverton, Oregon (Nike 2001b).

Nike founder Phil Knight is still CEO and chairman of the board. Given Nike's tremendous success, Mr Knight is considered "one of the marketing wizards of the 1980s and 90s" ("Just doing it": 30). His company's success is in part attributable to superior product design, clever marketing, and commitment to athletic excellence. Another factor conducive to Nike's rise from a small importer of Japanese sneakers to the leading athletic shoe company is that people in the United States value physical fitness, which creates a ready market for Nike's products ("Fitting the world in sport shoes: 73; Rhodes 1981: 52). Nike's success can also be put down to its organization as a marketing and design company rather than a production company. Nike has always outsourced production, systematically shifting production from country to country, always looking for the region with the lowest wages. In its early days, Nike subcontracted to Japan only. Later on, in the late 1970s, it moved production to South Korea and Taiwan, as labor costs in Japan had become too high. Nike had some of its sneakers produced in the United States as well, primarily in its plant in Exeter, New Hampshire, which opened in 1974 (Nike 2001b; Rhodes 1981: 52). Nike subsequently established additional plants in New England, yet closed all of them down later on as a result of rising labor costs in the United States ("Nike layoffs": 1; "Nike to close two plants": 1). To keep up with increasingly fierce competition in the athletic shoe industry, Nike moved production back to countries in Asia where wages were considerably lower than in the United States. In the 1980s Japan, Hong Kong, South Korea, Taiwan, Malaysia, and the

Philippines lost their cost-efficiency and by the mid-1990s the company had moved its manufacturing to contract suppliers in Indonesia, China, and Viet Nam, and Thailand (Goldman and Papson 1998: 6; Clifford 1994: 68).

6.1.1.2 Nike's Corporate Icons and Symbols

Nike has managed to construct a company philosophy with its empowering slogan "Just do it" (Goldman and Papson 1998: 173; 169). Nike's iconic slogan "Just do it" was first aired in 1988 and became "the slogan of the 1990s" (Griggs 1998: 28). At its core, Nike is a company "created by athletes for athletes" (Rhodes 1981: 52) and the idea of winning is thus deeply rooted in the company (Rhodes 1981: 52). Nike has become synonymous with sports culture (Goldman and Papson 1998: 36), which makes its "Just do it" slogan a perfect fit, given that

> "nothing touches the heart of traditional American ideologies of individual achievement more than sports conceptualized as a level playing field for competition, because when the playing field is level, the individual may prevail" (Goldman and Papson 1998: 20).

Nike's logo was created in 1971, when Mr Knight had a logo designed for his first line of running shoes. He was looking for a "design that suggested movement" (Nike 2001a) and the graphic designer he had hired came up with a logo that is now known as the Swoosh (see Figure 7) (Nike 2001a).

Figure 7: Examples of the Swoosh

Nike managed to attach meaning and value to its logo through its advertisements (Goldman and Papson 1998: 17). After decades of ubiquity in sports marketing, the Swoosh has gigantic marketing clout, symbolizing "athletic excellence, a spirit of determination, hip authenticity, and playful self-awareness" (Goldman and Papson 1998: 1). Or, as *Marketing* magazine puts it:

> "It has gone on to become the most powerful global marketing logo of the century. The swoosh has succeeded in communicating Nike's brand value and philosophy to countries and cultures around the world without saying a single word. ... The Nike swoosh became synonymous with the brand and is 'Just do it' advertising campaign. It is regarded as shorthand for winning, achieving, excellence" ("The century's masters": 24).

Nike and its logo have become so closely intertwined that Nike's advertisements do not even include the company name anymore but only its logo, and the business press refers to the company simply as "the swoosh machine" (Harris 1999: 13) or just "the swoosh" (Meyer 1998: 24; Harari 1998: 39; Lefton 1999: 1A).

Prominent symbols and logos are prone to overuse and exactly this happened to Nike's logo and slogan in the late 1990s. Goldman and Papson (1998) coined the term overswooshification for this phenomenon as "a metaphor for the loss of value due to oversaturation and overcommercialization" (Goldman and Papson 1998: 178). For years, Nike was on *Young & Rubicam's* list of preferred labels among teenagers, but in 1997 Nike did not make it on the list for the first time and has been struggling to reposition its brand ever since. The company's loss of appeal cannot be put down solely to overuse of the Swoosh and the "Just do it" slogan but also to overseas labor issues, lackluster ads and fashion miscues (Lee 2000: 128). Declining sales, increasing inventory and a slipping stock price gave the impetus for Nike to distance itself from its slogan. Early in 1998, it replaced the iconic "Just do it" slogan with "I can" in an effort to reposition its brand (Jensen 1997: 3; Garfield 1998: 47; Jenkins 1998: A19). Nike now tries to use the Swoosh logo more selectively in order not to completely dilute the logo (Lee 2000: 128).

6.1.1.3 Nike's Image Threats

6.1.1.3.1 Operation PUSH

In summer 1990, Operation PUSH, a Chicago-based civil-rights group, called a nationwide "Say No to Nike" boycott. The group accused Nike of investing too little in the black community and having no African-American top executives, although African-Americans were a market segment that generated 30% of Nike's annual sales. Operation PUSH also managed to win the support of African-American pastors and radio stations (Johnson 1990: B1; Wynter 1990: n.p.; "Operation PUSH": C15).

In response to these charges, Nike pointed out that only 15% of its sales stem from African-American customers, but nevertheless announced a set of new goals for the near term. These goals included appointing a minority board member and a minority vice president within a year and raising the number of non-white department heads by 10% within 12 months. Operation PUSH deemed these goals inadequate and demanded that Nike also use banks, advertising agencies and other service companies that are owned by African-

Americans ("Operation PUSH": C15). Despite all its efforts, Operation PUSH remained largely ineffectual in getting consumers to boycott Nike. Consumers did not heed its call to boycott the company and so Nike's image was left only mildly tarnished (Wynter 1990: n.p.).

6.1.1.3.2 Labor Issues in Asia

Nike has always outsourced production to Asian factories to capitalize on lower labor costs overseas. It was not until the 1990s that this strategic move started to backfire when Nike's subcontractors in Asia, particularly in Indonesia and Vietnam, were accused of maintaining sweatshop conditions ("Nike's Asia lesson": 1; "Just don't": 1-2). The ensuing media exposure of these labor issues fueled an onslaught of additional criticism from public-interest groups.

A 1991 report by the *Asian-American Free Labor Institute* (AAFLI) charged that Nike's Indonesian subcontractors paid their workers below the minimum wage, overworked them and employed children. The report also blamed Nike's system of subcontracting production factories for such labor violations. Nike's general manager in Jakarta maintained that Nike had no control over working conditions at the factories it sourced from and did not feel it was within Nike's scope to investigate alleged labor violations. According to local labor unions, workers at these Indonesian factories had repeatedly protested against these labor violations (Schwarz 1991: 16).

In 1992 Nike hit the headlines again with labor issues in Indonesia. Nike subcontracted factories in Serang, West Java, which were owned by a South-Korean firm. The workers in these factories felt underpaid and went on strike. They were granted the pay increase they demanded (Clifford 1992: 56), but working conditions did not improve, although Nike had introduced a code of conduct in 1993 (Clifford 1996b: 56). Ill-treatment of workers at these very factories in Serang was again reported in 1994 ("Doing it, earning it": 63) and 1996 (Clifford 1996a: 24). Allegedly, excessively long working hours, very low wages, corporal punishment and humiliations were standard practice. Given the fast population growth in Indonesia, there was no shortage of people willing to put up with such working conditions. In 1994 another strike eventually caused the Indonesian government to increase the minimum wage ("Doing it, earning it": 63). However, this did not help these workers, as the subcontractors had "secured an exemption from a minimum-wage increase" (Clifford 1996a: 24). The following passage is an extract from an article that appeared in *Business Week* in July 1996. At that time, Nike sought to distance itself from these labor issues, arguing that it did not own the overseas plants that produced Nike shoes.

"Nike Chief Executive Philip H. Knight defends the Indonesian operations, saying that sneaker assemblers in Indonesia earn an average of double the minimum wage. But that's because they have no choice but to do overtime. As for how subcontractors treat the workers, Knight says, 'There's some things we can control and some things we can't control' " (Clifford 1996a: 24).

This cold attitude towards labor conditions set off an even worse firestorm of criticism of Nike's overseas sourcing in the late 1990s. In response, Nike placed ads in major newspapers, set up a toll-free number, and spoke out on the issues on its Web site (Rasmusson 1997: 22). Not only did Nike not feel responsible for the conditions at its subcontracted factories, but it also did not allow independent monitors into these factories (Clifford 1996a: 24). Instead, it referred to the audit Ernst & Young performed in 1994, which revealed that occupational health and safety standards were poor. Nike responded by forcing its subcontractors to provide their workers with protective gloves and masks and to equip their factories with fire extinguishers (Clifford 1996a: 25).

Throughout the early 1990s, Nike had claimed that labor conditions in overseas factories were beyond its control, since it did not run these production facilities. In late 1996, Nike finally accepted responsibility for working conditions in its subcontracted factories and responded more sympathetically to criticism (Oakley 1999: 27). For example, it accepted responsibility for child labor in the Pakistani soccer-ball industry, where child labor is endemic because most stitching work is done in private homes. Nike established stitching centers, introduced a minimum-age standard and prohibited homework (Clifford 1996b: 56; Bernstein 1996: 22; Knight 1998: n.p.). In October 1996, Nike also established a labor practices department at headquarters to handle its labor affairs and institutionalize overseas monitoring (Clifford 1996b: 56). In spring 1997, Nike appointed Andrew Young, former US ambassador to the United Nations, to scrutinize production facilities in Asia. He criticized that only few managers knew of Nike's code of conduct, although Nike had time and again used its code of conduct to defend itself against allegations regarding working conditions in Asia (Goldman and Papson 1998: 12). Overall, Andrew Young's report was only "mildly critical" (Bernstein 1997a: 47).

To keep its critics at bay, Nike also had *Ernst & Young* audit factories in Vietnam in 1997. The audit indeed revealed that these factories had a poor record of occupational health and safety, including overtime violations and hazardous fumes in the workplace (Bernstein 1997b: 10). The two independent audits were intended to underline Nike's commitment to improving labor standards at its overseas subcontracted factories. However, the ensuing media coverage made the company worse off than before the audit (Bernstein 1997b: 10). Nike's image was even more severely hurt when CorpWatch, a San Francisco human-rights group, in November 1997 disclosed a confidential audit report of a Vietnam factory, which had been compiled as part of the *Ernst &*

Young audit. The results of this audit did not correspond to the picture painted in Andrew Young's report, but turned up dismal working conditions at this Vietnamese factory. This incident was a serious embarrassment for Nike and just made matters worse (Bernstein 1997a: 47; Corpwatch 2002). To shed more light on the wage situation, Nike appointed a group of MBA students from Dartmouth College as independent auditors for Nike's subcontracted factories in Indonesia and Vietnam in 1997. Surprisingly, their study revealed that workers at these factories did earn a living wage, which Nike's critics considered doubtful (Oakley 1999: 27).

In 1998 Nike announced a series of improvements. The company started to send labor inspectors to each factory once a month to check the factory floor. Plus, Nike said it would hire full-time Nike production managers for each factory (Saywell 1998: 46). In May 1998, in the aftermath of the media scandal, Nike CEO Phil Knight announced a set of additional measures to improve working conditions. He made such lofty promises as raising the minimum hiring age to 16 for apparel production and 18 for footwear production, improving air quality in plants by switching to water-based glues, providing free after-hours education to workers, and providing financial assistance to workers' families for education or starting businesses of their own. He also announced that Nike would open factory floors to monitoring by independent, local organizations in addition to monitoring by accounting firms. Though U.S. labor groups deemed these improvements a breakthrough, they disliked the idea that Nike would open its subcontracted factories to monitoring by local NGOs only. They would have preferred monitoring by both local and foreign NGOs. But for the most part, Nike managed to disarm its critics with these vows and restored its image to some extent (Richards 1998: B10; "The power of publicity": 14; Herbert 1998: A33; Gilley 1998: 66). In Fall 1998, Nike was one of the founding members of the Fair Labor Association (FLA), an organization made up of human-rights groups and companies, including Nike, Reebok, Liz Claiborne, Kathie Lee Gifford, Patagonia, L.L. Bean, Nicole Miller and Phillips-Van Heusen (Bernstein 1999: 110).

U.S. student protests in 1999 demanded that Nike release the locations of its Asian factories. Nike was at first reluctant to do so, because it feared it would be put at a competitive disadvantage if it disclosed the locations of its factories. In October 1999, eventually, Nike released the locations of 42 of its 365 factories. The company ran advertisements in the press titled "Here's your chance to criticize us more accurately", which listed these 42 locations (Bernstein 1999: 110-112). In July 2001 Nike temporarily beefed up its Web site with a 12-minute online video featuring Nike's contracted factories in Vietnam, China and Thailand. The video's host, Nike director of labor Dusty Kidd, took the viewers on a factory tour. The message conveyed in the video was that Nike was dedicated to improving working conditions and the well-being of workers, e.g. by providing free food, free accommodation, classes after work and healthcare. The video was online for 90 days only ("Nike-cam": 55).

Overall, it seems that Nike did not respond particularly well to the charges it faced. Rather, it conveyed the impression it had something to hide. Nike would have needed more staff to deal with the labor issue and should have launched a Web site dedicated to labor issues much earlier (Marshall 1997: n.p.). Even CEO Phil Knight admitted that the company did not handle these issues successfully, when he made the following statement:

> "Corporate responsibility and the perception relating to it is important. And we have not done a very good job in getting our message out to date" ("Just doing it": 31).

In addition, Nike has acknowledged that it failed to hire local managers right from the beginning of its outsourcing activities, which could have prevented the scandal outright ("Just don't": 1-2).

A theme commonly found in the anti-Nike press is that of juxtaposing the millions of dollars Nike paid to Michael Jordan against the rock-bottom wages of the manufacturing workers (Clifford 1996a: 24; Goldman and Papson 1998: 14). The antagonistic press on Nike's labor issues certainly tarnished the corporate image, but not its sales. Paradoxically, in 1997, the year when the public outcry reached its peak, Nike generated record sales (Marhsall 1997: n.p.), which suggests that consumers are largely unconcerned about labor issues. The news media also played with Nike's slogan to create headline puns for their reports on Nike's labor issues. For example, headlines of articles on Nike's labor issues read "Just do it—or else"[9], "Just don't"[10] and "Nike's Asia lesson: Just don't do it"[11]. Nike's slogan has also been ridiculed as a punch line in a cartoon on child labor. Figure 8 shows a cartoon by John Ambrosavage, which appeared in the *Washington Free Press* in 1998. The omnipresent Swoosh identifies the plant as Nike's.

---

[9] Ballinger, J. (1995): "Just do it—or else", *Multinational Monitor*, June 1995: 7.
[10] "Just don't", *Business Asia*, 28 July 1997: 1-2.
[11] "Nike's Asia lesson: Just don't do it", *Crossborder Monitor*, 1 October 1997: 8.

Figure 8: "Just do it" as a Punch Line
(Source: <http://www.speakeasy.org/wfp/31/Nike.html>, 14 January 2002)

6.1.1.3.3 Anti-Nike Campaigns on the Internet

The World Wide Web seems like ideal medium for campaigning, for it provides an enormous reach at low cost coupled with the capabilities of hypermedia technology. Its effectiveness is however difficult to assess. Unsurprisingly, anti-Nike Web sites have sprung up on the World Wide Web, providing detailed accounts of Nike's labor issues at its subcontractors' plants in Asia. Typically, these sites also provide links to other anti-Nike Web sites, some of which have already become obsolete, e.g. <www.nikewages.com> and <www.nikewatch.org>, presumably because they were closed down on legal grounds or because the anti-Nike campaigns have simply fizzled out. The anti-Nike Web sites listed below are current as of January 2002.

- <http://www.caa.org.au/campaigns/nike/index.html> is run by Oxfam Community Aid Abroad, a member of Oxfam International. Their Web site is intended to support their "Just stop it" campaign against Nike's subcontracted sweatshops (Oxfam Community Aid Abroad 2002).
- <http://www.nikeworkers.org> is maintained by a pressure group called Press for Change and provides information on the inhumane production practices of Nike's subcontractors in Indonesia (Press for Change 2002). The site's URL is strikingly similar to <http://www.nikeworkers.com>, one of Nike's official sites.

- <http://www.nikewages.org> charges that Nike's wages are insufficient to meet basic needs and seeks to put pressure on Nike and its subcontractors to pay living wages. Figure 9 illustrates this point, by comparing Tiger Woods' daily sponsoring income and CEO Phil Knight's net worth with a factory worker's daily wage in US dollars and Indian rupees (NikeWages.org 2001).

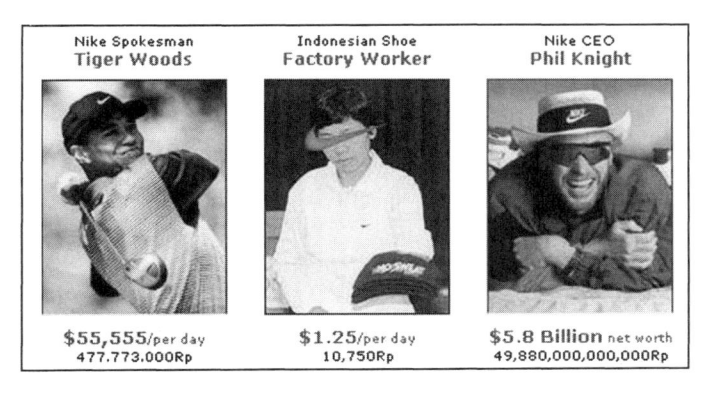

Nike Spokesman Tiger Woods	Indonesian Shoe Factory Worker	Nike CEO Phil Knight
$55,555/per day 477.773.000Rp	$1.25/per day 10,750Rp	$5.8 Billion net worth 49,880,000,000,000Rp

Figure 9: What Does Nike Pay its People?
(Source: NikeWages.org 2001)

- <http://www.saigon.com/~nike> focuses on sweatshop conditions at Nike's subcontracted production plants in Vietnam (Vietnam Labor Watch 2002).
- <http://www.geocities.com/Athens/Acropolis/5232>, an anonymous Web site, calls Nike boycotts in Canada, sells anti-Nike merchandise, and hosts an anti-Nike Internet message board. As the site has not been updated since 1999, its timeliness is doubtful (Just do it! 2002).
- <http://www.nikesweatshop.net> is a bogus Nike site sporting the colors, fonts, and graphics of Nike's corporate design. It is a perfect representation of Nike's corporate design standards, except for the broken Swoosh in the top-left corner, yet it links to other anti-Nike Web sites instead of Nike pages.

Figure 10 shows a selection of anti-Nike logos found on the anti-Nike Web sites listed above. All logos use or abuse the Swoosh in some form.

Figure 10: Anti-Nike Logos

(Sources: Clean Clothes 2002; Just do it! 2002)

In June 2000, hackers gained control of Nike's web site and redirected Nike's traffic to a Web site run by S11, a Melbourne-based anti-capitalism coalition, for a few hours. The hackers behind the Internet hijack, also referred to as i-jack, remained unidentified and also S11 claimed it did not know anything about the redirect ("Nike website is hijacked", 2000).

6.1.2 Discourse Analysis

Nike's Web site at <http://www.nike.com> or <http://www.nikeworkers.com> is geared at those interested in Nike's products. The link *About Nike* takes users to <www.nikebiz.com>, which contains comprehensive information on Nike. A selection of the pages in the ethics section of this Web site was used as a corpus for the discourse analysis.

6.1.2.1 The Ideational Function

Nike's ethical discourse focuses mainly on corporate philanthropy, environmental protection, and labor issues. The latter is dealt with so comprehensively that its discussion is divided into sections on the code of conduct, factory compliance and monitoring, case studies, child labor, and collegiate licensing.

Corporate Philanthropy

Nike confines its giving activities to *communities where our employees live and work*, i.e. communities where Nike has operations. The company boasts that *giving back to the community isn't tired, uninspired corporate rhetoric — it's who we are*. Nike thus involves its employees in its giving program and encourages them to do volunteer work at nonprofit organizations. Nike values every employee volunteer hour at USD 10 and gives an amount equivalent to the hours its employees donated to charitable organizations. Also, Nike matches all financial donations made by employees dollar-for-dollar. This Employee Matching Gift Program, as Nike calls it, creates the impression that Nike is looking for a way to justify its giving activities by making its employees responsible for the amount Nike gives away.

Apart from its Employee Matching Gift Program, the Nike Foundation administers all corporate giving. The main goal of the Nike Foundation is to *increase the participation of young people in physical activity*. Further, Nike states it funds nonprofits *whose programs increase physical movement among youth in the communities where Nike has a significant market presence*. Although encouraging young people to do sports is a worthwhile cause, one cannot fail to notice that this is directly related to the sale of sports gear and equipment. What's more, Nike's involvement in such activities inevitably raises Nike's brand awareness among young people. Also the fact that Nike supports youth only in communities where it has a strong presence makes it obvious that Nike's giving is purely self-serving.

Nike's grantmaking guidelines are quite stringent. It gives exclusively to *nonprofit organizations as defined under Section 501(c)(3) of the Internal Revenue Code*. Nike funds the organizations *through invitational programs* but mainly funds projects that is has *proactively* launched with these nonprofit organizations. Nike points out that it reviews unsolicited applications from nonprofits, but seldom funds them.

Nike gives detailed accounts of its contributions. It lists all cash and non-cash contributions that Nike and the Nike Foundation donated in the fiscal year 2001. Although Nike claims *it's always more than just money*, it mentions twice in the corpus that its donations amounted to USD 29 million in 2001. Nike also displays a bar chart showing its donations and employee volunteer hours of the past three years. In the subheading on one of its community-affairs pages, Nike pledges to donate 3% of its pre-tax profit to non-profit organizations worldwide. The text, however, does not elaborate on this 3% contribution. Based on the income before tax taken from Nike's annual reports, a rough calculation for the past three years shows that Nike's donations should have amounted to USD 27 million in FY 2001, 27 million in FY 2000 and USD 22 million in FY 1999. According to Nike's bar chart, its actual donations amounted to over USD 29 million in FY 2001, approx. USD 18 million in FY 2000 and approx. 27 million in FY 1999. Evidently, Nike's contributions match this 3% target only in FY 2001, but grossly fell short of this target in FY 2000 and exceeded their target in FY 1999. This suggests that Nike's commitment to donating 3% of untaxed earnings was introduced fairly recently.

Environment
Nike admits that it had not acknowledged its environmental responsibility and had only complied with legal regulations by the late 1980s. Then a group of employees formed an environmental task force, which became the Nike Environmental Action Team, a separate department, in 1993. In 1994, Nike launched its Reuse-A-Shoe program, which it still has in place today. The goal of the program is to collect old athletic shoes and reuses the rubber from the sole. In 1998, Nike adopted its Corporate Environmental Policy, which centers on the sustainability of Nike's business practices, in particular throughout the product life cycle. Nike's commitments also include *securing quality of life* and *restoring the environment.* The term *sustainability* is the key term on Nike's environmental pages, as the examples below demonstrate:

(1) "to drive sustainability in everything we do"

(2) "The reach of sustainability extends into nearly every corner of Nike operations."

(3) "Our long-term goal is for sustainability to"

(4) "the company-wide pursuit of sustainable business practices"

(5) "Through the adoption of sustainable business practices"

(6) "Integrate principles of sustainability into all major business decisions"

(7) "according to the fundamental principles of sustainability"

(8) "to support our goal of achieving sustainability"

(9) "to integrate sustainability into various parts of the company"

The idea of sustainability is also expressed in its commitment *to securing intergenerational quality of life*. Nike lists ten measures it pledges to undertake to achieve sustainability. These measures include vague goals such as reporting, monitoring, education of employees and business partners, continuous improvement, etc. Among these goals is also compliance with environmental legislation around the world, which is actually the least one would expect of a company.

Social Reporting
In 2001 Nike issued its first Corporate Responsibility Report, which is available for download on Nike's Web site. The report covers the same areas as Nike's ethics Web pages but is more comprehensive. It contains, for example, an introductory statement by CEO Phil Knight and a section on Nike's stakeholders, which the Web site does not include. Also, the report is full of graphic images and photographs, whereas the Nike Web site uses visual elements sparsely. The report itself is a manifestation of CSR, as Nike tries to project an image of a socially concerned company to the general public. Nike describes its social report on its Web site as follows:

(10) "It is our intent and hope that this report will help to outline the challenges facing us - and what we're doing to make a difference."

The words *intent* and *hope* convey the impression that the report is a desperate attempt to restore the company image. The phrase *challenges facing us* seems to euphemize public criticism.

Nike's Code of Conduct
The page that contains Nike's Code of Conduct starts off with the heading *Nike was founded on a handshake,* using *handshake* as a metaphor for honesty and trustworthiness. Nike then continues in the text: *Implicit in that act was the determination that we would build our business with all of our partners based on trust, teamwork, honesty and mutual respect*. These seem to be Nike's values or core principles, although Nike does not label them as such. Similarly, the next sentence reads:

(11) "At the core of the NIKE corporate ethic is the belief that we are a company comprised of many different kinds of people, appreciating individual diversity, and dedicated to equal opportunity for each individual"

This statement is actually the only place where Nike uses the term *ethic*. Still, it does not really fit in at this place, because the page focuses on the relationship between Nike and its contractors, who do not belong to the company as such.

Nike's Code of Conduct, which Nike deems *the spirit of our partnership*, is posted in English on the Web site and can be downloaded in 15 other languages. Nike adopted its first code of conduct in January 1992, as it points out and *was among the industry's first to establish a manufacturing Code of Conduct*. It was seemingly not the first to come up with this idea, but does not want to appear as a follower, hence the use of *among the first*. The Nike Code of Conduct contains stipulations on forced labor, child labor, wages, working hours, occupational health and safety, environmental protection and factory inspection. Nike more or less imposes its own standards on foreign suppliers and requires compliance with local legislation only to its own advantage. Working hours and age limits, for example, are determined by Nike's policies or local laws, depending on which one sets higher standards:

(12) "the Nike or legal age limit, whichever is higher"

(13) "complies with legally mandated work hours"

(14) "complies with local limits if they are lower" [working hours]

(15) "compliance with this Code of Conduct and required laws" [factory inspection]

The selectivity with which Nike approaches local norms is best illustrated by its wage policy. Nike does not force its suppliers to pay more than the legal minimum wage or the prevailing industry wage and only requires them to pay their workers the benefits they are entitled to by law:

(16) "at least the minimum wage, or the prevailing industry wage, whichever is higher"

(17) "fully compensated according to local law"

(18) "all legally mandated benefits"

Paradoxically, it states on the same page that *we are driven to do not only what is required by law, but what is expected of a leader*. Here, Nike claims that its understanding of responsible business conduct goes beyond the letter of the law. Still, it adheres to local legislation and local wage levels when it comes to compensation and does not force its contractors to pay wages above the industry level, irrespective of how low these wages are. Nike is not bothered whether these wages are living wages, presumably because paying higher wages would only increase Nike's manufacturing costs. Also, industry level in the context of athletic shoe production and athletic apparel is probably determined by multinationals like Nike anyway, as local companies are unlikely to deal in athletic shoes or apparel. Evidently, Nike takes advantage of its own standards, by keeping wages low and appearing culturally sensitive, while at the same time imposing its own age standards to protect its image at home.

Child Labor
Part of the compliance subsection is a page on child labor. Nike communicates its stance on child labor with a lot of pathos: *For Nike, and to many in the industrialized world, no two words evoke more emotion, empathy and resolve than child labor.* Similarly, it states that *we abhor child labor.* Considering that Nike did not feel this way in the mid-1990s when it tolerated child labor and put the blame for it on its contractors, these firm assertions lack credibility. However, Nike is quite frank about the mistakes it has made and claims it has learned from them:

(19) "Out of ignorance and not researching regional business practices, we made a huge, unmitigated mistake"

(20) "But we've learned from our mistakes"

(21) "But we've learned some tough lessons along the way"

As a result of these mistakes, Nike introduced its anti-child-labor policy on May 12, 1998, which it calls *our rigid standards* that *are among the highest in the industry.* It gives the exact date of when it introduced these standards, presumably to back up the argument with factual information. However, in the paragraph following this date, Nike recalls the soccer-production incident in Pakistan of 1995/1996, which happened more than two years before Nike introduced it anti-child labor policy. Nike calls the incident its *most sobering experience with child labor*, yet does not explain the two-year delay between the *sobering experience* and the introduction of its *rigid standards*.

Nike's standards include a clause stipulating that workers have to be 16 years of age for apparel production and 18 years for footwear production. Nike acknowledges that child labor is standard practice in many less developed countries and that many families there depend on their children's income, but its 16/18 age limit *is, we believe, the right thing to do.* Presumably to anticipate charges that there are still children in Nike's contracted factories, Nike gives reasons why there might still be children making Nike products. It admits that the implementation of its policies was not successful immediately (*didn't exactly work out that way*). One of the reasons Nike gives is the production of counterfeits with child labor, which Nike is not responsible for. Further, Nike says it did not dismiss children who were 14 years of age when it introduced its 16/18 age policy. Therefore, there might still be workers younger than Nike's minimum age in Nike's contracted factories.

Factory Compliance and Monitoring

Nike points out that it has always outsourced production and has always just marketed the products. It says this business model *has helped provide jobs* for 600,000 people in 700 contract factories in 50 countries, *including the United States*. The page does not give a regional breakdown of employment figures, but the *Company Overview* (Nike 2002) does. Seemingly, Nike has 13,000 manufacturing workers in the United States, which translates to a modest 2.16% of all employees. Hence, highlighting production in the U.S. is superfluous, as its extent is hardly noticeable. The figure of 600,000 workers seems to be inexact anyway, as adding up the regional figures given on the *Company Overview* (Nike 2002) makes a total of only 484,500 workers. Even when allowing for this inaccuracy, U.S. workers still account for just 2.68%, which is equally insignificant. The reference to the United States as a location of manufacturing is apparently intended to mitigate the fact that Nike exports jobs to take advantage of cheap labor in Asia by mentioning that the company also produces in its high-wage home country.

Nike stresses that *We don't own these factories, but we take pride in our relationships with them*. The use of *but* actually calls for a starker contrast than just pride in these business relations. Instead, one would expect something like a clear recognition of responsibilities and a firm commitment to improvements. Nike's pride takes the form of a code of conduct and audits performed by *independent* third parties. Nike acknowledges its responsibilities in its *mission*, though: *To make responsible sourcing a business reality that enhances workers* [sic!] *lives*. This is phrased as a mission rather than a firm commitment, presumably because not all of Nike's contracted factories fully comply with Nike's standards, as Nike even admits: *none are perfect*. Nike's goal is therefore continuous improvement rather than full compliance and Nike *expects the same commitment to continuous improvement from every one of them* [the factories]. This improvement mainly involves training and education in the factories to facilitate the implementation of Nike's labor policies.

Nike uses forceful language to describe its stance on labor violations:

(22) "We work strenuously to improve"

(23) "a set of rigorous labor, health and environmental standards"

(24) "we take rigorous steps to"

(25) "we do the utmost to ensure those standards are met"

(26) "Our rigid standards"

Despite the determination conveyed in these examples, Nike treats cases of non-compliance with surprisingly little rigor. If a violation is detected, Nike will first *work with those owners* of the factories. If violations continue, Nike levies fines, which are used to improve working conditions. The next disciplinary step is putting the contractor on probation. If non-compliance persists, Nike gives notice to the contractor and eventually discontinues doing business, but Nike points out that *those situations are rare*. To some extent, this procedure suggests that Nike does not want to terminate business relations with contractors, presumably to avoid the costs of searching for new partners. Also, it could be that the majority of contractors violate Nike's policies and so a more forceful procedure would jeopardize supply. Still, this lax procedure raises the question of how much sense stringent policies make if non-compliance is sanctioned so weakly.

Nike uses internal and external monitoring to audit its factories. As a *charter member* of the Fair Labor Association (FLA), Nike strongly relies on the FLA for policy setting and external monitoring. To enhance the third-party credibility of FLA monitoring, Nike points out that the FLA's members include companies, consumer groups and universities. Formerly, Nike also used PriceWaterhouse Coopers (PwC) for factory audits, but now uses Global Social Compliance, a company founded by former PwC employees. Nike also prides itself on being a founding member of the Global Alliance for Workers and Communities (GAWC), which focuses on improving monitoring processes. The GAWC's members also include unidentified *private, public and non-profit organizations*. Together with the Center for Economic Studies and International Applications at the University of Ho Chi Minh, the GAWC conducts audits of Nike's contracted factories in Vietnam.

In addition, Nike has given students the opportunity to visit overseas factories and to publish their uncensored findings on Nike's Web site. It makes eleven such reports available for download. These reports bring *to light things that are working well in the factories, as well as areas that need improvement*. These reports may well be uncensored and seemingly even contain unfavorable information, yet the fact remains that Nike is the one to decide which report to publish and which not. Together with these reports, Nike also makes a document containing factory locations available for download.

Case Studies
Nike makes four case studies of working conditions in its subcontracted factories available for download and gives a short summary of or comment on each of these four case studies. The introductory paragraph on the case-study page reads:

> (27) "We won't insist that you simply take our word for how we operate within the world of global manufacturing and what impact we've had in the regions where Nike products are made. We urge you to

examine these case studies for third-party perspectives of Nike's manufacturing practices."

Nike uses the negation *we won't* to challenge the audience's presupposition that Nike's assertions are untrue. Also, Nike uses the direct address *you* as a way to add authenticity and intimacy to the message, thereby establishing a closer relationship with its audience. Considering that there are only nine instances of the direct address in the whole corpus — three of which occur in the instructions on how to view the responsibility report — they make this paragraph stand out. The authors of these four case studies are *Verité*, a professor of Business Administration at the University of Michigan, students of Dartmouth's Amos Tuck School and journalists from *Sports Marketing Quarterly*.

Nike publishes these case studies to support its claims with objective findings from third parties. However, these case studies are doubtful evidence, as Nike clearly selected only case studies that draw a positive or mildly negative picture of factory conditions. *Verité was commissioned by Nike* to take a look at a factory in Vietnam, which is very likely to have positively impacted the outcome of the report. As for the Dartmouth student report, Nike's only comment is that *They find that Nike contract factories offer an economically attractive alternative for entry-level workers* but says nothing about manufacturing practices. Similarly, according to Nike, the *Sports Marketing Quarterly* report *concludes that some of the criticisms of Nike have been unfair*, which implies that most of the criticisms were fair. By presenting seemingly biased and subjective material as on objective assessment of the company's practices Nike whitewashes the fact that its contracted manufacturing plants are not up to Western standards.

Collegiate Licensing
Although collegiate licensing accounts for only 1% of its business, Nike still dedicates a separate page to it and implicitly gives the reason for it: *Perhaps nowhere are Nike's labor practices more hotly debated than on American college and university campuses*. Nike also takes up the issue of disclosing factory locations (see Section 6.1.1.3.2), but reverses the picture when talking about *our offering of conditional disclosure*. The term *offering* suggests that Nike came up with the idea of disclosing its factory locations, yet in reality student protests had demanded that the company disclose the locations of its Asian contractors.

6.1.2.2 The Interpersonal Function

Nike
Nike uses first-person pronouns more often than the company name or the company when referring to itself. However, the factor by which first-person pronouns outnumber nouns (viz. *Nike* and *company*) and *it/its* is not a very large one, as is evident from Table 11. We is never used inclusively, but always includes only Nike. Nike frequently mixes *Nike* and first-person possessive adjectives within sentences, e.g. as in *Nike strives to not only bring value to our business*.

	Subject	Object	Genitive	Adjective	TOTAL
we / us / our	82	4	n.a.	88	**174**
Nike	39	21	24	41	**125**
company	1	4	2	-	**7**
it / its	1	-	n.a.	4	**5**

Table 11: Breakdown of References to Nike

Nike considers itself a *global citizen* rather than a global company and is *committed to being a responsible corporate citizen*. Also, its link on its home page that directs visitors to its ethics section bears the name *Global Citizenship*. Nike obviously equates *citizenship* with ethical and socially responsible business conduct, but does not use ethics-related terminology like *ethical*, *moral* or *integrity* on its Web pages at all. Instead, the company uses equally vague business jargon, e.g. *continuous improvement*, *sustainability* or *best practices* to praise its business conduct. Nike probably deliberately avoids moral concepts, as it does not want to appear hypocritical, given that its past behavior and attitude do not match its current stance. Still, Nike uses *honesty* once and *respect* five times, so its discourse it not completely free from ethics terminology.

Nike's Stakeholders
The stakeholder groups mentioned in the corpus include customers, shareholders, communities, employees, workers and business partners. Shareholders are only mentioned once on one of the environment pages: *Nike is committed to securing quality of life, restoring the environment and increasing value for our customers, shareholders and business partners*. Customers appear only once more in the corpus among Nike's environmental goals: *Educate our employees, customers, and business partners to support our goal of achieving*

sustainability. Nike devotes more attention to the remaining four stakeholder groups, which are discussed below in separate sections.

Communities

Nike commits itself to *proudly and actively* supporting communities around the globe by giving away 3% of its income before tax to non-profit organizations. These communities are communities *where the company has an employee or retail presence* or *where our employees live and work.* The Nike Foundation, in turn, gives only to nonprofits in the United States, but also only *in communities where Nike has a significant market presence and where our Nike employees live and work.* These are mainly in Orgeon, where Nike is headquartered, and Tennessee, where it has a major distribution center.

As a founding member of the Global Alliance for Workers and Communities (GAWC), Nike pretends it wants to improve the communities where its contractors' plants are located. Nike claims it is *incumbent upon our company ... to increasingly shoulder more of the social responsibilities in countries just beginning to develop market economies.* Nike constructs a relationship of paternalism and patronage with these communities. Considering that Nike is always in search of cheap labor markets, it does not seem plausible that Nike wants to foster economic development in these communities, as this would inevitably lead to higher wages.

Business Partners

Nike's business partners include suppliers, contractors, distributors and retailers, as Nike points out in its Code of Conduct: *Nike considers every member of our supply chain as partners in our business.* Nike requires its business partners to adhere to all of Nike's policies, be it its Code of Conduct, its environmental principles, or general principles like trust, teamwork, honesty and mutual respect. It makes compliance with Nike's standards a condition for doing business with Nike. Nike expresses this requirement in the following phrases:

- (28) "contractors' obligations to workers and to us"
- (29) "we bind our contractors to these principles"
- (30) "we also bind our partners to specific standards of conduct"
- (31) "NIKE partners with contractors who share our commitment"
- (32) "seek business partnerships with suppliers who operate in a manner consistent with our values."

(33) "we expect all of our business partners to operate on the same principles"

(34) "We expect our business partners to do the same."

Nike imposes its own standards on all entities in the supply chain, thereby taking control of working conditions and environmental standards of its suppliers and contractors. It seems that past media scandals have taught Nike to accept responsibility for conditions outside of its own factories and to ensure that its contractors meet standards expected by Western consumers.

The paragraphs preceding the Code of Conduct use modal verbs expressing strong obligation for Nike's business partners, e.g. *contractors must* or *There shall be no*, while the code itself does not contain any modals. It uses exclusively verbs in simple present tense, e.g. *the contractor maintains, the contractor complies, the contractor provides*. Also, negative assertions in present tense (*does not*) occur five times. This categorical present tense sounds less admonitory and creates the impression that these conditions stipulated are already met.

Employees and Workers

Nike proudly presents its employees as generous and committed to doing good. It gives exact figures of how many volunteer hours they have worked in the past and much money they have donated. Nike expresses its appreciation of its ethnically and culturally diverse workforce by supporting them in establishing *Employee Networks* for minority groups, including African Americans, Native Americans, Latinos, gays and lesbians, and disabled employees. These networks seek to build awareness of minorities among employees and to educate them about minority cultures. Through these networks, Nike seeks to *realize an overall vision for Diversity*.

Nike distinguishes between employees and workers. *Worker(s)* and *employee(s)* occur 48 times in the corpus each. Although this exact match seems to be due to mere chance, it still suggests that Nike devotes equal attention to both groups on its ethics pages. While *employee(s)* mainly refers to its U.S.-based staff, *worker(s)* refers to its laborers in production facilities abroad. Nike also uses the term *employee* to refer to foreign manufacturing workers when it stipulates employment conditions for contractors and their workers:

(35) "The contractor provides each employee at least the minimum wage"

(36) "Contractors must recognize the dignity of each employee"

(37) "Contractors must post this Code in all major workspaces, translated into the language of the employee"

Apart from these examples, *employee(s)* is always taken to mean white-collar staff in Nike's U.S. bases. In this context, the use of *employees* collocates with *Nike* (eleven times), *our* (three times), *its* (once) or *our Nike* (once) to establish a direct relationship between the company and its employees. Conversely, foreign manufacturing workers are just referred to as *workers* without any possessive adjectives, obviously to distance them from Nike. Nike does not even make it explicit that these workers are employed by its subcontractors. Only three times does Nike establish a connection between workers and Nike in the following phrases:

(38) "workers making our products"

(39) "workers who make Nike goods"

(40) "people who manufacture Nike products"

Still, these phrases do not suggest that Nike is responsible for their well-being in any way. Visually, Nike seeks to convey the impression that its contract workers in Asia work on well-lit, modern factory floors, wear neat uniforms, and are happy with their jobs by decorating its Web site with pictures in order to appeal to people's emotions. It is worth noting that this impression is only created subtly through visual cues. There is no corresponding text to strengthen the impression created in the pictures.

Nike Critics

Nike invites comments and questions from concerned individuals. It has an FAQ database, including questions and answers arranged according to topic ranging from products to labor issues. Users can browse by category or search by keyword. The link to this FAQ page is a menu item on the menus in the sections *Community Affairs*, *Environment* and *Manufacturing Practices*. These menus also contain an item *Contact Us*, which allows users to submit questions or comments. Nike then sends e-mail replies.

6.1.2.3 The Textual Function

Nike's ethics section can be reached via the link *Global Citizenship* on its home page <http://www.nikebiz.com>. The home page links to the page on the responsibility report. To make its Web site cohesive, Nike uses mainly menus. It has an ethics menu including five items: *Community Affairs, Diversity,*

Environment, Manufacturing Practices and *Reporting*. Nike has submenus for four of these items. Figure 11 illustrates how menus connect the ethics pages included in the corpus.

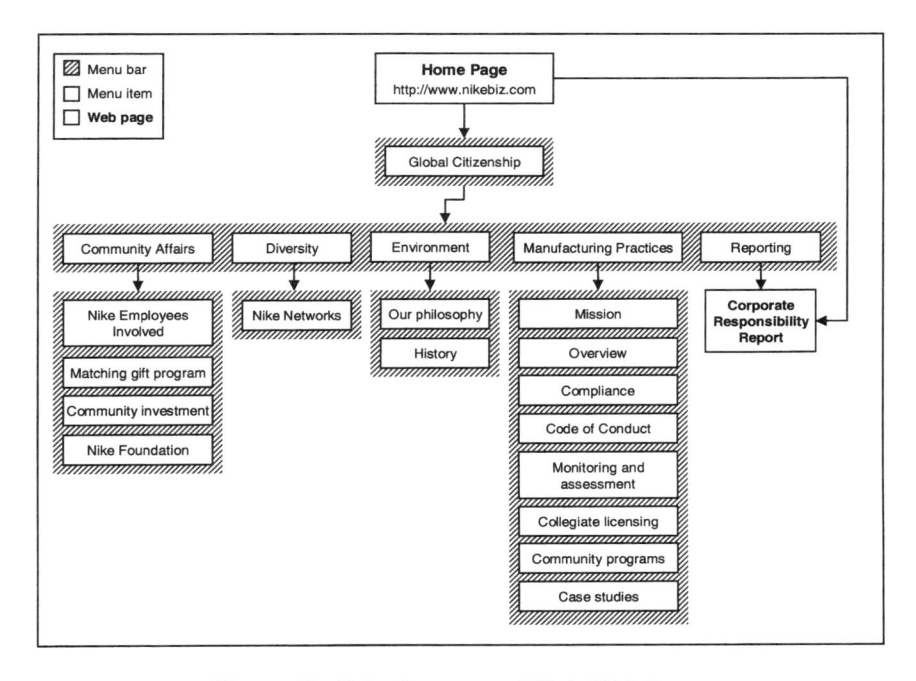

Figure 11: Cohesion among Nike's Web Pages

Nike's ethics pages contain solely three crosslinks, which point from the Code of Conduct to related pages, e.g. *Child labor*. These latter pages cannot be reached via the ethics menu. The small number of crosslinks is surprising, as especially the contents of the pages in the subsection *Manufacturing Practices* are often closely related, which calls for crosslinking.

Visually, Nike's Web site follows a consistent design — white background and gray/black font. All sections have big headings, indicating the title of the subsection, e.g. *environment*. Below the section heading is the page heading in light-gray italics, sometimes followed by a summary lead or other introductory statements in boldface before the real text of the page starts. Images, if any, are typically in the top right corner of the page. The top-level menu and the ethics menu span vertically across the page, while the menus of the ethics subsections always appear in a frame on the left. The headings and the menu items help users keep track of where they are and what they have seen already.

6.2 Case 6: *Levi Strauss & Co.*

6.2.1 Background to the Company

6.2.1.1 Company Profile

Born in Bavaria in 1829, Levi Strauss emigrated from Germany to New York in 1847 to join the dry-goods business of his half-brothers. A few years later he moved to San Francisco to open a wholesale dry-goods business of his own. In 1863 his brother-in-law joined the business and the company was renamed "Levi Strauss & Co.". In 1873 Levi Strauss and Jacob Davis applied for a patent for strengthening the jeans with metal rivets at the points of strain, e.g. the pocket corners, creating pants that are now known as jeans all over the world (Levi Strauss & Co. 2001a). The patent expired in 1891 and soon other clothing manufacturers copied the idea of riveted jeans. Around the same time Levi Strauss assigned number 501 to these jeans, which are Levi Strauss & Co.'s best selling jeans today (Levi Strauss & Co. 2001m). The word "Levi's" was registered as a trademark in 1928 only (Levi Strauss & Co. 2001c). In 1936 Levi Strauss & Co. started to attach a red tab device to the Levi's ® 501 ® jeans to help better identify the jeans (Levi Strauss & Co. 2001k).

In the 1940s Levi's ® jeans and jackets became known outside of North America when U.S. soldiers wore them overseas (Levi Strauss & Co. 2001e). Jeans were still called waist overalls then. The name jeans became established in the 1960s only (Levi Strauss & Co. 2001k). It was not until the 1960s that Levi Strauss & Co. set up shop abroad, when it established subsidiaries in Europe and Asia to expand its global market reach. At around the same time Levi Strauss & Co.'s first TV commercials were aired (Levi Strauss & Co. 2001g). After years of tremendous growth, Levi Strauss & Co. went public in 1971. The company included its values statement in its stock prospectus, which was an unusual thing to do at that time (Levi Strauss & Co. 2002h). Levi Strauss & Co. remained a public corporation for fourteen years only. In 1984 Levi-Strauss-descendant Bob Haas became CEO. He closed dozens of manufacturing plants in the U.S., expanded abroad and redirected the company's focus onto its core products (Munk 1999: n.p.). In the same year, Mr Haas made the company private in a leveraged buyout to make the company a family business again (Levi Strauss & Co. 2001h and 2001i; "A comfortable fit": 71). After the 1985 takeover Mr Haas managed to relaunch the 501 ® jeans by means of heavy advertising, which helped double sales in the United States ("A comfortable fit": 71). He also launched Dockers®, a category of business-casual khakis (Levi Strauss & Co. 2002o). Despite Levi Strauss & Co.'s success, the jeans industry remained a declining industry, as the urban cowboy look did not sell well anymore (Pouschine 1992: 78). During the 1990s, Levi Strauss & Co. saw its market share in the U.S. slip from 31% in 1990 to just under 17% in 1998 (Voight 1999: 28). After several unsuccessful product launches and flopped marketing campaigns, Mr Haas bought Levi Strauss & Co. together with three family members in a second leveraged buyout to gain even more control of the firm (Munk 1999: n.p.). In the 1998 and 1999, Levi Strauss & Co. closed half of its plants in North America and Europe, thereby slashing over 16,000 jobs (Munk 1999: n.p.; Quick 1999: A6; "Levi Strauss is likely to cut additional jobs": n.p). Levi Strauss & Co. got squeezed primarily as a result of marketing missteps and fierce competition from designer labels, such Ralph Lauren, Calvin Klein, and Tommy Hilfiger ("Levi Strauss & Co.: Yearly sales dropped": B4; Bounds 1998: B1). Levi's jeans were classic and original, but they were popular among the people of the baby-boom generation rather than their teenage children. In 1998 only, Levi Strauss & Co. launched the Levi's silver-tab brand to accommodate the taste of teenagers and regain market share among teenage consumers (Bounds 1998: B1; Kane 1998: D11). In view of the bleak outlook, Mr Haas resigned as CEO in 1999 but remained as chairman of the board (Levi Strauss & Co. 2001j; Colvin 1999: n.p.). Levi Strauss & Co.'s downfall is in part attributable to its organization as a closely held corporation, which means that Levi Strauss & Co. is accountable to no one, apart from its family owners and does not divulge financials either ("Levi Strauss & Co.: Yearly sales dropped": B4; Munk 1999: n.p.). Things might have developed differently, if the company had been accountable to a large number of external shareholders.

6.2.1.2 Levi Strauss & Co.'s Corporate Symbols and Icons

Since the 1930s Levi Strauss & Co. has been using the American cowboy as the brand icon for its 501® jeans. Conveying the image of "rugged individualism" (Levi Strauss & Co. 2001d), the cowboy was also *en vogue* in Hollywood then, which was a vital factor behind this decision (Levi Strauss & Co. 2001d). In the 1930s, *Vogue* magazine was the first to realize that Levi's jeans were more than just work pants worn by the working class. Although Levi's jeans were the uniform of laborers and cowboys then, Vogue still considered them fashionable (Voight 1999: 32). This might have been the impetus for the steady growth of the jeans industry in the ensuing decades. By the 1960s young people had chosen blue jeans as their anti-establishment uniform (Collins 1981: n.p.; Goll and Zuckermann 1993: A18). In particular Levi's 501® jeans "became a political statement" (Voight 1999: 32). Since the 1960s, the jeans industry has grown to a billion-dollar industry and Levi's jeans established themselves as an American icon, not least because of heavy advertising (Voight 1999: 29; 32; Kane 1998: D11; Collins 1981: n.p.). The company describes its jeans brand as follows:

> "Levi's® jeans embody freedom and individuality. ... They are a symbol of frontier independence, democratic idealism, social change and fun" (Levi Strauss & Co. 2001b).

Levi's 501® jeans are the company's best selling product and come in 108 sizes and 20 fabrics (Levi Strauss & Co. 2001k).

6.2.1.3 Social Responsibility at Levi Strauss & Co.

In 1991, *The Economist* deemed Levi Strauss & Co. "a family firm which for over a century has succeeded in mixing profits with philanthropy" ("A comfortable fit": 71). Although the past decade was Levi Strauss & Co.'s least successful one, it has still not abandoned its philanthropic roots that trace back to company founder Levi Strauss. Allegedly, Levi Strauss believed that business had the responsibility to give back to society. Accordingly, he regularly donated to orphanages, schools, and local charities. He even endowed 28 scholarships at the University of California at Berkeley, which the company still endows today (Levi Strauss & Co. 2001a). After his death, the company continued to uphold his values. During the Depression in the 1930s when demand dwindled, Levi Strauss & Co. kept all its manufacturing workers, thereby gaining a reputation for paternalism. The staff worked reduced hours or was given other tasks in the company ("A comfortable fit": 72; Levi Strauss & Co. 2001d; Rapaport 1993). Levi Strauss & Co. was a pioneer in integrating factories in the 1940s when most factories in the United States were still segregated (Levi Strauss & Co. 2001e). In 1952, the Levi Strauss Foundation was set up to administer corporate philanthropy (Levi Strauss & Co. 2001f). Community involvement was institutionalized at Levi Strauss & Co.'s in 1968 with the establishment of the Community Affairs Department (Levi Strauss & Co. 2001g). In the 1980s, Levi Strauss & Co. started to devote special attention to AIDS and formed AIDS support groups at headquarters (Levi Strauss & Co. 2001i; Rapaport 1993). CEO Bob Haas summarizes the company's ethics policy as follows:

> "At Levi Strauss & Co., we're integrating ethics and other corporate values (such as empowerment and diversity) into every aspect of our business — from our human-resources programs to our vendor relationship" (Haas 1994: 380).

In 1987 it formalized its values in drawing up "The Mission and Aspirations Statement" (Levi Strauss & Co. 2001i). Interestingly, Levi Strauss & Co. refers to its Mission and Aspirations Statement in the company-history section on its Web site, but does not publish this statement on its Web site.

6.2.1.4 Levi Strauss & Co.'s Image Threats

In December 1991, Levi Strauss & Co. was in the news for the first time in connection with labor issues. NBC broadcast a news report on Levi Strauss & Co.'s contractor in Saipan, a small U.S.-territory island in the Pacific Ocean, a few thousands miles off the Californian coast. The contractor's factories maintained sweatshop conditions, underpaid their workers, and put them up in padlocked quarters, which clearly violated U.S. laws. In response, Levi Strauss & Co. immediately discontinued business relations with its Saipan supplier. After an investigation by the U.S. Department of Labor, the contractor was fined to pay USD 9 million in damages and back wages to the workers ("Ethical shopping. Human rights": 66; Rapaport 1993).

In early 1992, Levi Strauss & Co. began to audit its 400 operations worldwide, which it does not own, but contracts. About 25% of the audited factories qualified as sweatshops. To improve working conditions at its contractors' factories, in early 1992 the company established stringent global sourcing guidelines to ensure that their contractors' operations abided by Levi Strauss & Co.'s business principles. The guidelines pertained to child labor, prison labor, health and safety standards, wages, and the environment (Haas 1994: 381). By 1993 Levi Strauss & Co. had cancelled contracts with 5% of its 600 suppliers and had forced 25% of its suppliers to implement changes to improve labor conditions ("Ethical shopping. Human rights": 66). Levi Strauss & Co. was quite frank about the rationale behind establishing such guidelines. The company admitted that the guidelines had not been drawn up out of pure altruism but rather to protect the company's brand image in the U.S., because most consumers disapproved of products made by forced labor or child labor ("Exporting jobs and ethics": 10; Levi Strauss & Co. 2001j; Rapaport 1993).

When Levi Strauss & Co. discovered that some of its contractors in Bangladesh employed children, it found itself in an ethical dilemma. Child labor was incompatible with its corporate values and would not go down well with consumers at home, so this practice had to be eradicated. Firing the children, on the other hand, would be in compliance with Levi Strauss & Co.'s sourcing guidelines, but would make the children and their families worse off, which the company did not want either. Levi Strauss & Co. escaped the ethical dilemma by working out an unconventional solution. It persuaded its contractors to pay these children their regular wages, while they attended school full-time. As soon as the children were old enough to work, the contractor would offer them regular jobs, which the children were not required to accept. This solution squeezed Levi Strauss & Co.'s margins, since the contractors passed on the payroll costs for these children. To Levi Strauss & Co. this solution was sensible, not only because the company could retain its Bangladeshi contractors but also because it could protect its image that way (Haas 1994: 382). The stakes for Levi Strauss

& Co. were high and apparently, the company was willing to pay a very high price for maintaining the credibility of its values-driven business approach.

Levi Strauss & Co.'s guidelines did not apply to individual contractors but to countries as a whole. CEO Bob Haas pointed out that the company would not source in countries with pervasive human-rights violations, as this "would run counter to our [the company's] values and have an adverse effect on our [the company's] global brand image" (Haas 1994: 381). In 1992, Levi Strauss & Co. pulled out of Myanmar due to serious human-rights violations (Miller 1993: 10). An onslaught of public criticism from all over the world had led a number of other U.S.-based multinationals to withdraw from Myanmar as well, including Liz Claiborne, Eddie Bauer and PepsiCo ("The power of publicity": 13-14). Myanmar was not the only country where Levi Strauss & Co. encountered human-rights violations that were incompatible with its ethical principles. In 1992, after allegations of prison labor in China, Levi Strauss & Co. started to audit its Chinese factories and established sourcing guidelines to prevent the use of forced prison labor for their products (Borrus 1992: 15). These efforts notwithstanding, in 1993, Levi Strauss decided to discontinue manufacturing in China as a sign of protest against persistent human-rights abuse in China ("A fashion statement": 5; Miller 1993: 10; Goll and Zuckermann 1993: A18) and planned "to undertake a phased withdrawal from China" (Haas 1994: 381). Levi Strauss had not made any direct investment in China, but contracted 30 Chinese manufacturing companies. Therefore, the company reckoned that the withdrawal from China would take several years, as they had to wait for existing contracts to expire. It still intended to purchase cloth from Chinese manufacturers, though (Miller 1993: 10).

Levi Strauss & Co.'s decision to pull out of China fueled a public debate. The company's move to leave China was met with both approval and skepticism. For one, the decision to leave China was considered in accordance with Levi Strauss & Co.'s corporate ethical commitments (Goll and Zuckermann 1993: A18). At the same time, harsh criticism was voiced regarding the rationale for this decision, as critics deemed it doubtful that Levi Strauss & Co. withdrew its manufacturing from China on purely ethical grounds. Rather, it was assumed that the company expected its radical move to improve its image among U.S. consumers. Other critics contended that the company was forgoing a highly profitable business opportunity by pulling out of China, given that China was already an extremely fast growing market then. It was argued that Levi Strauss & Co. might find it difficult to reenter the Chinese market, once China's human-rights record had improved, as the company's withdrawal certainly did not go down well with the Chinese government. Hostility from the Chinese government was expected to hinder business deals with China in the future (Beaver 1995: 35; Goll and Zuckermann 1993: A18). Apparently, all other companies found these prospects too threatening and thus no other company followed suit. In 1996, Levi Strauss & Co. temporarily froze its phased withdrawal because the human-rights situation seemed to get better and also because no other company had joined the protest (Landler 1998: CA; D1). In 1998, five years after announcing its withdrawal from China, Levi's Strauss & Co. eventually decided to go back into China. In an interview to the *New York Times* on April 8, 1998, Peter Jacobi, President and Chief Operating Officer at Levi Strauss & Co., made it public that the company would expand manufacturing in China. Levi Strauss & Co. had, in fact, never fully withdrawn from China. It still manufactured 800,000 units of clothing there after the pullout. To put that in perspective, the company produced three million units there before the 1993 pullout. Mr Jacobi also disclosed that Levi Strauss & Co. would start selling clothing in China, which it had decided against in the course of the withdrawal. Arguably, the decision not to sell jeans in China was not prompted by human-rights violations but rather by China's huge market for counterfeit Levi's jeans, which would have rendered marketing original Levi's jeans in China pointless. In the *New York Times* interview, Mr Jacobi justified the company's decision to expand business in China by claiming that the human-rights situation had improved, but also stressed that Levi Strauss & Co. would continue to monitor its subcontractors. Mr Jacobi conceded that Levi Strauss & Co. withdrew from China because its reputation was at stake. He also admitted that the company expanded its presence in China in order not to forgo the enormous value of the Chinese market and acknowledged that "You're nowhere in Asia without being in China" (Landler 1998: CA; D1).

Levi Strauss & Co.'s announcement on April 8, 1998 that it would resume production in China triggered criticism from human-rights groups and labor-rights activists alike. The company's decision cast serious doubt on its integrity, as China was still well-known for its poor human-rights record then (Benjamin 1998). Medea Benjamin, co-director of Global Exchange, a San-Francisco-based human rights group, strongly opposes the company's move, claiming that China's human-rights record is poorer than ever before. She cites the example of freedom of association, which Levi Strauss & Co. requires its contractors to grant their workers. In China, however, independent unions are strictly prohibited, which makes Levi Strauss & Co.'s guidelines difficult to implement (Benjamin 1998; Christie 1999). Likewise, the National Labor Committee, a Washington-based advocacy group, reported that excessively long working hours are standard practice in China and thus likely to occur in Levi Strauss & Co.'s contracted factories as well (Landler 1998: CA; D1). To make factory compliance and monitoring more transparent, Levi Strauss & Co. joined the Fair Labor Association in October 1999 (Bernstein 1999: 110; "Levi Strauss & Co. joins Fair Labor Association": S11).

6.2.2 Discourse Analysis

Levi Strauss & Co. launched its first Web site in 1995 at <http://www.levi.com> (Levi Strauss & Co. 2001j). In the meantime, the company has launched a second Web site at <http://www.levistrauss.com>, which provides only company information, while <http://www.levi.com> now solely focuses on Levi's ® products.

6.2.2.1 The Ideational Function

The contents of Levi Strauss & Co.'s ethics pages focus on both business ethics and corporate social responsibility. The sections below discuss themes pertaining to both paradigms as well as the neutral themes *Reputation* and *History*.

Social Responsibility and Business Ethics

Levi Strauss & Co.'s ethics menu consists of three items, including (1) *Our commitment*, a sort of introduction, (2) *Levi Strauss Foundation* and (3) *Sourcing Guidelines*. The latter two point to pages on social responsibility (philanthropy) and business ethics (compliance), respectively. Evidently, Levi Strauss & Co. attaches equal importance to both paradigms. Levi Strauss & Co. repeatedly utters its commitment to both social responsibility and business ethics. For example:

(1) "Ethical conduct and social responsibility characterize our way of doing business."

(2) "Our commitment to ethical business practices and social responsibility"

Similarly, Levi Strauss & Co. claims that its values guide both the company's CSR activities and its BE efforts:

(3) "These values guide our foundation's giving programs, the support we provide to communities where we have a business presence, our employees' community-involvement programs, and our code of ethical conduct."

Also, when listing examples of its ethics-related activities, Levi Strauss & Co. cites examples of both CSR and BE, including employee volunteerism and its sourcing guidelines.

Compliance and Monitoring
Levi Strauss & Co.'s business-ethics efforts are confined to its overseas supply chain. It seeks to prevent labor issues by implementing a manufacturing code of conduct, referred to as Global Sourcing and Operating Guidelines. This two-part code of conduct consists of the Country Assessment Guidelines and the Business Partner Terms of Engagement. They stipulate the criteria according to which Levi Strauss & Co. selects countries and business partners. It Levi Strauss & Co. seeks business partners whose ethical standards are *not incompatible with our own*. This condition is a reflection of ethical imperialism, as overseas contractors are required to adopt the standards mandated by Levi Strauss & Co. The rationale behind imposing ethical standards is not necessarily the company's cultural insensitivity but rather the expectations of Westerns consumers.

The company publishes three *Success Stories*, which serve as examples of how its policies have benefited contracted factories and their workers. In a Mexican factory, the additional emergency exits Levi Strauss & Co. had demanded saved employees' lives during an earthquake. In an Indian factory, the implementation of the Terms of Engagement allegedly helped to raise employee morale and productivity. Further, Levi Strauss & Co. claims that factory owners in Greece and Tunisia have received national prizes for their environmental efforts regarding wastewater treatment and energy minimization, which Levi Strauss & Co.'s Terms of Engagement had required.

The company prides itself on having received the America's Corporate Conscience Award for International Commitment from the Council on Economic Priorities for the development of its code of conduct. Levi Strauss & Co. also points to its participation in labor-related NGOs such as the Fair Labor Association (FLA) and the Ethical Trading Initiative and provides an e-mail address for more information on its code of conduct. In early 2002, the company also mentioned the U.S. China Business Principles Working Group on its Web site, but has removed this reference from its Web site in the meantime. Levi Strauss & Co. does not make any other reference to the China issue either but rather deliberately avoids it. The company history, which was not included in the corpus, lists a few additional awards the company received, e.g. the Lawrence A. Wien Prize in Corporate Social Responsibility in 1984 and *Business Ethics* magazine's "Excellence in Ethics" award in 1993 (Levi Strauss & Co. 2001j). Interestingly, it fails to mention that it received the latter award "for its leadership in the area of human rights" ("Business ethics awards": 14) — obviously for its withdrawal from China in 1993. The fact that the company does not point this out and does not refer to this prize on its ethics pages suggests that it seeks to evade the China issue altogether. Obviously, the company still wants to capitalize on the award for PR and thus leaves out the controversial details. At least, the company is honest enough to list China among the countries where it manufactures jeans (Levi Strauss & Co. 2001n).

Philanthropy and Community Involvement

Philanthropy at Levi Strauss & Co. is based on the aspiration to eliminate discrimination and empower socially or economically disadvantaged people. Further, the company participates in *socially responsible initiatives that are ... consistent with the values of LS&CO*. Accordingly, it supports projects and organizations that focus on either of the following issues: *AIDS Prevention, Economic Empowerment, Social Justice* or *Youth Empowerment*. Levi Strauss & Co.'s philanthropy encompasses *strategic initiatives*, including grants made by the Levi Strauss Foundation, community projects and employee volunteerism. Levi Strauss & Co. describes its achievements in emotive platitudes such as the following:

(4) "Through our grantmaking, we support and lead social change. Through our employee community involvement, we strive to reinvigorate civic engagement and rebuild a sense of community locally and globally."

Levi Strauss & Co.'s monetary donations are administered by the Levi Strauss Foundation, which it calls *a catalyst for positive change*. In 2001, the Levi Strauss Foundation donated USD 16 million in close to 40 countries. It makes grants only to certified charities and rules out all other grant requests, using the anaphora *we do not* as a figure of speech:

(5) "We do not make grants to individuals. We do not make grants for capital campaigns, endowments, event sponsorships, or scholarships. We do not make product donations, except to preselected charities. We do not accept letters of inquiry or proposals seeking Community Involvement Team grants."

These repetitions perform not only an emphatic function but also a cohesive function, as they are basically a syntactically marked list, which is more cohesive than a mere bullet-point list.

Levi Strauss & Co. then outlines the application guidelines for organizations situated in North America and Latin America, Asia Pacific, and Europe and Africa. It also provides names and e-mail addresses for contacting the relevant offices in these regions. The company seemingly encourages its employees to do volunteer work in their communities, e.g. by participating in charitable NGOs or by joining the company's Community Involvement Teams. Levi Strauss cites the example of its headquarters staff participating in a *company volunteer day* to clean up the environment at sites in the San Francisco area. The Foundation also matches employee hours donated to NGOs financially. Likewise, the Foundation matches its employees' financial donations to U.S. 501(c)3 organizations.

The Value Statement

Levi Strauss & Co.'s business strategy is driven by its four core values that company founder Levi Strauss allegedly upheld. These values include *Empathy — Walking in Other People's Shoes, Originality — Being Authentic and Innovative, Integrity — Doing the Right Thing,* and *Courage — Standing Up For What We Believe*. These four values *form the foundation of Levi Strauss & Co.*, as the company points out on the home page. Having such clearly labeled values and trumpeting them on the very first page of the Web site, is a clear indication that the company wants to be recognized as a value-driven organization.

The values statement elaborates on these values and provides examples of how the company has enacted them. While *Originality* is strictly product-related, the other three values are related to ethics, albeit to different extents. *Integrity* is, as the name suggests, about ethical business conduct, including virtues such as honesty, trustworthiness and respect. Levi Strauss & Co. cites the examples of employee diversity and its code of conduct to provide evidence for the enactment of integrity. *Empathy* is mainly about meeting customer needs, which is a sheer necessity for every company and does actually not qualify as a value. Levi Strauss & Co. mentions the promotion of AIDS awareness among employees as an example of *Empathy*. *Courage* is the vaguest of all values and encompasses the idea of innovation. Among the examples given are *full medical benefits to domestic partners of employees*. The value statement ends with a three-part vision, which is not related to ethics but to marketing and sales only.

Levi Strauss & Co. repeatedly considers itself a commercially successful company, which is definitely an overstatement in view of the declining business in recent years. The company attributes its success to the values-driven business approach it has pursued for decades and also deems its socially responsible business conduct a critical factor behind its success.

(6) "As we look at our history, we see a story of how core values work together and are the source of our success".

(7) "it is this special relationship between our values, our consumers and our brands that is the basis of our success".

(8) "our 'profits through principles' approach to business is a point of competitive advantage"

(9) "The company's long-standing traditions of philanthropy, community involvement and employee volunteerism ... contribute to our commercial success."

(10) "This principle of responsible commercial success ... drives sustained, profitable growth and superior return on investment."

Levi Strauss & Co.'s reference to the correlation between ethics and financial success strongly suggests that the company strategically uses its ethics efforts to create a socially responsible image, which could translate into higher sales. Hence, its ethics efforts are unlikely to be driven by Levi Strauss' spirit and values but rather by mere profit motives.

Reputation

Levi Strauss & Co. mentions reputation in connection with ethical business conduct, but does not identify reputation as the rationale behind its corporate ethics efforts. The terms *reputation* and *image* appear only once each in the corpus.

(11) "Our Terms of Engagement are good for the people working on our behalf and good for the long-term reputation of our brands."

(12) "The Country Assessment Guidelines help us assess any issue that might present concern in light of the ethical principles we have set for ourselves. ... Specifically, we assess whether the ... Political, Economic and Social Environment would protect the company's interests and brand/corporate image."

Interestingly, *reputation* and *image* appear in connection with the Terms of Engagement and the Country Assessment Guidelines, which are the heart of corporate ethics. In both cases the company acknowledges that its image benefits from implementing these policies.

History

History and tradition are a frequent theme in the corpus. Levi Strauss & Co. never fails to emphasize that philanthropy has a long tradition in the company and that the corporate values have permeated the organization since its establishment. In this context, the company also prides itself on Levi Strauss' philanthropic mind.

(13) "Levi Strauss & Co. has a long history of conducting business in a responsible manner"

(14) "Our commitment ... traces back to the values of our founder, Levi Strauss"

(15) "Levi Strauss was both a merchant and a philanthropist"

(16) "The company's long-standing traditions of philanthropy"

(17) "As we look at our history, we see a story of how our core values work together."

(18) "Integrity is woven deeply into the fabric of our company."

The company positions itself as a responsible company by stressing that philanthropy and values-driven business practices have always been part of the company's business strategy. Levi Strauss & Co. seeks to emphasize that it has not just jumped on the bandwagon of responsible business conduct but points to the long tradition of doing good in order to make its claims about corporate ethics more credible.

6.2.2.2 The Interpersonal Function

Levi Strauss & Co.
Levi Strauss & Co. seeks to present itself as people rather than a company. As is evident from Table 12, the discrepancy between the three categories of self-reference is quite remarkable. *We/us/our* are used almost nine times as often as the company name or *company*. The company name always reads *Levi Strauss & Co.* or *LS&Co.*, presumably to avoid confusion with company founder Levi Strauss.

	Subject	Object	Genitive	Adjective	TOTAL
we / us / our	129	15	n.a.	130	**274**
Levi Strauss & Co.	11	7	3	9	**30**
company	1	5	5	4	**15**

Table 12: Breakdown of References to Levi Strauss & Co.

As regards products and marketing, Levi Strauss & Co. constructs itself an identity of superiority by using superlatives, quasi-superlatives or the numeral *first*:

(19) "we will market the most appealing ... casual clothing"

(20) "Dockers® khakis had become the fastest growing apparel brand in history"

(21) "the most popular clothing in the world — blue jeans"

(22) "We put quality in everything we do"

(23) "Levi's® Engineered Jeans™ were the first ergonomically designed jeans"

(24) "We were the first U.S. apparel company to use radio and television to market our products"

Levi Strauss & Co. presents itself as a pioneer and leader in the area of corporate social responsibility and business ethics again and again. To support its claims, Levi Strauss & Co. is always careful to include bullet lists of examples that demonstrate the company's leadership role. The following statements illustrate Levi Strauss & Co.'s attitude towards its own achievements in the field of corporate ethics.

(25) "Levi Strauss & Co. is recognized as a leader in corporate citizenship"

(26) "A Leader in Socially Responsible Worldwide Sourcing"

(27) "We quickly became a business leader in promoting AIDS awareness and education."

(28) "We have played a leadership role in educational programs and policies regarding AIDS in the workplace."

(29) "In 1991, we became the first worldwide company to establish a comprehensive ethical code of conduct"

(30) "In 1991, we became the first multinational company to establish a comprehensive ethical code of conduct"

(31) "In 1991, we were the first multinational company to develop a comprehensive code of conduct"

(32) "Our groundbreaking code"

(33) "In 1992, Levi Strauss & Co. became the first Fortune 500 company to extend full medical benefits to domestic partners of employees. ... [T]his action foreshadowed the widespread acceptance of this benefit and positioned us as a progressive employer with prospective talent."

(34) "that pioneering spirit permeates all aspects of our business — innovation in product and marketing, workplace practices and corporate citizenship."

(35) "In 1968, we pioneered an employee volunteer effort"

(36) "Our commitment to equal employment opportunity and diversity pre-dates today's programs."

(37) "Our commitment to equal employment opportunity and diversity predates the U.S. Civil Rights movement ... we led our industry by sending a strong message. ... Our approach changed attitudes and helped to open the way for integration in other companies and industries."

The examples above show that Levi Strauss & Co. believes they have set unparalleled standards in all areas of corporate ethics they are engaged in, e.g. employee volunteerism, diversity or global sourcing. Levi Strauss & Co. also mentions the U.S. President's Ron Brown Award for Corporate Leadership it received in 1998 *for outstanding achievements in employee and community relations.*

Stakeholders

Levi Strauss & Co.'s main stakeholders are the people they *serve*, as is evident from phrases like *giving back to the people we serve* and *the needs of those we serve*. Levi Strauss & Co. also recognizes the diversity of cultures and lifestyles around the world and among its employees in the phrase *we reflect the diverse world we serve*. These stakeholders are specified in the following statement: *those we serve, including customers, retail customers, shareholders, and each other as employees*. The use of the verb *serve* constructs an asymmetrical relationship of submissiveness.

Addressees are practically excluded from the discourse. There are only three instances of a personal address (*you, your*) in the whole corpus. They all appear on the page outlining the company's giving guidelines: *the country you are based in*, *Your letter*, and *you will be informed*. This page also contains a few verbs in imperative mood, e.g. *please read*, *please visit*, or *please send*. Although this is almost the only page that includes the readers in the discourse, it also excludes the agent by using passive constructions in several places, thereby removing either the grant applicant or the company from the grantmaking process, e.g. as in *can be mailed to* and *should be submitted* (removing the grant applicant) or *will be informed* and *will be reviewed* (removing Levi Strauss & Co.). The only other page that includes the readers is that on the Sourcing Guidelines, which invites readers to get in touch with the company: *For more information about our code of conduct, contact: Mo Rajan at mrajan@levi.com.*

Customers

Levi Strauss & Co. apparently wants to be responsive to customer needs and has customers dictate product design. This relational meaning is conveyed in phrases like

(38) "we walk in our customers' shoes"

(39) "responding to the ... needs of ... consumers around the world"

(40) "understanding and appreciating needs — consumer insight"

Levi Strauss & Co. not only considers customers as trusting but also claims the authority to know what they want and what values they espouse, as is evident from the confident assertions in examples 41 and 42:

(41) "consumers trust our brand"

(42) "our brands embody many of the core values that our consumers live by"

Both statements are unverifiable and lack substance. Also, the company equates itself with a person by claiming it upholds the same values as individuals. Although Levi Strauss & Co. asserts that its customers trust the company, it covertly hints at pressure from consumers regarding overseas manufacturing, when stating that *Increasingly, they* [consumers] *are holding corporations accountable not only for their products but also for how they are made*. This statement actually suggests the opposite of trust, and this is why Levi Strauss & Co. talks about *corporations* in general here and not about itself, as if it were not involved in such issues.

Shareholders

Levi Strauss & Co. describes its relationship with its shareholders as follows:

(43) "This principle of responsible commercial success is embedded in the company's experience. ... Our shareholders expect us to manage the company this way."

The relationship Levi Straus & Co. constructs suggests that the company has to fulfill its shareholders' expectations in order to keep them. Considering that Levi Strauss & Co. as a close corporation does not have any shareholders other than family members — as it claims on the Web site (Levi Strauss & Co. 2002o) — this statement is pure hypocrisy. The fact that Levi Strauss & Co. is family-owned may actually be the reason why it is able to implement its ethics policies and giving guidelines, given that it does not have to woo shareholders with high dividends.

Business Partners, Suppliers and Contractors

Levi Strauss & Co.'s sourcing pages deal with foreign business partners, also referred to as suppliers or contractors. The company insists on their compliance with its sourcing guidelines but gives them the opportunity of remedy before it discontinues doing business. Levi Strauss & Co. puts this unequivocally:

> (44) "If Levi Strauss & Co. determines that a business partner is not complying with our Terms of Engagement, we require that the partner implement a corrective action plan within a specified time period. If a contractor fails to meet the corrective action plan commitment, Levi Strauss & Co. will terminate the business relationship."

The strict tone of this statement makes it clear that Levi Strauss & Co. is not prepared to tolerate persistent violations of its guidelines. At the same time, the company points out that it intends to *effect change by working with our business partners to find long-term solutions* for the benefit of the laborers and their local communities. *Working with* and *long-term* imply that the company seeks to keep its contractors and does not terminate business relations that easily.

A striking feature of the Terms of Engagement is the frequent use of negatives in the section on employment standards. Instead of positively stipulating certain criteria for supplier selection, Levi Strauss & Co. chooses to prohibit conditions that do not comply with its own ethics policies. By using the negatives *no* and *not*, Levi Strauss & Co. essentially addresses the corresponding positive assertions and contests them. In view of the company's past labor issues, this is presumably intended to make its assertions more convincing. Examples of this negative selection include:

(45) "Use of child labor is not permissible"

(46) "not younger than ..."

(47) "seek business partners who do not exceed them"

(48) "ensure that workers ... are not the object of discrimination"

(49) "We will not utilize or purchase materials from ..."

(50) "We will not utilize prison or forced labor"

(51) "We will not utilize partners who ..."

(52) "We will not utilize business partners who ..."

(53) "we will not utilize contractors who ..."

Examples 49 to 53 repeat the phrase *we will not utilize* for effect. In addition to the negatives in the above examples, there are also double negatives in the phrases *ethical standards not incompatible with our own* and *Workers can be no less than 15 years of age.* Two negatives make a positive and could thus be easily avoided, but are used for special emphasis here. The remaining clauses of the Terms of Engagement typically stipulate positive selection criteria and sound less rigid, especially because of uncommitting verbs like *expect, seek* and *favor*, which appear in several places. The adverb *only* is sometimes used for accentuation. For example:

(54) "We will seek to identify and utilize business partners who"

(55) "We expect our business partners to"

(56) "We will favor business partners who"

(57) "We will only do business with partners who"

(58) "We will only utilize business partners who"

Interestingly, not even the section titled *Legal Requirements* in the Terms of Engagement is phrased as forcefully as the stipulations in the section on *Employment Standards*, although legal compliance is the minimum one would expect of a business relationship. The former clause reads: *We expect our business partners to be law abiding as individuals and to comply with legal requirements relevant to the conduct of all their business.* This difference in tone might be attributable to the fact that the company's image has been shattered by labor issues overseas, and the company therefore seeks to show its uncompromising attitude towards labor violations.

Three images on the sourcing page depict workers sewing in modern, well-equipped factories. Levi Strauss & Co. did not include Asian workers in these pictures, presumably to distance its products from low-wage labor in Asia. The workers are seemingly content with their work and the working conditions in the factory suggest the opposite of what Levi Strauss & Co. has been accused of.

Employees

Levi Strauss & Co. constructs a relationship with its employees only once when it declares *a willingness to do the right thing for our employees*, which conveys a sense of caring but also appears patronizing, as Levi Strauss & Co. claims the authority to know what is right for its employees. Speaking on behalf of its employees in the inclusive-*we* form, Levi Strauss & Co. pledges the following:

(59) "As colleagues, we also are committed to helping one another succeed. We are sensitive to each other's goals and interests, and we strive to ensure our mutual success through exceptional leadership, career development and supportive workplace practices."

Levi Strauss & Co. also gives the example of *full medical benefits to domestic partners of employees*, which it was the first company ever to introduce, as it claims. An incidence of positional meaning is that Levi Strauss & Co. seems to value its highly diverse workforce, when it states *our company workforce mirrors the marketplace in its diversity, helping us to* ...and *We value ethnic, cultural and lifestyle diversity*. To provide evidence for its commitment to diversity the company mentions that *Fortune* magazine ranked it number 2 among "America's 50 Best Companies for Minorities" in 2000.

The Communities

In the value statement, the public at large is also included among the stakeholders, e.g. in statements like *paying close attention to the world around us*, *paying attention to the world around us*, and *a willingness to do the right thing for ... society as a whole*. In the relationship established, Levi Strauss & Co. presents itself as a caring partner, but commits itself essentially to nothing, as *attention* and *thing* are too vague a term to express commitments. The notion of partnership also appears in the name of Levi Strauss & Co.'s giving program, which is called *Community Partnership Global Giving*.

Corporate grants aim at effecting change in *communities around the world* by addressing *critical social issues* and *critical local community issues*. Since Levi Strauss & Co. makes grants to organizations around the global, the phrase *the world around us* (see above) is not an overstatement. However, giving activities are confined to those *countries and communities where we have a business presence*. Thus, the definition of *world* obviously excludes communities and countries where its contractors are located.

Competitors

Competitors are hardly referred to in the corpus. *Competition* is brought up explicitly only once in the very first paragraph of the Value Statement: [Our values] *set us apart from the competition*. Similar assertions include

(60) "our 'profits through principles' approach to business is a point of competitive advantage" and

(61) "these attributes and values make the Levi's® brand unlike any other".

In all three statements, Levi Strauss & Co. suggests that it is the values that make the company and its brands superior to competitors.

6.2.2.3 The Textual Function

Themes
Levi Strauss & Co.'s value statement exhibits a noteworthy thematic structure. First, the most prominent theme is the company. Of 129 sentences, 35 (27%) start with *we* or *our*, while not a single one starts with *Levi Strauss & Co.* Presumably, Levi Strauss & Co. aims for sincerity and closeness, which is definitely achieved by starting a sentence with a personal pronoun rather than a noun. Second, time is also a common theme throughout the value statement, as the company frequently uses examples from the company history to support its claims. Examples of the thematic use of time include:

(62) "A year later, Dockers® khakis had become ..."
(63) "As early as 1926 ..."
(64) "In 1982, a group of company employees ..."
(65) "In 1991, we were the first ..."
(66) "In the 1930s, consumers complained that ..."
(67) "In 1992, Levi Strauss & Co. became ..."
(68) "In the 1950s, we combined ..."
(69) "In the 1980s, we took ..."
(70) "In the company's early years, that meant ..."
(71) "Now, it means ..."
(72) "Now, more than ever, ..."
(73) "Throughout the 1990s, we were ..."
(74) "Today, the Levi's® brand is ..."

This choice of theme suggests that Levi Strauss & Co. seeks to convey the impression that it has always been a socially responsible company.

Text Cohesion
Levi Strauss & Co. frequently uses bullet lists as a device to structure text. In particular, it uses bullet lists to provide examples of its socially responsible behavior and the enactment of its core values. These list items are not just keywords but rather complete sentences, stating what the company did and when. These examples are typically ordered chronologically, which stands to reason given that almost all examples contain a date. The lists appear without any strong lead-in sentence to introduce the list items and thus do not indicate the meaning or purpose of the lists. Levi Strauss & Co. uses either the heading

For example: or no heading at all, which makes the texts lack cohesion, as the connection between the lists and the paragraphs above them is not apparent. However, the fact that the items in the lists are examples suggests that Levi Strauss & Co. seeks to provide evidence for its asserted ethical behavior.

The list format makes the number of examples cited evident right away, which the straight text of normal paragraph format would not achieve. The cumulative effect of the examples listed seems to be more important than the examples per se, as Levi Strauss & Co. even uses the same examples in different lists. For example, the desegregation of factories is listed three times, and AIDS awareness and the code of conduct twice each.

Web Site Cohesion

Levi Strauss applies navigation interfaces very consistently. Every page has a horizontal menu bar on top. Depending on the menu item chosen, an additional vertical menu bar pops up on the left-hand side of the screen, providing links to related pages. The flowchart in Figure 12 depicts the site structure and the linkages between Levi Strauss & Co.'s ethics pages. The Web site includes only a total of nine pages on corporate ethics. As is evident from the flowchart, the pages are logically embedded in the whole Web site, which makes navigation very efficient. Overall, there are three crosslinks, two of which can be seen in the flowchart in Figure 12.

Levistrauss.com is a Web site dressed in pale colors. With its white background, black font, and gray headlines, the Web site does not remind one of a company selling mostly blue jeans. Also, the color red, as used for the jeans' red tabs, is hardly used. Levi Strauss & Co. has adopted the white/gray color scheme, which conveys a sense of purity and modesty. The color scheme and the formatting of text and headlines are applied consistently to all Web pages. If used at all, decorative devices are rather small in size and include photos rather than graphics.

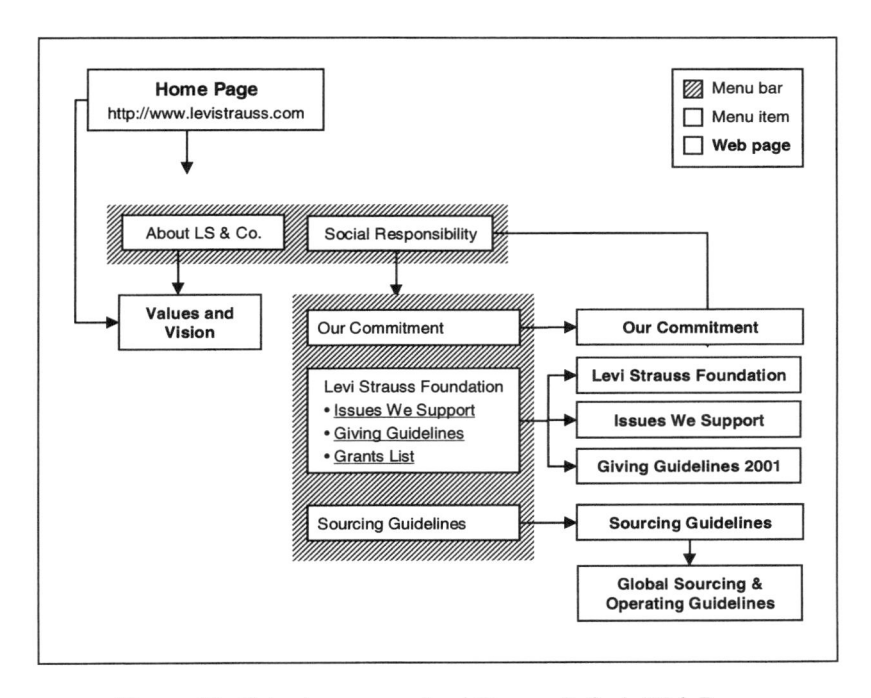

Figure 12: Cohesion among Levi Strauss & Co.'s Web Pages

6.3 Intra-Paradigm Analysis

Business Ethics and Social Responsibility

The structures of Nike's and Levi Strauss & Co.'s ethics menus show an equal distribution between social responsibility and business ethics. Nike's ethics submenu includes four CSR items (*Community Affairs, Diversity, Environment, Corporate Responsibility Report*) and one BE item (*Manufacturing Practices*). The corresponding subsections have their own submenu each. As the number of menu items on the manufacturing submenu roughly equals the number of items on the other four submenus, Nike seems to balance CSR and BE. Levi Strauss & Co. assigns virtually equal weight to BE and CSR, which is evident from the mere structure of its ethics menu. The menu contains just three items, including an introduction (*Our Commitment*), a CSR item (*Levi Strauss Foundation*) and a BE item (*Sourcing Guidelines*). Upon clicking either of the latter two, additional menu items appear.

Manifestations of the Business-Ethics Paradigm

Nike and Levi Strauss & Co. apply business ethics only to their overseas supply chains to combat the industry's stigma of sweatshop labor.

- Nike's code of conduct corresponds to Levi Strauss & Co.'s Business Partner Terms of Engagement. In addition to its manufacturing code of conduct, Levi Strauss & Co. has also drawn up Country Assessment Guidelines, whereas Nike has no corresponding policy statement. This suggests that Nike is in principle willing to move its production to any country with low labor costs irrespective of the political and legal environment. Both corporate codes aim at preventing harm by requiring foreign contractors to adhere to the standards stipulated by the companies. Harm in this context is taken to mean damage to the corporate reputation, which is inevitable if public-interest groups or the media discover ethical lapses, e.g. child labor or poor health and safety standards.
- Both companies participate in labor-related NGOs, e.g. Nike as a founding member of the Global Alliance for Workers and Communities (GAWC) and Levi Strauss & Co. in the Ethical Trading Initiative (ETI).
- Nike and Levi Strauss & Co. are members in the Fair Labor Association (FLA) and open their factories to FLA monitoring.

Manifestations of the Social-Responsibility Paradigm

Although their business-ethics approaches were almost identical, Nike's and Levi Strauss & Co.'s approaches to social responsibility differ in quite a few points.

- The only similarity is that the two companies claim to value employee diversity and present themselves as attractive employers for minorities.
- While Levi Strauss & Co.'s ethics centerpiece is its lengthy values and vision statement, Nike has no formal ethics statement. It spells out its values only implicitly.
- Nike dedicates a whole subsection of its ethics section to environmental protection and sustainability, whereas Levi Strauss & Co. mentions the environment only as part of employee volunteerism and in connection with foreign contractors but not as a corporate objective at headquarters.
- Their pages on philanthropy are similar in that they focus on their foundations and employee volunteerism. Both companies provide numerical evidence of their financial contributions, but with differing levels of detail. Nike's pages on philanthropy give thorough accounts of its contributions of the past three years, providing bar charts of company donations and employee volunteer hours. It also pledges to give away 3% of its pretax earnings. Levi Strauss only states the total of grants it made in the year 2001 but does not commit itself to donating a certain percentage of its profits.
- Nike also devotes a short page to its first Corporate Responsibility Report, which it makes available for download as well. Levi Strauss & Co. has no such social report.

7 Cross-Case Analysis

The current chapter sets out to answer the research questions posed in Section 2.1. The primary research question was how companies communicate their ethical stance on their Web sites. The subsidiary research questions match the ideational, the interpersonal and the textual functions looked at in the discourse analyses. The subsidiary research questions will be answered in the following sections by identifying both similarities and variation across cases.

7.1 The Ideational Function across Cases

The ideational cross-case analysis seeks to answer the first subsidiary research question: *What themes are addressed and what persuasive appeals are used in the messages?* This analysis focuses on content choice and persuasive appeals with regard to ethics.

7.1.1 Content

The five prominent subjects identified include reputation, image threats, ethics codes, ethics statements and philanthropy. Table 13 indicates whether these themes are realized in the case corpora.

	Reputation	Image Threat	Ethics Code	Ethics Statement	Philanthropy
BellSouth	✓	✗	✓✓	Values	✓✓
Lockheed Martin	✗	✗	✓✓	Values, principles	✓✓
Ben & Jerry's	✗	✓	✗	Mission	✓✓
McDonald's	✓	✗	✓	Values, vision	✓✓
Nike	✗	✓	✓✓	✗	✓✓
Levi Strauss & Co.	✓	✗	✓✓	Values, vision	✓✓

Table 13: Content across Cases

Explanation of Criteria:

- *Reputation* indicates whether corporate reputation/image/brand is mentioned in connection with corporate ethics efforts.
- *Image Threat* indicates whether the company addresses issues it has been criticized for.
- *Ethics Code* indicates whether the company has an ethics code. The second tick indicates that compliance is a major theme, too.
- *Ethics Statement* indicates what kind of ethics statement the company has.
- *Philanthropy* indicates whether the company has a giving program. The second tick indicates that giving is administered by a foundation.

7.1.1.1 Reputation

Some of the case companies are surprisingly frank about the rationales of their corporate-ethics initiatives. Reputation seems to be the driving force behind corporate ethics for half of the case companies examined. Below are the companies' statements about ethics and reputation:

- BellSouth: *to protect and enhance the company's reputation for integrity;*
- Levi Strauss & Co.: *good for the long-term reputation of our brands; would protect the company's interests and brand/corporate image;*
- McDonald's: *we also work to ... enhance McDonald's brand by being a leader in social responsibility;*

As the three companies that mention reputation belong to a different paradigm each, reputation seems to be a rationale for corporate ethics across all paradigms, even for internally-focused BE companies.

7.1.1.2 Image Threats

Understandably, there is a tendency to avoid issues that have shed a bad light on the company. Although companies do not specifically highlight issues they have faulted on, they all address their ethical lapses indirectly by stipulating standards and commitments that are intended to prevent such misconduct in the future.

- BellSouth does not take up specific issues that have hurt its image in the past and have made the company appear fraudulent. Rather, it stresses compliance with laws and regulations, in particular with the Federal Sentencing Guidelines. It includes issues such as proprietary information, insider information and hospitality in the scenarios of its ethics games, thereby relating to the scandals BellSouth has been involved in.
- In view of major violations of U.S. and foreign law in the past, Lockheed Martin points to legal compliance as a major goal of its ethics program. This might have prevented the Japanese bribery scandal, which cast a bad light on Lockheed Martin's business practices.
- Ben & Jerry's takes up the issue of food safety, when taking a stand on dioxin and rBGH and defends itself at great length against allegations that have had an unfavorable effect on its image.
- McDonald's implicitly responds to a variety of issues it has been criticized for, in particular by McSpotlight.org. Its ethical discourse includes commitments to the conservation of rainforests, waste reduction and the humane treatment of animals, all of which are charges by McSpotlight. To counter its McJob image, McDonald's also pledges to offer its employees opportunities for learning, growth and development and to pay them competitive wages.
- Nike dedicates a whole section of its Web site to overseas manufacturing, giving a detailed account of its monitoring and compliance efforts in countries like Thailand, Vietnam and Indonesia. Further, the company points to the Pakistan child-labor scandal.
- Levi Strauss & Co.'s stringent labor policies are an obvious response to its overseas labor issues. However, Levi Strauss & Co. does not refer to its withdrawal from and re-entry into China, not even in the company history and even removed the reference to the U.S. China Business Principles Working Group from its Web site.

7.1.1.3 Ethics Codes

The discourse analyses have confirmed the general impression that ethics codes and their implementation are a central concern for companies in the BE paradigm and in the BE & CSR paradigm and of less significance to companies in the CSR paradigm.
- BellSouth has a code of conduct, but it is untypical in terms of content: The code sounds more like a mission or aspirations statement, as it lays

down the company's responsibilities to its various stakeholder groups. However, BellSouth's *Commitment Booklet* has a number of other pages which complement the code, and together they represent a typical ethics code. Lockheed Martin, too, has a comprehensive ethics code that serves as a guideline for its employees.
- Ben & Jerry's does not have an ethics code, and deliberately so, as was pointed out in the section *Context of the Discourse*. McDonald's, on the other hand, has a code of conduct for suppliers, which is, however, superfluous for most of its suppliers. This shows that companies in the CSR paradigm may have ethics codes, albeit of little significance.
- Nike and Levi Strauss & Co. both have ethics codes directed at their overseas subcontractors. Their codes are implemented particularly in countries where employment legislation is non-existent or poorly enforced. Thus, their codes contain stipulations that U.S. legislation would render unnecessary, e.g. child labor or non-discrimination. Both companies also have NGOs monitor the implementation of these codes.

7.1.1.4 Ethics Statements

The ethics statements drawn up by the case companies include vision statements, mission statements and value statements. It is worth noting that all companies use the terms vision, mission and values correctly.
- BellSouth's value statement contains five values, viz. *Our Customers*, *Our People*, *Our Communities*, *Excellence* and *Integrity*.
- Lockheed Martin has both a value statement and ethical principles, which overlap to some extent. Its values are *Ethics*, *Excellence*, *"Can-Do"*, *Integrity*, *People* and *Teamwork*, while its ethical principles include *Honesty*, *Integrity*, *Responsibility*, *Trust*, *Respect* and *Citizenship*.
- Ben & Jerry's has a Statement of Mission, which describes the company's *Product Mission*, *Economic Mission* and *Social Mission*.
- McDonald's has a very brief value statement in the form of its *People Promise*. It also has vision statement, called *People Vision*.
- Levi Strauss & Co. has a lengthy value statement, which outlines the company's four core values and describes how the company enacts them. These values include *Empathy*, *Originality*, *Integrity* and *Courage*. This value statement also contains Levi Strauss & Co.'s vision, which is unrelated to ethics, though.

- Nike has no formal ethics statement. However, it spells out one-sentence missions for manufacturing practices and the environment and talks about its *vision for diversity*. It also brings up *our values* in the text but does not state them in a formal document.

7.1.1.5 Philanthropy

Similar to ethics codes, philanthropy also seems to be an activity companies from all three paradigms engage in. Employee volunteerism and foundations seem to have become *de rigueur* for large corporations. McDonald's and Ben & Jerry's, the two companies in the CSR paradigm, put most weight on their foundations, while the two companies in the BE paradigm dedicate only a little space to their foundations on their Web sites.

Ben & Jerry's and Nike point out that their foundations give exclusively to 501(c)3 organizations, while Levi Strauss & Co. refers to these organizations only in connection with employee gift matching. Donations made to these tax-exempt 501(c)3 organizations are tax-deductible for the donor (Casey 2000), which explains why the companies prefer to donate to 501(c)3 charities.

The recipients of the grants are educational institutions in the case of BellSouth and Lockheed Martin, social projects in the case of Ben & Jerry's and Levi Strauss & Co., and children and adolescents in the case of McDonald's and Nike. As has been argued earlier, grants dedicated to education and youth projects are not purely altruistic, as they are possibly intended to raise brand awareness among an uncritical audience.

7.1.2 Persuasive Appeals

The discourse analyses have identified an array of means of persuasion companies use to construct credible arguments. In this analysis, persuasive appeals are categorized according to Aristotle's three argumentative appeals: the appeal to source credibility (*ethos*); the appeal to the audience's emotions (*pathos*); and the appeal to reason (*logos*) (Cragan and Shields 1998: 237).

7.1.2.1 Appeal to Source Credibility

The most influential factor in affecting public opinion is the speaker's ability to present himself as trustworthy, knowledgeable and truthful (Cragan and Shields 1998: 237). As for ethics-related communication, companies seemingly consider a long-standing tradition of ethics as well as membership in ethics associations to be conducive to their credibility.

7.1.2.1.1 Integrity as a Heritage

Claiming that integrity is a heritage is obviously intended to convey the impression that corporate ethics is not just a recent fad but has always driven the company's business conduct.

- Despite BellSouth's short history of 19 years the company points out that it has a *heritage of integrity*, which it seeks to *pass on*.
- McDonald's mentions the *heritage of giving back to the communities* and points to its legacy of *doing the right thing*. McDonald's also quotes company founder Ray Kroc who said that the company is obliged to give to the communities.
- Levi Strauss & Co. also claims that ethical business conduct has a long tradition that was started by company founder Levi Strauss, whose values allegedly still guide corporate conduct.
- Lockheed Martin does not claim that ethics is a heritage in the company, and is right to do so, given that the company was founded in 1995 only and that the founding companies were a result of several mergers and reorganizations. Hence, the founders' sprits have long been extinguished and the corporate culture is probably still not very distinct. Speaking of heritage in connection with company values or ethical principles would therefore not be credible.
- Ben & Jerry's does not make this heritage claim either. The only reference to history in connection with corporate ethics is that its Statement of Mission was introduced as early as 1988. It does not even mention company founders Ben Cohen and Jerry Greenfield in connection with corporate ethics, although the two were the founders of Caring Capitalism, as the context of the discourse has revealed. This aspect could have been exploited more in the company discourse, considering what prominent figures the two are in the United States.

- Nike is right not to label corporate ethics as a heritage considering its past stance on outsourced labor. Its labor policies of 1998 do certainly not qualify as a heritage either.

7.1.2.1.2 Membership in Ethics-Related Associations

The two companies from the BE paradigm are members of the *Ethics Officer Association* (EOA), but they do not mention this on their ethics pages. They only provide hyperlinks to the EOA. To join the EOA, prospective members must have a comprehensive ethics program in place. Prior to their accession, companies are audited by the EOA to check whether they qualify for membership (EOA 2002c). Thus, by pointing to their membership in the EOA, BellSouth and Lockheed Martin could indicate that their ethics programs are sophisticated enough to qualify for EOA membership, which could lend their claims more credibility.

Ben & Jerry's and McDonald's are members of *Business for Social Responsibility* (BSR), which they both do not point out. They could capitalize on their affiliation with BSR, especially since Ben & Jerry's is a founding member.

Nike and Levi Strauss & Co. pride themselves on their membership in the *Fair Labor Association* (FLA). Companies participating in the FLA need to make sure that their subcontractors adhere to the Association's code of conduct and must open their subcontracted production facilities to outside monitoring (Fair Labor Association 2002). Thus, their membership in the FLA suggests that Nike and Levi Strauss & Co. have implemented effective compliance programs along their overseas supply chain.

7.1.2.2 Appeal to Reason

Appeals to reason found on the case companies' ethics Web pages include statements by CEOs, ethics awards, concrete examples of ethical conduct, external monitoring reports, feedback mechanisms and external ethics links (see Table 14).

Case Company	CEO Statement	Ethics Awards	Concrete Examples	External Monitoring	Alignment with Science	Feedback Mechanism	External Links [12]
BellSouth	✓	✗	✓	✗	✗	✓	4
Lockheed Martin	✓	✗	✗	✗	✗	✓	17
Ben & Jerry's	✗	✗	✓	✓	✓	✗	9
McDonald's [13]	✓	✓	✗	✓	✗	✗	✗
Nike	✗	✗	✓	✓	✓	✓	1
Levi Strauss & Co.	✗	✓	✓	✗	✗	✓	4

Table 14: Appeals to Reason across Cases

7.1.2.2.1 CEO Statements

Statements on ethics by CEOs appear to be an attempt to add credibility to the messages, as they signal that top management is concerned with corporate ethics. Also, a statement made by an identifiable individual weighs probably more than one by a faceless institution.

- BellSouth uses a letter from CEO Duane Ackerman as an introduction to its electronic ethics booklet. The CEO's commitment is also reinforced by the fact that the ethics office reports directly to the CEO, as BellSouth points out.
- Lockheed Martin posts a letter from CEO Vance D. Coffman on its Web site to make its suppliers aware of how seriously Lockheed Martin takes ethics.
- McDonald's page on social responsibility quotes incumbent CEO Jack Greenberg, who asserts that McDonald's is *a socially responsible company* and wants to make the world *a better place*. The page also shows a picture of the CEO to add a human touch to the statement.

---

[12] Links to company foundations do not qualify as external links, even if these foundations have a separate Web address.
[13] Shortly before this analysis was completed, McDonald's redesigned its Web site and now has an online feedback and four external links to ethics NGOs, including *Business for Social Responsibility*.

- Ben & Jerry's does not have a CEO statement on its Web site, which may be put down the fact that Ben Cohen and Jerry Greenfield resigned in 1995 and were succeeded by two CEOs before the company was eventually taken over by Unilever in 2000.
- Similarly, Levi Strauss & Co.'s long-time CEO Rob Haas stepped down in 1999 and the new CEO is not as high-profile as company heir Haas, so his commitment to ethics would not make for higher credibility.
- Nike does not have a CEO statement on any of its ethics pages. In view of the harsh criticism Nike and its CEO Phil Knight have faced, a commitment to ethics endorsed by Phil Knight would not enhance the credibility of the message.

7.1.2.2.2 Honors, Awards and Magazine Rankings

Awards from ethics organizations and rankings by renowned magazines, e.g. *Fortune*, have the credibility of an objective third-party endorsement. This outside evaluation of corporate conduct could lend credibility to the companies' claims. However, companies seem to make use of this credibility appeal to a very small extent only.

- McDonald's has a separate page dedicated to recognitions it has received for its socially responsible business conduct. These include, for example, a *Fortune* magazine ranking and honors from the U.S. Environmental Protection Agency, the U.S. Consumer Product Safety Commission and Audubon Society. McDonald's is the only company that makes full use of its ethics awards and rankings by listing them on a separate page, which smacks of self-congratulations, though. Mentioning these rankings in the context of the relevant commitments would have been less obvious.
- Levi Strauss & Co.'s ethics pages mention a ranking by *Fortune* magazine in 2000 and two ethics awards it has received, including America's Corporate Conscience Award from the Council on Economic Priorities and the U.S. President's Ron Brown Award for Corporate Leadership.
- The two companies in the business-ethics paradigm do not list any ethics awards or rankings at all. They might not have received any, in view of the internal focus of their ethics efforts and the non-visibility of these efforts in the media.
- Ben & Jerry's has received a number of awards, but does not mention them on its ethics pages. They are listed in the rather lengthy company

history only. This does not appear to be very effective, as the company history's length and level of detail might deter readers from reading it in the first place. Ben & Jerry's seemingly does not fully exploit the third-party credibility that awards provide.
- Nike has obviously not received any awards, which is readily understandable against the backdrop of the unfavorable media coverage of its overseas labor issues.

7.1.2.2.3 Concrete Examples

Supporting general arguments with details and facts makes claims more acceptable. Some of the case companies seek to win acceptance of their assertions by using concrete examples from corporate reality. The examples the companies cite are not verifiable for people outside of the company, but still suggest that the company fulfills its commitments, whereas the absence of such examples gives the impression that the company does not live up to its commitments.

- BellSouth gives details on when it established its ethics office and its compliance policy board and outlines their responsibilities. It is probably difficult for a company in the business-ethics paradigm to cite examples of ethical conduct, as its ethics efforts take place within the organization only, but it could have stated the number of people who have received ethics training, the number of people who were dismissed or otherwise penalized for ethical misconduct, or the number of calls the hotline has received.
- Ben & Jerry's has launched social campaigns, e.g. against the use of rBG hormones, and urges its audience to join these campaigns. This form of social activism is an enactment of Ben & Jerry's social mission and serves well to enhance the credibility of its Statement of Mission.
- Levi Strauss & Co. gives bullet lists of examples of events to illustrate how it enacts its core values and ethical commitments. The three *Success Stories* illustrate how Levi Strauss & Co. has effected change at its suppliers' facilities, but omit details regarding date and place. Furthermore, the company posts its grant list for the year 2000, specifying which organization received how much money.
- Nike gives exact figures of its monetary donations and the dates when certain ethics policies were adopted. It also points out that it was a

founding member of the Global Alliance for Workers and Communities (GAWC).

That examples are a very credible form of communication is best illustrated by the case of Ben & Jerry's. The company does not provide vague information like values and commitments, as opposed to McDonald's. Instead, its ethics-related pages focus mostly on campaigns it has initiated. This activism is probably the reason why its reputation for ethical behavior is said to be sterling[14], which again proves that actions speak louder than words.

7.1.2.2.4 External Monitoring and Auditing

Inviting external parties to scrutinize company practices suggests that the company has nothing to hide and that it seeks an objective evaluation of its practices. To add credibility to their ethical commitments, companies cite third-party reports on their ethics pages and sometimes make these reports available for download as well. These reports offer a seemingly independent perspective on company dealings, yet one has to bear in mind that companies would clearly not publish them on the WWW, if they contained a substantial amount of negative information. What is more, the third-party status of the authors is not always verifiable either.

- Nike has incorporated by far the greatest number of external sources into its Web pages. It publishes eleven student monitoring reports and four case studies prepared by external parties. The student reports are evidently intended to present the perspective of an extremely critical, anti-corporate audience. However, the sincerity of these reports is difficult to judge from the outside, as the identity of these individuals cannot be proved easily. These reports suggest that Nike is desperately seeking to repair its shattered image. Furthermore, Nike hired Global Social Compliance, a PriceWaterhouseCoopers spin-off for external monitoring. The Fair Labor Association oversees the monitoring process.
- Ben & Jerry's makes two CERES reports and three social-audit reports available for download.
- McDonald's used third-party auditing to prepare its *Shareholders' Report on Supplier Social Compliance*.

---

[14] cf. Gardberg and Fombrun 2002:385-391.

7.1.2.2.5 Alignment with Science

Companies also appeal to the authority of academia or other research institutions to back their claims with seemingly scientific evidence.

- Ben & Jerry's refers to the U.S. Environmental Protection Agency Dioxin Reassessment report. The report acknowledges that dioxin is a global problem, which makes the fact that Ben & Jerry's ice cream contains dioxin sound less threatening. As an antipole to the authority of the EPA, Ben & Jerry's mentions junkscience.com, a Web site that has originally brought up the issue of dioxin in ice cream. By juxtaposing the two, Ben & Jerry's obviously seeks to reduce the credibility of junkscience.com.
- Nike points out that the Global Alliance for Workers and Communities, which it is a member of, cooperates with the Center for Economic Studies and International Applications at the University of Ho Chi Minh to monitor Nike's contracted factories in Vietnam. Furthermore, one of the four case studies Nike makes available was prepared by a professor from the University of Michigan.

7.1.2.2.6 Feedback Mechanisms

Inviting questions and feedback suggests that the company has nothing to hide and that it is willing to enter into a direct dialogue with its stakeholders. The case companies invite feedback on their ethics pages in the following ways:

- BellSouth includes the phone number of its ethics hotline and its e-mail address ethics@bellsouth.com, but points out that these are available to employees only.
- Lockheed Martin posts the number of its ethics hotline (1-800-LM-ETHIC), but does not restrict it to any particular group.
- Levi Strauss & Co.'s Web pages give a contact e-mail address for more information on the company's code of conduct: mrajan@levi.com.
- Nike has an FAQ database and a *Contact Us* e-mail form. Nike seems to make most of the WWW's capability for interaction by providing a comprehensive set of questions and answers and by soliciting comments and questions. Presumably, Nike was flooded with inquiries during the peak of its labor issues and then set up this sophisticated feedback mechanism to handle the large number of inquiries.
- Ben & Jerry's has no feedback mechanism on its ethics pages, but a general *Contact Us* page for submitting questions and a database of

frequently asked questions and answers. However, there is neither a link from any ethics page nor from the home page to the *Contact Us* page.

7.1.2.2.7 Links to External Ethics Sites

External links, i.e. outward-pointing links, to NGOs in the field of corporate ethics or U.S. government sites demonstrate a company's affiliation with them. Five of the six companies use external links to NGOs, albeit to varying extents. BellSouth and Lockheed Martin have separate pages listing these external links. McDonald's does not provide external links at all, while Ben & Jerry's, Nike and Levi Strauss & Co. use external links in the texts.

7.1.2.3 Appeal to Emotions

Appeal to emotions appears to be the least important of the three argumentative appeals when companies communicate their ethical stance. In some places they all use emotive language, avoid negatives and neutralize or euphemize certain terms in order to appeal to their audiences' emotions. Conversely, they all do not shy away from using unambiguous and sometimes even negative language either. Thus, emotional appeal is not a principal objective of these company messages. This is readily understandable in view of the "public mistrust of the business community" (Pinkham 1998: 34), which is more likely to be reduced by appealing to reason than to emotions.

In addition to word choice, graphic images are also a mechanism for appealing to the audience through emotions. Examples of such images include Lockheed Martin's pictures of people at work, Ben & Jerry's comic-style images, McDonald's pictures of grazing cows and happy employees, Nike's pictures of happy workers, and Levi Strauss & Co.'s pictures of happy employees in a high-tech sewing factory.

7.2 The Interpersonal Function across Cases

The second subsidiary research question posed in Section 2.1 reads: *In what form do companies include their stakeholders in these messages?* The cross-case analysis of the interpersonal function focusing on personal address forms, addressees and viewpoints has yielded the results shown in Table 15.

Case Company	Personal Address	Addressees	Viewpoint Ratio	Subject Ratio
BellSouth	115 / 2.00%	employees	2.45	7
Lockheed Martin	10 / 0.53%	employees	2.29	3.4
Ben & Jerry's	61 / 1.29%	general public, grant applicants	2.62	4.18
McDonald's	4 / 0.14%	employees	2.3	2.16
Nike	9 / 0.15%	general public	1.27	2
Levi Strauss & Co.	3 / 0.06%	grant applicants	6.09	10.75

Table 15: The Interpersonal Function across Cases

Explanation of criteria:

- *Personal Address* gives the frequency of *you/your* and their relative frequencies in the corpora.
- *Addressees* indicate at whom the personal addresses are directed.
- *Viewpoint Ratio* is the ratio dividing all instances of *we*, *us* and *our* by all instances of the company name, *company*, *corporation* and *it/its*. For example, a ratio of 4 means that the company uses the first-person perspective four times as often as the neutral third-person perspective.
- *Subject Ratio* is the ratio between *we* as the subject of the clause and the company as the subject of the clause (e.g. *the company*, *it* or the company name).

7.2.1 Personal Address

As for the personal address, the findings strongly suggest that business-ethics companies communicate mainly with their employees on their ethics Web pages, despite the fact that their Web sites are open to every Internet user. This confirms that the business-ethics approach to corporate ethics is internally oriented, but used for PR as well. As McDonald's personal addresses occur only in the *People Promise* and the *People Vision*, they are not comparable to the personal addresses in the other corpora. The frequency of the personal address is apparently independent of the paradigm, as comparisons of BellSouth with Lockheed Martin and Ben & Jerry's with McDonald's demonstrate. Rather, the use of personal addresses seems to be a trait of the corporate personality.

7.2.2 Viewpoint

The six case companies have in common that they use the first-person perspective far more often than the neutral third-person perspective when talking about themselves. This creates the impression that they communicate opinions and beliefs, whereas a third-person viewpoint would suggest a certain level of factuality and impersonality. There seems to be no obvious explanation for the more or less identical results for the two BE companies and the two CSR companies and the varied results for the two BE & CSR companies. The results can only be put down to the different ways the companies operate and present themselves.

7.2.3 Stakeholders

Irrespective of the paradigm they belong to, all companies recognize that they have responsibilities toward multiple constituencies and therefore include them in their ethical discourses. An analysis across all cases has revealed that all six companies acknowledge that their business activities have a bearing on their stakeholders (see Table 16):

	Employees	Customers	Suppliers[15]	Stockholders	Community
BellSouth	✓	✓	✓	✓	✓
Lockheed Martin	✓	✓	✓	✓	✓
Ben & Jerry's	✓	✓	✗	✓	✓
McDonald's	✓	✓	✓	✓	✓
Nike	✓	✓	✓	✓	✓
Levi Strauss & Co.	✓	✓	✓	✓	✓

Table 16: Stakeholders across Cases

The illustrative statements below are intended to demonstrate that the case companies voice ethical commitments to the groups ticked in the above grid.

---

[15] Suppliers include business partners, contractors, vendors and agents.

- Lockheed Martin: *To have the courage to speak our truth, and to be absolutely forthright in all cases, with our customers, co-workers, suppliers, communities, and shareholders*;
- BellSouth: *our responsibilities to our customers, our owners, our vendors and suppliers, our families, the communities where we live and work, and to each other;*
- Ben & Jerry's: *career opportunities and financial rewards for our employees; increasing value for our shareholders; to improve the quality of life of a broad community — local, national, and international; Ben & Jerry's cares about its customers*;
- McDonald's: *honest and forthright communications with our customers, shareholders, suppliers and employees; an obligation to give back to the communities;*
- Nike: *Nike is committed to ... increasing value for our customers, shareholders and business partners; We proudly and actively support the communities where our employees live and work; supporting all Nike employees with tools and resources*;
- Levi Strauss & Co.: *meeting the needs of those we serve, including consumers, retail customers, shareholders and each other as employees; a willingness to do the right thing for ... society as a whole; Our goal is to achieve positive results and effect change by working with our business partners to find long-term solutions*;

The emphasis the companies put on each stakeholder group in their discourses varies according to the paradigms they belong to. BellSouth and Lockheed Martin direct most of their ethics-related Web pages to their employees, which is evident from the comprehensive ethics support they offer to their employees on their Web sites. Communities play a significant role in the discourses of the other four companies, while employees are mostly referred to in connection with employee volunteerism.

7.3 The Textual Function across Cases

On Web sites, cohesive devices are hyperlinks rather than textual elements. Table 17 gives an overview of the criteria considered in the cross-case analysis.

Case Company	Link on Home Page	Name of Link on Home Page	Ethics Menu	Crosslinks
BellSouth	✘	*About us (→ Ethics & Compliance)*	✓	6
Lockheed Martin	✘	*About us (→ Ethics)*	✓	✘
Ben & Jerry's	✓	*We care about, Foundation info PartnerShops, Company Info*	✘	9
McDonald's	✓	*Social Responsibility, RMHC, People Promise*	✓	6
Nike	✓	*Global Citizenship, Corporate Responsibility Report*	✓	3
Levi Strauss & Co.	✓	*Social Responsibility*	✓	3

Table 17: The Textual Function across Cases

Explanation of criteria:

- *Link on Home Page* indicates whether the company has a link from its home page, i.e. the opening page, to its ethics section.
- *Name of Link on Home Page* gives the name of the home-page link.
- *Ethics Menu* indicates that the company has a separate ethics menu to organize its ethics pages.
- *Crosslinks* indicate the number of inward-pointing hyperlinks **in the texts**, i.e. hyperlinks pointing to other pages of the corporate Web site. Crosslinks exclude menu items and links within pages.

7.3.1 Links on Home Page

Whether or not a company has a link on its home page to its corporate-ethics subsection is a clear indication of how important the company deems the issue. Interestingly, home-page links have proved to be influenced by the ethics paradigms the companies belong to.

- BellSouth and Lockheed Martin both do not have ethics links on their home pages, but the menu item *About Us* takes users to a submenu with the items *Ethics & Compliance* (BellSouth) and *Ethics* (Lockheed Martin). For BellSouth and Lockheed Martin, ethics is apparently not a central element of the image they seek to project. Also, the fact that the companies label these menu items *ethics* and *ethics & compliance* is a reflection of the business-ethics paradigm.
- Ben & Jerry's has several links on the home page that take users to pages on social responsibility, including *We care about*, *PartnerShop*, *Company info* and *Foundation info*. McDonald's has home-page links named *Social Responsibility*, *People Promise* and *RMHC* (Ronald McDonald House Charities). It is worth highlighting that both McDonald's and Ben & Jerry's have links to their foundations on their home pages, which shows how much importance CSR companies assign to their charity foundations.
- Nike and Levi Strauss & Co. have links on their home pages named *Global Citizenship* and *Social Responsibility*, respectively, so ethics is obviously a key issue in their self-presentations on the Web. Also, Nike's home-page link to its social report suggests that its ethical discourse serves PR purposes.

7.3.2 Menus

Apart from Ben & Jerry's, all companies have ethics menus. These ethics menus provide an overview of the ethics-related pages and serve as a cohesive device. Some companies even have submenus for different sections of their ethics pages. Lockheed Martin, for example, has a submenu specifically for its ethics statements, including its code of conduct, its ethical principles and its value statement. Ben & Jerry's Web site lacks cohesion, as it has several comprehensive menus instead of one top-level menu with sub-menus. It has no menu item subsuming all its ethics-related pages either.

7.3.3 Crosslinks

The absence of a separate ethics menu necessitates crosslinks to create cohesion, as can be seen from Ben & Jerry's, which does not have an ethics menu but has more crosslinks than the other case companies. The other case companies exploit the capabilities of hypertext for cross-referencing to a surprisingly small extent. The reason for this might not only be that they use ethics menus instead of crosslinks as a cohesive device but also that they have only few, rather long pages, often amounting to several pages of printouts. Thus, the contents of these long pages are largely unrelated, which renders crosslinking unnecessary. However, pages should not be larger than one screen in order to reduce the need for scrolling, as was pointed out by Nielsen (2000) (see Section 2.2). For the sake of readability and clarity, the company Web sites analyzed could be improved by breaking up longer text into multiple pages to make them fit into one screen.

8 Conclusion

The multiple-case design of this book was intended to illuminate the phenomenon of corporate Web sites as a vehicle to communicate corporate ethics. The six case studies and the three intra-paradigm analyses have also added to the understanding of the paradigms. The three-paradigm approach and the number of cases have made for systematic variety among the sample, thereby giving a broader picture of the phenomenon studied. Although this variation in the sample makes findings more valid, generalization is of course limited to similar cases in a similar context. A series of inferences can be drawn from the research conducted:

- The communicative strategies seem to be largely independent of the paradigm. Persuasive appeals, self-reference, audience address and the hypertextual organization of the messages are realized similarly across paradigms. Also, codes of conduct, value statements, corporate foundations and employee volunteerism seem to transcend the borders of the paradigms.
- As for persuasion methods, companies use predominantly appeals to reason to support their messages, while appeal to the credibility of the speaker and appeal to emotion are used to a far lesser extent. Although commonly used in product advertising or corporate advertising, emotional appeals are not widely used on ethics pages, although companies essentially advertise themselves on their Web pages. Companies seem to be aware that their messages face low credibility, so that they do not use appeals to the credibility of the speaker extensively.
- Companies communicate with *all* their stakeholder groups via their Web sites. However, their audiences are potentially heterogeneous in terms of nationality, mother tongue, age, education and personal stake in the company, unlike for example the readers of annual reports. In this sense, Web sites are directed at an amorphous but critical mass, which makes Web communication a complex task. Although the companies relate to both internal and external audiences, their main target audience must be an external one, otherwise the material would not be on the WWW for everyone to see but on the corporate intranet only. Putting something up for everyone to see means that it is intended to enhance corporate reputation and anticipate criticism.
- Companies display little creativity when it comes to exploiting the sheer endless possibilities the World Wide Web provides for multimedia presentations and interactivity to support their messages on their ethics pages. They make mainly use of the classic hypertext features — text, links and

images. BellSouth's games and Nike's FAQ database seem to be the exceptions to the rule.

- Comparing the content of the Web sites with the public image of the companies, one may conclude that a Web site is not enough to create and promote an ethical image. Ben & Jerry's, for example, has a reputation as an ethical company, yet its Web site does not convey this image to the same extent. Conversely, Nike's Web site contains an overabundance of information on its labor policies, but Nike's public image is still shattered from its labor issues in Asia. This suggests that Web-site communication is next to ineffectual for building an ethical image, presumably because the audience targeted does not read a company's ethics-related Web pages.

Bibliography

ADBUSTERS (2002a): *Grease.* <http://adbusters.org/spoofads/food/grease>. Retrieved: 2 January 2002.

ADBUSTERS (2002b): *Big Mac attack.* <http://adbusters.org/spoofads/food/bigmac>. Retrieved: 2 January 2002.

ADBUSTERS (2002c): *Information.* <http://adbusters.org/information>. Retrieved: 2 Jan 2002.

ALLEN, R.L. (1998): "Kroc, Monaghan exemplify industry's charity as season of good will nears", *Nation's Restaurant News*, 12 October 1998: 33.

ALSOP, R. (2002): "For a company, charitable works are best carried out discreetly", *Wall Street Journal* (Online edition), 16 January 2002.

ALTCULTURE (2001): *McJob.* <http://www.plastic.com/altculture/01/04/09/2029209.shtml>. Retrieved: 10 September 2001.

ALTHAM, J. (2001): "Business ethics versus corporate social responsibility: Competing or complementary approaches?", *International Business Ethics Review*, Spring 2001: 10-12.

The American heritage dictionary of the English language. 4th ed. Boston: Houghton Mifflin, 2000.

ARNOLD, M. (2001): "Is Ben & Jerry's losing its bohemian appeal?", *Marketing*, 3 May 2001: 17.

ASSOCIATED PRESS (2000a): "A surprise with your fries?", *ABC News*, 28 August 2000. <http://more.abcnews.go.com/sections/world/dailynews/mcdonalds000828.html>. Retrieved: 20 January 2002.

ASSOCIATED PRESS (2000b): "China: McDonald's fires underage workers", *CorpWatch*, 4 September 2000. <http://www.corpwatch.org/news/PND.jsp?articleid=583>. Retrieved: 20 January 2002.

ATKINS, R. (1997): "The lessons of the McLibel case", *International Commercial Litigation*, July/August 1997: 33-35.

BAKER, L.W. (1993): *The credibility factor. Putting ethics to work in public relations.* Homewood: Irwin.

BANKOWSKI, E. (1997): "Ethics must come from the top down", *Compensation and Benefits Review*, March/April 1997: 25-26.

BEAVER, W. (1995): "Levi's leaving China", *Business Horizons*, March 1995: 35-40.

BELL ATLANTIC (2001): *Our vision statement.* <http://www.bell-atl.com/about/vision.htm>. Retrieved: 30 January 2001.

BELLSOUTH (2001a): *BellSouth Corporation.* 31 December 2001. <http://www.bellsouth.com/whoweare/corp.vtml>. Retrieved: 2 April 2002.

BELLSOUTH (2001b): *Business profile.* 31 December 2001. <http://www.bellsouth.com/investor/ir_businessprofile.shtml>. Retrieved: 2 April 2002.

BELLSOUTH (2001c): *History.* 31 December 2001. <http://www.bellsouth.com/investor/history_bellsouth.shtml>. Retrieved: 2 April 2002.

BELLSOUTH (2002): *Federal sales division.* <http://www.bellsouth.com/federal/>. Retrieved: 27 March 2002.

BEN & JERRY'S (1999): *Annual Report.* <http://lib.benjerry.com/fin/1999/10K.html>. Retrieved: 1 June 2002.

BEN & JERRY'S (2000): *Where in the world are we?* <http://www.benjerry.com/international/index.html>. Retrieved: 13 July 2001.

BEN & JERRY'S (2001): *Ben & Jerry's timeline.* <http://lib.benjerry.com/timeline.html>. Retrieved: 13 July 2001.

BEN & JERRY'S (2002): <http://www.benjerry.com>. Retrieved: 2 February 2002.

"Ben & Jerry's to raise its UK profile", *Marketing Week*, 5 April 1996: 12.

"Ben & Jerry's: Will 'caring capitalism' yield to creamy profits?", *CNN.com*, 26 January 2000, <http://cnn.org/2000/US/01/26/ben.jerry.takeover/index.html>. Retrieved: 24 July 2001.

BENJAMIN, M. (1998): "A riveting announcement", *San Francisco Bay Guardian*, 10 June 1998: n.p. Also available at <http://www.cleanclothes.org/companies/levi10-6-98-2.htm>. Retrieved: 8 February 2002.

BENSON, G.C.S. (1982): *Business ethics in America.* Lexington: Lexington Books.

BERNSTEIN, A. (1996): "Vendors and soccer council call child labor out of bounds", *Sporting Goods Business*, June 1996: 22.

BERNSTEIN, A. (1997a): "A potent weapon in the war against sweatshops", *Business Week*, 1 December 1997.

BERNSTEIN, A. (1997b): "Nike labor issues front page news", *Sporting Goods Business*, 15 December 1997: 10.

BERNSTEIN, A. (1999): "Sweatshops: No more excuses", *Business Week*, 8 Nov 1999: 110-112.

BORRUS, A. (1992): "Stanching the flow of China's gulag exports", *Business Week*, 13 April 1992: 15-16.

BOUNDS, W. (1998): "Inside Levi's race to restore a tarnished brand", *Wall Street Journal*, 4 August 1998: B1.

BOWIE, N.E. (1978): "Business codes of ethics: Window dressing or legitimate alternative to government regulation?", *Ethical theory and business.* Eds. Tom L. Beauchamp and Norman E. Bowie. 1979. Englewood Cliffs: Prentice-Hall. 234-239.

BRANCACCIO, D. (2000): "Selling out for fun and profit", *The Wall Street Journal* (Eastern edition), 17 April 2000: A34.

BRENNER, S.N. (1992): "Ethics programs and their dimensions", *Journal of Business Ethics* 11: 391-399.

BRIGLEY, S. (1995): "Business ethics in context: Researching with case studies", *Journal of Business Ethics* 14: 219-226.

"Bring me the rating of Ronald McDonald", *Brandweek*, 21 April 1997: 26.

BROMLEY, D.B. (1993): *Reputation, image and impression management*. Chichester: Wiley.

BROOKS, L.J. (1989): "Corporate codes of ethics", *Journal of Business Ethics* 8: 117-129.

BOUNDS, W. (1998): "Inside Levi's race to restore a tarnished brand", *Wall Street Journal*, 4 August 1998: B1.

BUCHHOLZ, R.A. (1995): *Business environment and public policy. Implications for management*. 5th ed. Englewood Cliffs: Prentice Hall.

BUCHHOLZ, R.A. and ROSENTHAL, S.B. (1998): *Business ethics: the pragmatic path beyond principles to process*. Upper Saddle River: Prentice Hall.

"Business: Fat and thin", *The Economist*, 15 April 2000: 63-64.

"Business ethics awards", *Business Ethics*, November/December 1998: 14.

BUSINESS FOR SOCIAL RESPONSIBILITY (2002a): *Volunteerism*. <http://www.bsr.org/BSRLibrary/TOdetail.cfm?DocumentID=158>. Retrieved: 15 March 2002.

BUSINESS FOR SOCIAL RESPONSIBILITY (2002b): *Mission, vision, values*. <http://www.bsr.org/BSRLibrary/TOdetail.cfm?DocumentID=267>. Retrieved: 15 March 2002.

BUSINESS FOR SOCIAL RESPONSIBILITY (2002c): *BSR history*. <http://www.bsr.org/Meta/about/BSRHistory.cfm>. Retrieved: 18 May 2002.

BUSINESS FOR SOCIAL RESPONSIBILITY (2002d): *Illustrative list of BSR members*. <http://www.bsr.org/Meta/MemberList.cfm>. Retrieved: 18 May 2002.

CAMPELL, L., GULAS, C.S., and GRUCA, T.S. (1999): "Corporate giving behavior and decision-maker social consciousness", *Journal of Business Ethics* 19: 375-383.

CAREY, R. (1998): "The ethics challenge", *Successful Meetings*, April 1998: 57-58.

CARRINGTON, T. (1986): "Lockheed's withholding of labor data led to big C-5 overcharge, Pentagon says", *Wall Street Journal* (Eastern edition), 29 August 1986: 1.

CARROLL, A.B. (1989): *Business & society. Ethics & stakeholder management*. Cincinnati: South-Western Publishing.

CASEY, A.M. (2000): "Demystifying the United States Federal 501(c)3 application process: A self-help discussion", *Wildlife Rehabilitation* 22, Summer 2000: n.p.

CENTER FOR BUSINESS ETHICS (1992): "Instilling ethical values in large corporations", *Journal of Business Ethics* 11: 863-867.

"The century's masters", *Marketing*, 25 November 1999: 22-25.

CHINOY, M. (2000): "Activists claim McDonald's toys made with child labor", *CNN*, 6 Sept 2000. <http://www.cnn.com/2000/ASIANOW/east/09/05/mcdonalds.child.labor/>. Retrieved: 20 January 2002.

CHRISTIE, R. (1999): "Manufacturers sign up to foreign workers' bill of rights", *Financial Times* (London edition), 3 June 1999: n.p.

CLIFFORD, M. (1992): "Spring in their step", *Far Eastern Economic Review*, 5 November 1992: 56-57.

CLIFFORD, M. (1994): "Walk, don't run", *Far Eastern Economic Review*, 9 June 1994: 68.

CLIFFORD, M. (1996a): "Pangs of conscience. Sweatshops haunt U.S. consumers", *Business Week*, 29 July 1996: 24-25.

CLIFFORD, M. (1996b): "Keep the heat on sweatshops", *Business Week*, 23 Dec 1996: 56.

COHEN, D.V., and NELSON, K.A. (1994): "Multinational ethics programs: Cases in corporate practice", *Emerging global business ethics*. Eds. W. Michael Hoffman et al. London: Quorum. 151-200.

COLLINS, W. (1981): "Hustlers of the bottom line", *Canadian Business*, October 1981: 78-82.

Collins Cobuild English Usage. London: Harper Collins, 1992.

Collins Cobuild English Language Dictionary. London: Harper Collins, 1987.

COLVIN, G. (1999): "Levi Strauss", *Fortune*, 11 October 1999: n.p.

"A comfortable fit", *The Economist*, 22 June 1991: 71-72.

CONDON, B. (1992): "A nap a day may keep the doctor away", *Los Angeles Times*, n.d. April 1992: n.p.

"Conviction upheld in Lockheed case", *Wall Street Journal* (Eastern edition), 15 May 1986: 1.

CORNING, B. (1999): "Great reputations", *Accountancy International*, March 1999: 38-39.

CORPWATCH (2002): *About CorpWatch*. <http://www.corpwach.org/about/PAM.jsp>. Retrieved: 10 February 2002.

COTTRILL, K. (1996): "Global codes of conduct", *Journal of Business Strategy*, May/June 1996: 55-59.

CRAGAN, J.F. and SHIELDS, D.C. (1998): *Understanding communication theory. The communicative forces for human action*. Boston: Allyn and Bacon.

"Culture shock is shaking the Bell System", *Business Week*, 26 September 1983: 112-115.

"Culturing change", *The Economist*, 7 July 1990: 65.

CZERNIAWSKA, F. (1997): *Corporate speak: The use of language in business*. Basingstoke: Macmillan.

DAILEY, P.B. (2001): "On fry detail", *Restaurants & Institutions*, 15 June 2001: 12.

DAVIS, B. (1988): "Scandal threatens federal phone project—Dispute highlights bitterness between firms", *Wall Street Journal* (Eastern edition), 20 January 1988: 1.

DE CENZO, D.A. and ROBBINS, S.P. (1994): *Human resource management*. 4th ed. New York: Wiley.

DEGEORGE, R.T. (1987): "The status of business ethics: Past and future", *Journal of Business Ethics* 6: 201-211.

DELONG, B. (2001): *Carnegie*. <http://econ161.berkeley.edu/TCEH/andrewcarnegie.html>. Retrieved: 12 August 2001.

THE DEFENSE INDUSTRY INITIATIVE ON BUSINESS ETHICS AND CONDUCT (2000): *2000 annual report to the public and the defense industry.* Available from: <http://www.dii.org/annual/2000/_Toc506801356>. Retrieved: 18 February 2002.

DELANEY, J.T, and SOCKELL, D. (1992): "Do company ethics training programs make a difference? An empirical analysis", *Journal of Business Ethics* 11: 719-727.

DIENHART, J.W., and CURNUTT, J. (1998): *Business ethics: A reference handbook.* Santa Barbara: ABC-CLIO.

"Doing it, earning it", *The Economist*, 26 February 1994: 63-64.

DUFFY, J. (2002): "How Ronald got le boot", *BBC News*, 22 January 2002, <http://news.bbc.co.uk/hi/english/uk/newsid_1775000/1775381.stm>. Retrieved: 11 February 2002.

DUIMERING, P.R., and SAFAYENI, F. (1998): "The role of language and formal structure in the construction and maintenance of organizational images", *International Studies in Management and Organization*, Fall 1998: 57-85.

DUNFEE, T.W. and WERHANE, P. (1997): "Report on business ethics in North America", *Journal of Business Ethics* 16: 1589-1595.

DUPONT (2001): *DuPont Vision Statement.* <http://www.dupont.com/corp/gbl-company/statement.html>. Retrieved 30 Jan 2001.

EISENHART, T. (1990): "McRecycle USA: Golden Arches offers marketers a golden payoff", *Business Marketing*, November 1990: 25-26.

EISMANN, R. (1992): "Sweet charity", *Incentive*, December 1992: 24-26.

ENTINE, J. (1995): "Rain-forest *chic*", *The Globe and Mail — Report on Business*, October 1995: 41-45: n.p.

"Environmentally conscious carton", *Dairy Foods*, May 1999: 48.

EOA (2002a): *Ethics Officer Association.* <http://www.eoa.org>. Retrieved: 18 May 20002.

EOA (2002b): *Mission, vision & values.* <http://www.eoa.org/mission/list.html>. Retrieved: 18 May 2002.

EOA (2002c): *How to join the EOA.* <http://www.eoa.org/Join/join.html>. Retrieved: 1 June 2002.

"Ethical shopping. Human rights", *The Economist*, 3 June 1995: 66-71.

EVANS, S. (2001): "McDonald's grilled over 'veggie fries' ", *BBC News*, 24 May 2001, <http://news.bbc.co.uk/hi/english/world/newsid_1348296.stm>. Retrieved 11 Feb 2002.

"Exporting jobs and ethics", *Fortune*, 5 October 1992: 10.

FAIR LABOR ASSOCIATION (2002): *Participating companies.* <http://www.fairlabor.org/html/affiliates/corporate.html>. Retrieved: 1 June 2002.

FAIRCLOUGH, N. (1989): *Language and power.* London: Longman.

FAIRCLOUGH, N. (1992): *Discourse and social change.* Cambridge: Polity Press.

FAIRCLOUGH, N. (2001): *New Labour, new language?* London: Routledge.

FAIRCLOUGH, N. and WODAK, R. (1997): "Critical discourse analysis", *Discourse Studies Volume 2: Discourse as Social Interaction*. Ed. Teun A. van Dijk. London: Sage. 258-283.

FAIRCLOUGH, N. (2001): *Language and power*. 2nd ed. London: Longman.

FARRELL, H. and FARRELL, B.J. (1998): "The language of business codes of ethics: Implications of knowledge and power", *Journal of Business Ethics* 17: 587-601.

"A fashion statement", *Far Eastern Economic Review*, 20 May 1993: 5.

FERRELL, O.C., and FRAEDRICH, J. (1997): *Business ethics. Ethical decision making and cases*. 3rd ed. Boston: Mifflin.

FERRELL, O.C. and GABLE, T. (1997): "Ben & Jerry's Homemade balances social responsibility and growth", *Business Ethics. Ethical decision making and cases*. 3rd ed. Eds. Ferrell, O.C. and Fraedrich, J. Boston: Mifflin. 275-279.

"Fitting the world in sport shoes", *Business Week*, 25 January 1982: 73-74.

FOMBRUN, C.J. (1996): *Reputation. Realizing value from the corporate image*. Boston: Harvard Business School Press.

"Foot-and-mouth hits McDonald's", *BBC News*, 19 April 2001, <http://news.bbc.co.uk/hi/english/business/newsid:1285000/1285860.stm>. Retrieved: 11 February 2002.

"Former GSA worker enters guilty plea in BellSouth Case", *Wall Street Journal* (Eastern edition), 23 May 1989: 1.

FRANCE, M. (1996): "Ethics for hire", *Business Week*, 15 July 1996: 26-28.

FRANZ, N. (2000): "Dioxin debate turns icy", *Chemical Week*, 29 March 2000: 76.

FREDERICK, W.C., DAVIS, K., and POST, J.E. (1988): *Business and society. Corporate strategy, public policy, ethics*. 6th ed. New York: McGraw-Hill.

FREEMAN, E. and REED, D. (1983): "Stockholders and stakeholders: A new perspective on corporate governance", *Corporate governance: A definitive exploration of the issue*. Los Angeles: UCLA Extension Press.

FRIEDMAN, M. (1970): "The social responsibility of business is to increase its profits", *New York Times Magazine*, 13 September 1970: 122-126.

GAINES, S. (1994): "Handing out halos", *Business Ethics*, March/April 1994: 20-24.

GARBETT, T. (1988): *How to build a corporation's identity and project its image*. New York: Lexington.

GARFIELD, B. (1998): "Nike's new 'I can' just doesn't do it as well", *Advertising Age*, 19 January 1998: 47.

GEORGAKOPOULOU, A. and DIONYSIS, G. (1997): *Discourse analysis. An introduction*. Edinburgh: Edinburgh University Press.

GILLEY, B. (1998): "Sweating it out", *Far Eastern Economic Review*, 10 Dec 1998: 66-67.

GISSEN, J. (1983): "Bells, bells, bells", *Forbes*, 21 November 1983: 286-287.

GOLDMAN, R., and PAPSON, S. (1998): *Nike culture. The sign of the swoosh*. London: Sage.

GOLL, S.D. and ZUCKERMANN, L. (1993): "Levi Strauss, leaving China, passes crowd of firms going the other way", *Wall Street Journal*, 5 May 1993: A18.

GOODMAN, M.B. (1998): *Corporate communications for executives*. Albany: State University of New York Press.

GRAY, J.G. (1986): *Managing the corporate image. The key to public trust*. Westport: Quorum.

GRAY, S. (1996): "Audit your ethics", *Association Management*, September 1996: 188.

GREENBAUM, S. and QUIRK, R. (1990): *A student's grammar of the English language*. Harlow: Longman.

GREENGARD, S. (1997a): "Lockheed Martin is game for ethics", *Workforce*, October 1997: 51.

GREENGARD, S. (1997b): "50% of your employees are lying, cheating & stealing", *Workforce*, October 1997: 44-53.

GRIGGS, R. (1999): "Simple Nike slogan becomes '90s anthem", *Advertising Age* 14: 28.

GROSSMAN, S.R., and KING, M.J. (1993): "Where vision statements go wrong", *Across the Board*, June 1993: 56.

GUSTAFSON, K. (1985): "McDonald's turns them out at Hamburger University", *Corporate Design & Realty*, January/February 1985: 142-150.

GUTTENPLAN (1996): "McLibel", *Columbia Journalism Review*, July/August 1996: 13-14.

HAAS, R.D. (1994): "Ethics in trenches", *Management across cultures. Insights from fiction and practice*. Ed. Sheila Puffer. 1996. Cambridge: Blackwell. 380-384.

HALLIDAY, M.A.K. (1978): *Language as social semiotic: The social interpretation of language and meaning*. London: Edward Arnold.

HALLIDAY, M.A.K. (1994): *An introduction to functional grammar*. 2nd ed. London: Edward Arnold.

HALLIDAY, M.A.K. and HASAN, R. (1976): *Cohesion in English*. London: Longman.

HAMSTRA, M. (1998): "McDonald's co-founder dead at 89", *Nation's Restaurant News*, July 27, 1998: 74.

HARARI, O. (1998): "Lessons from the Swoosh", *Management Review*, July 1998: 39-42.

HARRIS, K. (1999): "Majors spin Web around Nike site", *Sporting Goods Business*, 8 March 1999: 13-15.

HARRIS, R.J and RICKS, T.E. (1994): "Lockheed faces possible suspension on Air Force contracts after indictment", *Wall Street Journal* (Eastern edition), 24 June 1994: A12.

HARRISON, S.R. (1995): "The most natural thing to do", *Management Accounting*, March 1995: 22.

HARTMAN, L.P. (1998): *Perspectives in business ethics*. Chicago: McGraw-Hill.

HARTUNG, W.D. (2000): *Corporate profile: Lockheed Martin*. World Policy Institute. Availaible from International Network on Disarmament and Globalization: <http://www.indg.org/Lockhee2.htm>. Retrieved: 27 March 2002.

HARTUNG, W.D. and CIARROCCA. M. (2000): "Nuclear Missile Deception: Corruption and conflicts of interest in the National Missile Defense (NMD) Test Program", *World Policy Institute Special Issue Brief*, 17 July 2000. <http://www.worldpolicy.org/projects/arms/updates/nmdtitle.htm>. Retrieved: 20 January 2002.

HERBERT, B. (1998): "In America: Nike blinks", *New York Times*, 21 May 1998: A33.

HILL, J.W., METZGER, M.B., and DALTON, D.R. (1992): "How ethical is your company?", *Management Accounting*, July 1992: n.p.

HODGE, R. and KRESS, G. (1993): *Language as ideology*. 2nd ed. London: Routledge.

HOFMAN, M. (2001): "Ben Cohen: Ben & Jerry Homemade Inc., established in 1978", *Inc*, 30 April 2001: 68.

HOFFMAN, W. Michael (Director of the Center for Business Ethics at Bentley College, Waltham, Massachusetts). Personal interview, 15 August 2001.

HOOGHIEMSTRA, R. (2000): "Corporate communication and impression management — New perspectives why companies engage in corporate social reporting", *Journal of Business Ethics* 27: 55-68.

HORTON, J.L. (1995): *Integrating corporate communications. The cost-effective use of message and medium*. Westport: Quorum.

HOWARD, S. (1998): *Corporate image management. A marketing discipline for the 21st century*. Singapore: Butterworth-Heinemann Asia.

HUBERMANN, A.M. and MILES, M.B. (1994): "Data management and analysis methods", *Handbook of qualitative research*, Eds. Norman K. Denzin and Yvonna S. Lincoln. Thousand Oaks: Sage. 428-444.

HUME, S. (1990): "How Big Mac made it to Moscow", *Advertising Age*, 22 Jan 1990: 16-17.

HUME, S. (1991): "The green revolution: McDonald's", *Advertising Age*, 29 Jan 1991: 32.

HUME, S. (1993): "When it comes to burgers, we crave for beef, not McLean", *Advertising Age*, 1 March 1993: 3-4.

IACOCCA, L. (2001): "Henry Ford", *TIME 100. The most important people of the 20th century*. <http://www.time.com/time/time100/builder/profile/ford.html>. Retrieved: 12 Aug 2001.

"The ice-man goeth", *The Economist*, 18 June 1994: 70.

IZRAELI, D. and BARNIR, A. (1998): "Promoting ethics through ethics officers: A proposed profile and an application", *Journal of Business Ethics* 17: 1189-1196.

JACKSON, W. (2001): *The Ben & Jerry's story*. <http://www.woodyjackson.com/bennjerry.html>. Retrieved: 30 December 2001.

JARDINE, A. (1999): "McDonald's still facing a McLibel backlash", *Marketing*, 16 September 1999: 15-16.

JENKINS, H.W. (1998): "Business World: The rise and stumble of Nike", *Wall Street Journal* (Eastern edition), 3 June 1998: A19.

JENSEN, J. (1997): "Nike eyes new 'I can' tag for '98 brand ads", *Advertising Age*, 17 November 1997: 3; 86.

JOHNSON, C. (1990): "Rights group to kick harder at sneaker firm's policies", *Wall Street Journal*, 17 August 1990: B1.

JOSE, A. and THIBODEAUX, M.S. (1999): "Institutionalization of ethics: The perspective of managers", *Journal of Business Ethics* 22: 133-143.

"Just doing it", *Accountancy International*, March 1999: 30-31.

"Just don't", *Business Asia*, 28 July 1997: 1-2.

KAMEN, R. (1993): "Values: For show or for real?", *Working Woman*, August 1993: 10.

KANE, C. (1998): "Levi Strauss is trying to regain market share for its jeans, especially among your consumers", *New York Times*, 5 May 1998: D11.

KELLER, L. (1997): "Dilbert does ethics", *Successful Meetings*, June 1997: 19.

KELLY, S.C. (1997): "Environmental issues in public relations: A matter of credibility", *The handbook of strategic public relations and integrated communications*. Ed. Clarke L. Caywood. New York: McGraw-Hill. 207-221.

KNIGHT, P. (1998): "Global manufacturing: The Nike story is just good business", *Vital Speeches of the Day*, 1 August 1998: 637-640.

KOTCHIAN, A.C. (1977): "The payoff — Lockheed's 70-day mission to Tokyo", *Saturday Review*, 9 July 1977: 7.

KOTEN, J.A. (1997): "The strategic uses of corporate philanthropy", *The handbook of strategic public relations and integrated communications*. Ed. Clarke L. Caywood. New York: McGraw-Hill. 149-172.

KRAMER (1998): "Ronald McDonald, new kids character share center stage", *Advertising Age*, 2 March 1998: 1; 40.

LAABS, J.J. (1992): "Ben & Jerry's caring capitalism", *Personnel Journal*, November 1992: 50-54.

LAABS, J.J. (1995): "CEO prompts Ben & Jerry's to raise salary cap", *Personnel Journal*, January 1995: 12.

LABERIS, B. (1999): "Image is everything", *MC Technology Marketing Intelligence*, February 1999: 20.

LANDLER, M. (1998): "Reversing course, Levi Strauss will expand its output in China", *New York Times*, 9 April 1998: CA, D1.

LANGLOIS, C.C. and SCHLEGELMILCH, B.B. (1990): "Do corporate codes of ethics reflect national character?", *Journal of International Business Studies* 4: 519-536.

LEE, L. (2000): "Take our Swoosh. Please", *Business Week*, 21 February 2000: 128.

LEHMAN BROTHERS (2002): *Mission Statement*. <http://www.lehman.com/who/mission/>. Retrieved: 18 March 2002.

LEFTON, T. (1999): "Swoosh switch", *Brandweek*, 24 May 1999: 1A.

"Levi Strauss & Co. joins Fair Labor Association", *HR Focus*, October 1999: S11.

LEVI STRAUSS & CO. (2001a): *About LS & Co. / Timeline: 19th century.* <http://www.levistrauss.com/about/history/noflash/1800.htm>. Retrieved: 7 Feb 2002.

LEVI STRAUSS & CO. (2001b): *Vision & values.* <http://www.levistrauss.com/about/vision/>. Retrieved: 4 April 2002.

LEVI STRAUSS & CO. (2001c): *About LS & Co. / Timeline: 1920s.* <http://www.levistrauss.com/about/history/noflash/1920s.htm>. Retrieved: 7 Feb 2002.

LEVI STRAUSS & CO. (2001d): *About LS & Co. / Timeline: 1930s.* <http://www.levistrauss.com/about/history/noflash/1930s.htm>. Retrieved: 7 Feb 2002.

LEVI STRAUSS & CO. (2001e): *About LS & Co. / Timeline: 1940s.* <http://www.levistrauss.com/about/history/noflash/1940s.htm>. Retrieved: 7 Feb 2002.

LEVI STRAUSS & CO. (2001f): *About LS & Co. / Timeline: 1950s.* <http://www.levistrauss.com/about/history/noflash/1950s.htm>. Retrieved: 7 Feb 2002.

LEVI STRAUSS & CO. (2001g): *About LS & Co. / Timeline: 1960s.* <http://www.levistrauss.com/about/history/noflash/1960s.htm>. Retrieved: 7 Feb 2002.

LEVI STRAUSS & CO. (2001h): *About LS & Co. / Timeline: 1970s.* <http://www.levistrauss.com/about/history/noflash/1970s.htm>. Retrieved: 7 Feb 2002.

LEVI STRAUSS & CO. (2001i): *About LS & Co. / Timeline: 1980s.* <http://www.levistrauss.com/about/history/noflash/1980s.htm>. Retrieved: 7 Feb 2002.

LEVI STRAUSS & CO. (2001j): *About LS & Co. / Timeline: 1990s.* <http://www.levistrauss.com/about/history/noflash/1990s.htm>. Retrieved: 7 Feb 2002.

LEVI STRAUSS & CO. (2001k): *About LS & Co. / Levi's® 501® jeans facts.* <http://www.levistrauss.com/about/history/501s.htm>. Retrieved: 7 February 2002.

LEVI STRAUSS & CO. (2001l): *About LS & Co. / A history of denim.* <http://www.levistrauss.com/about/history/denim.htm>. Retrieved: 7 February 2002.

LEVI STRAUSS & CO. (2001m): *About LS & Co. / Invention of Levi's ® 501® jeans.* <http://www.levistrauss.com/about/history/jeans.htm>. Retrieved: 7 February 2002.

LEVI STRAUSS & CO. (2001n): *About LS & Co. / Asia Pacific.* <http://www.levistrauss.com/about/apd>. Retrieved: 10 February 2002.

"Levi Strauss & Co.: Yearly sales dropped 4%, first decline in a decade", *Wall Street Journal*, 11 February 1998: B4.

"Levi Strauss is likely to cut additional jobs in move to trim costs", *Wall Street Journal* (Eastern edition), 17 July 1998: n.p.

LEXMARK (2001): *Lexmark vision and values.* <http://www.lexmark.com/US/corporate/vision_values.html>. Retrieved: 30 January 2001.

LOCKHEED MARTIN (2000a): *At a glance.* <http://www.lockheedmartin.com/about/ataglance.html>. Retrieved: 20 January 2002.

LOCKHEED MARTIN (2000b): *History.* <http://www.lockheedmartin.com/about/history.html>. Retrieved: 20 January 2002.

LOCKHEED MARTIN (2000c): *Setting the standard.* <http://www.lockheedmartin.com/about/ethics/standard.html>. Retrieved: 20 January 2002.

LOCKHEED MARTIN (2001): *Lockheed Martin fact sheet.* <http://www.lockheedmartin.com/investor/annualreport/factsheet.pdf>. Retrieved: 20 January 2002.

LOCKHEED MARTIN (2002): *Proxy statement. Notice of 2002 Annual Meeting of Stockholders.* 25 April 2002.

"Lockheed Martin agrees to pay $13 million to end U.S. government export complaint", *Satellite News,* 19 June 2000: 1.

LUTHANS, F., HODGETTS, R.M., and THOMPSON, K.R. (1990): *Social issues in business: Strategic and public policy perspectives.* 6th ed. New York: Macmillan.

LUXNER, L. (1993): "Florida probes Southern Bell executives in ongoing fraud case", *Telephony,* 25 January 1993: 8.

MALKIN, E. (1996): "Cleanup at the maquiladora", *Business Week,* 29 July 1996: 26.

MARSHALL, S. (1997): "Nike Inc.'s golden image is tarnished as problems in Asia pose PR challenge", *Wall Street Journal,* 26 September 1997: n.p.

MATHEWS, M.R. (1995): "Social and environmental accounting: A practical demonstration of ethical concern?", *Journal of Business Ethics* 14: 663-671.

MAZUR, L. (2001): "The trouble with takeovers", *Marketing,* 8 February 2001: 26-27.

MCCARTHY, M.J. (1999): "How one firm tracks ethics electronically", *Wall Street Journal* (Eastern edition), 21 October 1999: B1.

MCDONALD, G. (2000): "Business ethics: Practical proposals for organisations", *Journal of Business Ethics,* May 2000: 169-184.

MCDONALD, G.M. and DONLEAVY, G.D. (1995): "Objections to the teaching of business ethics", *Journal of Business Ethics* 14: 839-853.

MCDONALD'S (2001a): *McDonald's history.* <http://www.mcdonalds.com/corporate/info/history/history.html>. Retrieved: 24 July 2001.

MCDONALD'S (2001b): *Commitment to RMHC.* <http://www.mcdonalds.com/corporate/social/rmhc/rmhc.html>. Retrieved: 24 July 2001.

MCDONALD'S (2001c): *Our people promise.* <http://www.mcdonalds.com/corporate/promise/people/people.html>. Retrieved: 24 July 2001.

MCDONALD'S (2001d): *People history.* <http://www.mcdonalds.com/corporate/promise/history/history.html>. Retrieved: 24 July 2001.

MCDONALD'S (2001e): *McDonald's timeline.* <http://www.media.mcdonalds.com/secured/company/history/timeline/>. Retrieved: 10 September 2001.

MCDONALD'S (2001f): *McDonald's franchising.* <http://www.mcdonalds.com/corporate/franchise/franchise.html>. Retrieved: 24 July 2001.

MCDONALD'S USA (2001a): *Frequently asked questions.* <http://www.mcdonalds.com/countries/usa/corporate/info/faq/faq.html>. Retrieved: 24 July 2001.

McDonald's USA (2001b): *Oil alliances.* <http://www.mcdonalds.com/countries/usa/corporate/alliances/oil_alliance.html>. Retrieved: 24 July 2001.

McDonald's (2002a): *Apology related to French fry litigation settlement.* <http://www.mcdonalds.com/countries/usa/whatsnew/pressrelease/2002/06012002/>. Retrieved: 8 May 2002.

McDonald's (2002b): *Restaurants by country listing.* <http://www.mcdonalds.com/corporate/investor/financialinfo/systemrest/index.html>. Retrieved: 10 June 2002.

"McDonald's cuts ties with Chinese factory", *BBC News*, 8 September 2000, <http://news.bbc.co.uk/hi/english/world/asia-pacific/newsid_915000/915839.stm>. Retrieved: 11 February 2002.

"McDonald's dumps GM-fed meat", *BBC News*, 19 November 2000, <http://news.bbc.co.uk/hi/English/uk/newsid_1031000/1031182.stm>. Retrieved: 11 Feb 2002.

"McDonald's heiress donates $80 million to salvation army", *Wall Street Journal*, 24 September 1998: B8.

"McDonald's hit by mad-cow fears", *BBC News*, 24 July 2001, <http://news.bbc.co.uk/hi/English/business/newsid_14554000/1454771.stm>. Retrieved: 11 February 2002.

"McDonald's spends big on recycling", *World Wastes*, June 1993: 124.

"McDonald's takes on Asterix", 20 December 2001, *BBC News*, <http://news.bbc.co.uk/hi/english/entertainment/showbiz/newsid_1721000/1721029.stm>. Retrieved: 11 Feb 2002.

"McDonald's to give more information about its ingredients", *Wall Street Journal*, 14 August 2001: C13.

McDonaldization.com (2001a): *About us.* <http://www.McDonaldization.com/aboutus.shtml>. Retrieved: 17 January 2002.

McDonaldization.com (2001b): *What is it?* <http://www.McDonaldization.com/whatisit.shtml>. Retrieved: 17 January 2002.

McDonaldization.com (2001c): *McDonaldization.* <http://www.McDonaldization.com/main.shtml>. Retrieved: 17 January 2002.

McEnry, T. and Wilson, A. (1996): *Corpus Linguistics.* Edinburgh: Edinburgh Univ. Press.

"McLibel support campaign: McLibel trial becomes the longest civil case in British history", *M2 Presswire*, 11 December 1995: 1.

McMahon, T.F. (1999): "A brief history of American business ethics", *A companion to business ethics*. Ed. Robert F. Frederick. Malden: Blackwell.

McSpotlight (2001a): *The issues.* <http://www.mcspotlight.org/issues/intro.html>. Retrieved: 31 December 2001.

McSpotlight (2001b): *McSpotlight.* <http://www.mcspotlight.org>. Retrieved: 31 Dec 2001.

McSpotlight (2001c): *Contact us.* <http://www.mcspotlight.org/people/biogs/mcinfo.html>. Retrieved: 31 December 2001.

McSPOTLIGHT (2001d): *McSpotlight FAQ*. <http://www.mcspotlight.org/campaigns/current/mcspotlight/faq.html>. Retrieved: 31 December 2001.

MEAD, R. (1998): *International management: Cross-cultural dimensions*. 2nd ed. Oxford: Blackwell.

MENDELSON, S. (1996): "Research gone awry", *Supermarket Business*, November 1996: 43.

MEYER, P. (1998): "Learning from the Swoosh", *Brandweek*, 20 April 1998: 24-25.

MILLER, C. (1993): "Levi to sever link with China; critics contend it's just a PR move", *Marketing News*, 7 June 1993: 10.

MILES, M.B. and HUBERMAN, A.M. (1994): *Qualitative data analysis: An expanded sourcebook*. 2nd ed. Thousand Oaks: Sage.

MILTON-SMITH, J. (1999): "The code of ethics as an instrument of strategic management", *Applied ethics in management. Towards new perspectives*. Eds. Shitangsu K. Chakraborty and Samir R. Chatterjee. Berlin: Springer. 18-36.

MITCHELL, A. (1997): "The power of ethical branding", *Marketing Week*, 22 May 1997: 26-27.

MOON, C. and BONNY, C. (2001): "Attitudes and approaches", *Business ethics. Facing up to the issue*. The Economist Books. London: Profile Books: 22-37.

MORF, D.A., SCHUMACHER, M.G., and VITELL, S.J. (1999): "A survey of ethics officers in large organizations", *Journal of Business Ethics* 20: 265-271.

MUNK, N. (1999): "How Levi's trashed a great American brand", *Fortune*, 12 April 1999: n.p.

MUNRO, I. (1997): "Codes of ethics. Some uses and abuses", *Current issues in business ethics*. Ed. Peter W.F. Davies. London: Routledge. 97-106.

MURPHY, P.E. (1998): *Eighty exemplary ethics statements*. Notre Dame: University of Notre Dame Press.

NAIM, M. (2001): "McAtlas shrugged", *Foreign Policy*, May/June 2001: 26-37.

NAVRAN, F. (1997): "12 steps to building a best-practices ethics program", *Workforce*, September 1997: 117-122.

NEWSOM, D., TURK, J.V., and KRUCKEBERG, D. (1999): *This is PR. The realities of public relations*. 7th ed. Belmont: Wadsworth.

NIELSEN, J. (2000): *Designing Web usability*. Indianapolis: New Riders.

NIKE (2001a): *The origin of the Swoosh*. <http://www.nikebiz.com/story/stry_swoosh.shtml>. Retrieved: 7 December 2001.

NIKE (2001b): *Our chronology*. <http://ww.nikebiz.com/story/chrono.shtml>. Retrieved: 7 December 2001.

"Nike-cam shows happy workers", *Asian Business*, September 2001: 55.

"Nike layoffs totaled about 400 in last year", *Wall Street Journal*, 8 February 1985: 1.

"Nike to close two plants in Maine, idling nearly 650", *Wall Street Journal*, 7 Nov 1985: 1.

"Nike website is hijacked", *BBC News*, 22 June 2000, <http://news.bb.co.uk/hi/english/sci/tech/newsid_801000/801334.stm>. Retrieved: 11 February 2002.

"Nike's Asia lesson: Just don't do it", *Crossborder Monitor*, 1 October 1997: 1-7.

NIKEWAGES.ORG (2001): *What does Nike pay its people?* <http://www.nikewages.org>. Retrieved 22 April 2001.

OAKLEY, J.G. (1999): "Child labor, sweatshops, and the corporate social responsibility of MNCs", *Global Outlook* 1: 19-32.

"Operation PUSH keeps up pressure of boycott on Nike", *Wall Street Journal*, 21 August 1990: C15.

OXFAM COMMUNITY AID ABROAD (2002): *About Oxfam Community Aid Abroad* <http://www.caa.org.au/about/index.html>. Retrieved: 13 January 2002.

PASZTOR, A. (1995): "Lockheed willing to plead guilty, pay fine in Egyptian plane sales", *Wall Street Journal* (Eastern edition), 20 January 1995: B3.

PASZTOR, A. and COLE, J. (1995): "Lockheed Martin faces 3 federal probes into possible payments for foreign sales", *Wall Street Journal* (Eastern edition), 5 September 1995: B6.

PATTEN, D.M. (1992): "Intra-industry environmental disclosures in response to the Alaskan oil spill: A note on legitimacy theory", *Accounting, Organisations, and Society* 17 (5): 471-475.

PEACH, L. (1987): "Corporate responsibility", *Effective corporate relations: Applying public relations in business and industry*. Ed. Norman A. Hart. London: McGraw-Hill. 191-204.

PEPIN, J. (1998): "Burger Meister: Ray Kroc", *Time*, 7 December 1998: 176-178.

PETERSON, T (1996): "Now it's Ronald McYuppie", *Business Week*, 20 May 1996: 43.

PIELKEN, W.G. (1995): "Corporate responsibility and reputation management in crisis situations", *Facing public interest. The ethical challenge to business policy and corporate communication*. Eds. Peter Ulrich and Charles Sarasin. Dordrecht: Kluwer. 137-148.

PINKHAM, D.G. (1998): "Corporate public affairs: Running faster, jumping higher", *Public Relations Quarterly*, Summer 1998: 33-37.

POST, J.E., LAWRENCE, A.T., and WEBER, J. (1999): *Business and society: Corporate strategy, public policy, ethics*. 9th ed. Boston: McGraw-Hill.

POUSCHINE, T. (1992): "Ridin' high", *Forbes*, 9 November 1992: 78.

"The power of publicity", *The Economist: Survey human-rights law*, 5 Dec 1998: 13-15.

PRESS FOR CHANGE (2002): *Nikeworkers.org* <http://www.nikeworkers.org/contact_us.html>. Retrieved: 13 January 2002.

PUZO, D. (1997): "Who will save McDonald's?", *Restaurants & Institutions*, 1 July 1997: 10.

QUICK, R. (1999): "Levi Strauss to close half of its plants in North America, slashing 5,900 jobs", *Wall Street Journal*, 23 February 1999: A6.

RAPAPORT, R. (1993): "Import jeans, export values", *Fast Company*, November 1993, <http://www.fastcompany.com/online/00/levi.html>. Retrieved: 10 February 2002.

RAPOPORT, C. (1995): "McLibel in London", *Fortune*, 20 March 1995: 15.

RASMUSSON, E. (1997): "Defending a brand name", *Sales & Marketing Management*, September 1997: 22.

RASMUSSON, E. (2001): "A sweet marketing campaign", *Sales & Marketing Management*, November 2001: 14.

REDEKER, J. (1990): "Code of conduct as corporate culture", *HR Magazine*, July 1990: 83-87.

REED, M. (1999): "Wide open to the web warriors", *Marketing*, 4 February 1999: 18-19.

REYES, S. (2001): "B&J gives movie fans a spotlight on 'cool' ", *Brandweek*, 28 May 2001: 7.

RHODES, L. (1981): "Winning is a state of mind at Nike", August 1981, *Inc*, 52-56.

RICHARDS, B. (1998): "Nike to increase minimum age in Asia for new hirings, improve air quality", *Wall Street Journal*, 13 May 1998: B10.

RIGBY, R. (1997): "Old McDonald had a great idea", *Management Today*, August 1997: 70.

RIGBY, R. (1998): "Tutti-frutti capitalists", *Management Today*, February 1998: 54-56.

RITZER, G. (2000): *The McDonaldization of Society*. Thousand Oaks: Pine Forge Press.

ROMEO, P. (1998): "Re-ordering Ray's kitchen", *Restaurant Business*, 15 February 1998: 6.

"Ruling ends 19-year-old Lockheed bribery case", *Japan Times* (Weekly international edition), 6 March 1995: 8.

SANDERSON, G.R. and VARNER, I.I. (1984): "What's wrong with corporate codes of conduct?", *Management Accounting*, July 1984: 28-35.

SAYWELL, T. (1998): "Staying alert", *Far Eastern Economic Review*, 29 January 1998: 46-48.

SCHLEGELMILCH, B.B. (1998): *Marketing ethics: An international perspective*. London: Thomson Business Press.

SCHLEGELMILCH, B.B. (2002): AIESEC Exchange Forum 2002, Panel discussion on corporate social responsibility at the Vienna University of Economics and Business Administration, Austria. 14 March 2002.

SCHLOSSER, E. (2001): *Fast food nation. What the all-American meal is doing to the world*. London: Penguin Press.

"Scoops of hypocrisy", *ABC News*, 3 November 2000, <http://abcnews.go.com/sections/2020/2020/2020_001103_gmab_icecream_feature.html>. Retrieved: 24 July 2001.

SCHWARZ, A. (1996): "Culture shock", *Far Eastern Economic Review*, 22 August 1996: 63.

SEEGER, M.W. (1997): *Ethics and organizational communication*. Cresskill: Hampton Press.

SETHI, S.P. (2000): "Codes of conduct for global business: Prospects and challenges of implementation", *Business ethics. Readings and cases in corporate morality*. 4th ed. Eds. W. Michael Hoffman, Robert E. Frederick, Mark S. Schwartz. Boston: McGraw-Hill. 487-493.

SHAW, W.H. (1991): *Business ethics*. Belmont: Wadsworth.

SHELLENBARGER, S. (1991): "McDonald's low-fat burger to go national", *Wall Street Journal*, 13 March 1991: B1.

SILVERS, D.I. (1995): "Vision—Not just for CEOs", *Management Quarterly*, Winter 1994/1995: 10-14.

SIMS, R.R. (1991): "The institutionalization of organizational ethics", *Journal of Business Ethics* 10: 493-506.

SMITH, G. (2000): "A famous brand on a rocky road", *Business Week*, 11 December 2000: 54.

SMITH, N.C. (1995): "Marketing strategies for the ethics era", *Sloan Management Review*, Summer 1995: 85-97.

SLOAN, P. (1995): "Yo! Ben & Jerry's finds a CEO with taste for verse", *Advertising Age*, 6 February 1995: 4.

STAKE, R.E. (1994): "Case studies", *Handbook of qualitative research*, Eds. Norman K. Denzin and Yvonna S. Lincoln. Thousand Oaks: Sage. 236-247.

STARLING, G. (1995): *The changing environment of business*. 4th ed. Cincinnati: South-Western College Publishing.

STEINER, G.A. and STEINER, J.F. (2000): *Business, government and society. A managerial perspective*. 9th ed. Boston: McGraw-Hill.

STEVENS, B. (1994): "An analysis of corporate ethical code studies: 'Where do we go from here?' ", *Journal of Business Ethics* 13: 63-69.

STEVENS, B. (1999): "Communicating ethical values: A study of employee perceptions", *Journal of Business Ethics* 20: 113-120.

STILLAR, G.F. (1998): *Analyzing everyday texts. Discourse, rhetoric, and social perspectives*. Thousand Oaks: Sage.

STONE, A. (1997): "Lean? No thanks", *Restaurants & Institutions*, 15 May 1997: 102-111.

STUDABAKER, A.W. (1984): "And then there were seven", *Madison Avenue*, Jan 1984: 70-74.

TAYLOR, A. (1997): "Yo, Ben! Yo, Jerry! It's just ice cream!", *Fortune*, 28 April 1997: 374.

"Ten years of the Big Mac index", *The Economist*, 11 April 1998: n.p.

THOMAS, A.S. and SIMERLY, R.L. (1994): "The chief executive officer and corporate social performance: An interdisciplinary examination", *Journal of Business Ethics* 13: 959-968.

TREVIÑO, L.K. & NELSON, K. (1999): *Managerial business ethics*. 2nd ed. New York: John Wiley.

"Unilever scoops up Ben & Jerry's", *BBC News / Business*, 12 April 2000, <http://news.bbc.co.uk/hi/english/business/newsid_710000/710694.stm>. Retrieved: 24 July 2001.

U.S. DEPARTMENT OF JUSTICE (2002): *Foreign Corrupt Practices Act. Antibribery provisions*. <http://www.usdoj.gov/criminal/fraud/fcpa/dojdocb.htm>. Retrieved: 18 May 2002.

U.S. DEPARTMENT OF STATE (2000): "Daily Press Briefing", *M2 Presswire*, 16 June 2000.

VAN BERKEL, A. and DE JONG, M. (1999): "Coherence phenomena in hypertextual environments", *Textproduktion: HyperText, Text, KonText*, Eds. Eva-Maria Jakobs et al. Frankfurt: Lang. 29-40.

VAN HOUTEN, B. (2001): "McFix", *Restaurant Business*, 15 December 2001: 12-13.

VERSCHOOR, C.C. (1998): "A study of the link between a corporation's financial performance and its commitment to ethics", *Journal of Business Ethics* 17: 1509-1516.

VIETNAM LABOR WATCH (2002): *Boycott Nike*. <http://www.saigon.com/~nike>. Retrieved: 13 January 2002.

"The view from Taft: Good ethics is good business", *Businessworld*, 8 October 1998: n.p.

VOGEL COMMUNICATIONS (2000): *Ethics management services*. <http://www.ethicsworld.com/services/index.html>. Retrieved: 28 May 2002.

VOIGHT, J. (1999): "Red, white and blue: An American icon fades away", *Adweek*, 26 April 1999: 28-35.

WALSH, J. (1998a): " 'McJob' image first target in burger recruitment war", *People Management*, 22 January 1998: 11.

WALSH, J. (1998b): "HR managers set to drive through big McMakeover", *People Management*, 1 October 1998: 16.

WEAVER, G.R., TREVIÑO, L.K., and COCHRAN, P.L. (1999): "Corporate ethics practices in the mid-1990s: An empirical study of the Fortune 1000", *Journal of Business Ethics* 18: 283-294.

WEBLEY, S. (1998): "The Interfaith Declaration: Context, issues and problems of applications of a code of ethics for international business among those of three major religions", *Ethics in international management*. Eds. Brij Nino Kumar and Horst Steinmann. Berlin: Walter de Gruyter. 439-454.

WHITE, B.J. and MONTGOMERY, B.R. (1980): "Corporate codes of conduct", *California Management Review*, Winter 1980: n.p.

WHITMAN, M. (1999): *New world, new rules. The changing role of the American corporation*. Boston: Harvard Business School Press.

"Who cares, wins", *The Economist*, 16 May 1992: 19-20.

WIESENDANGER, B. (1993): "Ben & Jerry scoop up credibility", *The Public Relations Journal*, August 1993: 20.

WILLIAMS, R.J. and BARRETT, J.D. (2000): "Corporate philanthropy, criminal activity, and firm reputation: Is there a link?", *Journal of Business Ethics* 26: 341-350.

WULFSON, M. (2001): "The ethics of corporate social responsibility and philanthropic ventures", *Journal of Business Ethics* 29: 135-145.

WYNTER, L. (1990): "Operation Push set to step up effort against Nike Inc.", *Wall Street Journal*, 9 November 1990: n.p.

YIN, R.K. (1984): *Case study research*. Beverly Hills: Sage.

YULE, G. (1996): *The study of language*. 2nd ed. Cambridge: Cambridge University Press.

Ursula Wrobel

Andere Länder – Andere Sites

Bewältigung von Tabudiskursen in Online-Produktwerbung mit Hilfe von Abschwächungsstrategien unter besonderer Berücksichtigung von Heding

Ein Vergleich US-amerikanischer und deutscher Websites im Kontext interkultureller und werblicher Kommunikation

Frankfurt/M., Berlin, Bern, Bruxelles, New York, Oxford, Wien, 2003.
X, 202 S., zahlr. Abb. und Tab.
Kulturwissenschaftliche Werbeforschung.
Herausgegeben von Hartmut Schröder. Bd. 2
ISBN 3-631-39354-7 · br. € 35.30*

Tabuprodukte verlangen differenzierte Werbung. Wie für Entlausungsshampoo oder Inkontinenzeinlagen werben? Wie einem Kunden ein Spray gegen Fußpilz oder Hämorrhoidenzäpfchen nahe bringen? Lange Zeit war es üblich, solche Produkte nur unter der Ladentheke zu verkaufen. Heute sind sie Werbegegenstand, nicht zuletzt im neuen Massenmedium Internet. Web-Advertising bietet sich für die Vermarktung tabubehafteter Produkte in besonderer Weise an. Doch welche Strategien setzen amerikanische und deutsche Marketing-Experten zur Bewältigung visueller und verbaler Tabudiskurse ein? Anhand dieser Frage untersucht die vorliegende Studie Websites, in denen Tabuprodukte angeboten werden. Basierend auf semiotischer Theorie wird ein integratives Modell zur Analyse von Websites entwickelt. Die Ergebnisse der empirischen Fallstudien zeigen: Regionale Kulturen leben! Die betrachteten Online-Tabudiskurse sind zum gegenwärtigen Zeitpunkt kulturspezifisch ausgestaltet. Werbefachleute adressieren Tabuthemen kuradäquat für regionale Zielgruppen – auch in global rezipierbaren Websites.

Aus dem Inhalt: Interkulturelle Kommunikation · Diskurs · Tabu · Website · Werbung · Heding · Web-Advertising · Online-Werbung

Frankfurt/M · Berlin · Bern · Bruxelles · New York · Oxford · Wien
Auslieferung: Verlag Peter Lang AG
Moosstr. 1, CH-2542 Pieterlen
Telefax 00 41 (0) 32 / 376 17 27

*inklusive der in Deutschland gültigen Mehrwertsteuer
Preisänderungen vorbehalten

Homepage http://www.peterlang.de